Kant and the Problem of God

For Susannah

Kant AND THE PROBLEM OF *God*

Gordon E. Michalson, Jr
New College of the University of South Florida

First published 1999

2   4   6   8   10   9   7   5   3   1

Blackwell Publishers Ltd
108 Cowley Road
Oxford OX4 1JF
UK

Blackwell Publishers Inc.
350 Main Street
Malden, Massachusetts 02148
USA

British Library Cataloguing in Publication Data

A CIP catalogue record for this book is available from the British Library.

Library of Congress Cataloging-in-Publication Data

Michalson, Gordon E., 1948–
    Kant and problem of God/Gordon E. Michalson, Jr.
        p. cm.
    Includes bibliographical references and index.
    ISBN 0–631–21219–1 (alk. paper).—ISBN 0–631–21220–5 (pbk.:
alm. paper)
    1. Kant, Immanuel, 1724–1804—Religion.   2. Religion—Philosophy.
I. Title.
ZA3225.C48   1998
210′.92—dc21   98–33148
                                                                             CIP

Typeset in 10 on 12 pt Sabon
by Pure Tech India Ltd, Pondicherry
http://www.puretech.com
Printed in Great Britain by
MPG Books, Victoria Square, Bodmin, Cornwall

This book is printed on acid-free paper

Contents

Preface

There are several different kinds of books on Kant. One very familiar kind is the highly technical specialized work intended mainly for fellow members of the Kant guild. Focused narrowly on matters of textual detail and argumentation, such books make up in philosophical rigor what they often lack in narrative richness. These works are the backbone of Kant studies, and major new turns in Kant interpretation emerge out of the interaction of such works from one generation of Kant scholars to the next. At the same time, such books can be daunting for the non-specialist to read.

Another kind of Kant book is the introductory text, reflecting the perennial need on the part of students and the general reading public for aids in the understanding of this monumental yet difficult thinker. These works might be general in nature, offering an overview of Kant's entire philosophy, or they might be focused on specific topics, usually having to do with Kant's moral philosophy. Typically, the aim of such books is to smooth the reader's pathway into his or her own reading of Kant's works, providing just enough interpretive support to aid in this process without attempting to substitute for the actual reading of Kant himself. When these books are well done, they are invaluable.

Yet another sort of Kant study attempts to relate Kant to some broader interpretive theme in our philosophical, religious, or cultural history. In the case of these works, the aim is to show how some aspect of Kant's philosophy both fits into and illuminates a larger story bearing on our understanding of the modern world. For the authors of such books, the challenge is to strike a proper balance between responsible commentary on Kant and the development of the wider interpretive theme: too much of the former, and the narrative thread ends up buried under specialized digressions reminiscent of the first sort of Kant book; yet too much of the latter, and suspicions are rightfully aroused that the reader is getting "potted" Kant, worked up to fit a grand interpretive scheme and not necessarily bearing much relation to the original. The challenge, in other words, is to fashion a book that is informed by the best of recent specialized studies but without so replicating that genre that the accessibility afforded by the broader interpretive interest is forfeited.

This study fits into the third category. In a nutshell, the aim of this book is to show that Kant's ties to nineteenth century post-Hegelian atheism are stronger than typically supposed, and that the consequences of this fact are deeply subversive with respect to the role Kant plays in the "mediating" theologies that have so strongly shaped modern Protestant thought. At one level, then, this book is intended simply to clarify Kant's relationship to the traditions of thought that follow him. More generally, I hope with this account to aid reflection on a series of issues forming a bridge between Kant's philosophical interests and Christian theology at the close of the millennium. In this regard, my intention is to draw attention to the way in which Kant's famous effort to emancipate reason from what he took to be its dogmatic captivity bears on the tense relationship between human autonomy, including intellectual autonomy, and belief in God. The theme of "emancipation" is crucial here, for a crude but useful way of contrasting what we call the "modern" Western world with its medieval predecessor is to describe a series of developments that release humanity from the hold of outmoded traditions and superstitions. The extent to which modern theology finds its own credibility at stake in this emancipation project is tellingly evident in its readiness to engage Marx, Nietzsche, Freud, and others who would claim that theism is incompatible in principle with human life lived to its fullest. In this context, Kant is typically viewed by mediating theologians as a quaint but friendly partner in the project of showing how one can embrace both transcendence and modernity, God and human freedom, the Bible and natural science. While interest in Kant's own moral religion for its own sake was perhaps short-lived or otherwise limited, Kant's broader conceptuality for holding together theism and intellectual respectability would become a highly influential template for later thinkers, especially within European Protestantism, attempting to maintain theism while also embracing the advances in knowledge and sensibility we associate with modernity.

In this regard, my effort to form a bridge between Kant and contemporary theology may create disappointment, for I intend to show that the inner momentum of his philosophy points beyond theism toward a fully emancipated theory of autonomous rationality. Roughly speaking, the part of Kant's thought that makes it "modern" effectively jettisons a traditional religious content, beginning with divine transcendence itself – notwithstanding Kant's own claim regarding the way morality leads inevitably to religion. In so far as this view of Kant may be accurate, we confront the possibility that the animating idea of mediating theology, which includes holding together tradition and modernity in a single outlook, might be fundamentally unstable from the start: as it turns out, the true Kantian template exposes the incoherence involved in retaining the reference to a Christian content once the modern ideal of autonomy is embraced. Obviously, the implications of such a possibility are deeply troublesome for a wide range of theological strategies that often betray their Kantian roots through their efforts to disclose areas of overlap between common human experience and Christian faith as a means of demonstrating that faith involves no sacrifice of the intellect. Such strategies once enjoyed a certain confidence and preeminence in academic settings, due largely to the social and cultural hegemony of their practitioners. Those days appear to be over, and the long-term implications for mediating theologies are as confused as the politics associated with new faculty appointments in leading divinity schools. The enormous impact of theological outlooks arising out of the experience of oppression, together with the persistence – if not actual resurgence – of the kinds of fundamentalisms people like Kant predicted would disappear, constitute odd but telling bookends for mediating theologians of the more traditional sort, who find their influence as diminished as their maneuvering room.

It will of course finally be for the reader to decide if my attempt to untangle Kant's views on autonomy and theism sheds any light on these contemporary difficulties. Basically, I think it will suffice if the reader concludes that we often carry with us an overly simplified picture of Kant's relation to modern theology by not sufficiently gauging the impact of what I call the "principle of immanence" running through his philosophical outlook. As the key aspect of this principle of immanence, Kant's remarkable theory of autonomy is no doubt the most fundamental sign of his standing as a philosopher of modernity. Regrettably, our subsequent discovery that the Kantian ideal of autonomy should itself be such a vexed – perhaps unsalvageable – notion means that there is no neat story to tell here about the "progression" from an outmoded theism to a fully liberated conception of human endeavor. Yet for any theology attempting to confront the intellectual challenges of our day with Kant's help, the damage is done. For at every important turn, beginning with his own moral argument for the existence of God, Kant's theistic commitment turns out upon inspection to be a subordination of divine transcendence to the undeniable prerogatives of autonomous rationality. In such moments, the very idea of the "modern" both comes to expression and is called into question, with discomfiting implications for any theology aspiring to mediate between the Christian tradition and a contemporary sensibility.

This project emerges out of the last chapter of a previous book on Kant, where I posed a question concerning the very different directions in which Kant's influence on modern religious thought might be traced. One of the options linked Kant with Marx rather than with post-Kantian Christian thought. Theologian Schubert Ogden subsequently sent me a lengthy response arguing the compatibility of Kant's position with Christian theology and with the general aims of the liberal mediating outlook. As I reflected on this response – and on Ogden's own major role in the contemporary effort to mediate between faith and culture – I gradually discerned the point of view that animates this book. I am deeply grateful to Professor Ogden for his critical prodding, even as I ultimately find myself subscribing to a different view of Kant and his legacy from the view he holds.

Any study of Kant depends heavily on the research of others. In this instance, I am happy to acknowledge particular indebtedness to the works of Yirmiahu Yovel, Dieter Henrich, Jerome Schneewind, Onora O'Neill, and Richard Velkley. It is in fact altogether fair to say that I have, in effect, adapted and integrated major interpretive themes from their studies of Kant, with a view to their relevance to the issues facing modern mediating theology. In addition, anyone pursuing a serious interest in Kant's philosophy of religion owes a profound intellectual debt to Allen Wood. Over a period of nearly thirty years, Wood's efforts to raise the level of philosophical inquiry into Kant's religious thought have helped to redefine a field of study. Certainly I count myself among those who have benefited enormously from his writings.

There are yet other ways in which this book is a collaborative effort, and I am happy to extend thanks to my New College colleagues, Douglas Langston and Jennifer Herdt, for their interest, encouragement, and astute feedback. Wayne Proudfoot commented helpfully on portions of an early version of this project, while Van Harvey was good enough to read an entire draft and provide valuable suggestions for improvement. A number of friends and colleagues have maintained gentle pressure on my research efforts by treating my extended exile in a Deanship with the studied indifference it doubtless deserved. In any case, warm thanks to – among others – Henry Levinson, Jeff Stout, and Gil Meilaender. The late Malcolm Diamond similarly helped me to maintain my scholarly focus, even as he was dealing with momentous issues of his own.

For a second time I have benefited from the editorial wisdom and oversight of Alex Wright. His commitment to this project over a fairly long period is greatly appreciated, as is his own sound editorial judgment. Other staff members at Blackwell, including Clare Woodford, Alison Dunnett, and Joanna Pyke, have been models of professionalism and efficiency in our collective effort to bring this project to the publication stage. My thanks as well to Margaret Aherne for a meticulous job of copy-editing.

Susannah and Elliott – spouse and son – know at first hand the effects on home life of lengthy writing projects. In their case, my gratitude knows no bounds.

CHAPTER ONE

Kant, Modernity, and Theism

INTRODUCTION

Immanuel Kant's unquestioned influence on Christian theology since 1800 takes many forms. Sometimes we capture this influence in the image of Kant as the "philosopher of Protestantism," an image bringing to mind his success in accommodating in a single vision both the modern scientific outlook and religious faith. By showing that faith and progressive intellectual inquiry do not have to be pitted against one another, Kant provides progressive theologians with a strategy for mediating between Christianity and the powerful new intellectual currents set in motion by the Enlightenment. Such an achievement proves to be particularly timely during a period of increasingly rapid developments in scientific and historical inquiry that are potentially disturbing to Christian faith, such as the effects of biblical criticism or of evolutionary theory.

Consequently, for theologians influenced by the Enlightenment ideal of critical thinking, Kant charts a course making it possible to embrace the intellectual standards of the day while retaining religious conviction. For this reason, the broadly "liberal" tradition of modern theology over the past two centuries has enjoyed in Kant an invaluable example of how to be both modern and religious with no sacrifice of the intellect. Kant thereby helps to invent and make respectable the very idea of "mediating theology," which relies heavily on corridors of intelligibility connecting Christian faith with the surrounding culture. Theologians who may never mention Kant's name are for this reason often deeply indebted to him.

As a result of this legacy, we naturally associate Kant with the effort to sustain theism within an often skeptical world. In what follows, however, I intend to offer quite a different reading of Kant, suggesting that his philosophy enjoys stronger continuity with nineteenth-century atheism than with constructive theology. I hope to make this case partly by distinguishing between a Kantian *conceptuality* for theology and the actual *content* of Kant's philosophy. A Kantian conceptuality or framework, which generates separate compartments for balancing a modern sensibility with biblical faith, is indeed amenable to theological exploitation. By contrast, the specific content of Kant's position leads in an altogether different direction, collapsing the wall of separation between divine transcendence and autonomous rationality by systematically subordinating the former to the latter. Notwithstanding Kant's own personal piety, the effect of his position is that language about God gradually becomes either redundant or a disguised version of language about ourselves, in a manner foreshadowing Ludwig Feuerbach's *Essence of Christianity*. By the reading that I am proposing, Kant in fact becomes a way station between Luther and Marx in the debate over otherworldliness, thereby sharing more in common with Feuerbach than with liberal theologians. The implications of such a view are not simply suggestive regarding Kant's relation to nineteenth-century thought, but potentially subversive with respect to the very idea of mediating theology. For it may be that, once mediation is defined in a way requiring the satisfaction of a modern concept of autonomy, it is doomed to failure. Certainly this is what I am claiming in Kant's own case.

In one sense, of course, Kant's relationship to nineteenth-century atheism has never been a secret. His devastating criticism of speculative metaphysics, natural theology, and the traditional proofs for God's existence in the *Critique of Pure Reason* are a familiar part of the story we tell when accounting for the radical secularity of much modern European thought.[1] Likewise, we typically acknowledge the role Kant's philosophy plays in creating the context surrounding the young Hegel, whose own philosophy stands in readily acknowledged continuity with an emergent atheism. The numerous dualisms characterizing Kant's thought – such as those between theoretical and practical reason, duty and inclination, and phenomena and noumena – clearly compound the sense of crisis already affecting Hegel through his encounter with the French revolution and with the fragmented and politically backward German states.[2] The implication is that Hegel's resolution of his deep and troubling sense of conflict and disunity in thought and culture would not have occurred without the stimulus of Kant's fundamentally dualistic thinking. In Hegel's view, Kant's dualisms signal a philosophical failure of nerve that brings philosophy to an abrupt halt at precisely the moment that serious speculation should begin. This failure helps in turn to inform Hegel's philosophical solution.

At this point, however, Kant's name usually drops out of the story as we describe Hegel's eventual attempt to resolve the problem of bifurcation through a dialectical movement toward an absolute unity. In the course of this progressive movement, conceptual insight supersedes the merely "representative" thinking of religion, implying an overcoming of religion itself by philosophical wisdom. The sense in which Hegel's thought may thus become a powerful impetus toward atheistic thinking is further reinforced by a profound and lingering confusion in his philosophy over the exact relation between transcendence and immanence, God and humanity. This confusion is most evident in Hegel's notoriously obscure concept of *Geist*, in which human consciousness and God's own consciousness commingle in ways that defy clear exposition.[3] In the years following Hegel's sudden death, Feuerbach exploits the confusion by emphasizing humanity's dependence on nature, thereby introducing a materialist corrective to Hegel's supposed otherworldly excess. Taking up this materialist clue, and emboldened by his own aggressive sense of dialectic, Karl Marx subsequently attempts to jettison the last remnants of an otherworldly idealism from a progressive conception of history and human action. Feuerbach's presumed halfway house yields to a more thoroughgoing materialism, with our sense of humanity's dependence on nature now informed by sophisticated economic analysis. Eliminating all references to God in this fresh depiction of human destiny is for Marx not simply a sign of progressive thinking, but a virtual ethical duty. In effect, theism must be discarded for the same reason that otherworldliness itself must be rejected. The perpetuation of either one distracts us from our real problems, as well as from our most authentic possibilities.[4]

At best, Kant is thought to be merely transitional with respect to this story. Presumably, his more genuine connection is with the liberal Protestantism that has so animated theological activity since the Enlightenment and has set the pattern for the accommodation of faith and culture that would be such a high priority for a wide range of Protestant thinkers. A standard reference work on nineteenth-century religious thought suggests that "Kant helped shape the period's religious thought in two ways."

> On the one hand, his critical philosophy – challenging as it did many of the fundamental assumptions of traditional theology and metaphysics – can be seen in retrospect to have set the agenda for the whole of the nineteenth-century, as well as for much of the twentieth. On the other hand, Kant's own attempt to find a new and firmer foundation for religion by grounding it in moral self-consciousness or "practical reason" pointed a way forward which belongs more genuinely to the nineteenth century than to the eighteenth century.[5]

Both sides of this influence are explicitly evident in avowedly Kantian thinkers, such as Albrecht Ritschl in Germany or W. T. Mansel in England. In cases such as these, Kant's suspicion of metaphysics is coupled with a commitment to a privileged zone of moral and religious awareness that is immune to theoretical criticism. The result is a fresh way of appealing to revelation by means of a heightened sense of "value" in human experience that is vulnerable neither to the epistemological difficulties associated with traditional metaphysics, nor to the ongoing results of historical or scientific inquiry. Christian faith thus thrives alongside deep skepticism about metaphysical knowledge. One commentator's description of Ritschl captures in a single image the cumulative impact of the Kantian legacy: "He was the 'characteristic' man of the period, the embodiment of the late nineteenth century's effort to hold together personal faith, scientific history, and ethical demand and so to present a view of Christianity intelligible and persuasive to modern culture."[6]

Closely related to these explicit forms of Kant's influence would be the subtle yet powerful role Kantianism played in the cultural optimism permeating the morally charged "culture Christianity" characterizing much nineteenth- and early twentieth-century Protestant thought. Whenever theologians spoke hopefully about a "kingdom of heaven on earth," Kantian influence was not far removed. Moreover, while the devastating experience of World War I largely discredited the progressive moral element in Kantian theology, Kant's influence would reemerge in implicit yet very powerful forms as the dialectical theologians of the twentieth century devised fresh ways for Christian faith and critical inquiry to co-exist peacefully. The Kantian conceptuality would be particularly crucial in the effort to maintain the integrity of Christian faith in the face of accelerating – and highly problematic – developments in biblical studies, such as form criticism. Once again, faith remained protected, even as the seemingly negative results concerning the Bible's historical accuracy continued to mount. Thus, despite the explicit disavowal of the ethical accent in Kant's own thinking, his broader conceptuality for holding together faith and a modern sensibility would perhaps never be so important.[7] The fact that Kantianism could retain such a powerful hold on theological method despite the elimination of its most characteristic element – namely, the moral element – is itself a significant sign of how deeply the Kantian conceptuality had sent its roots into modern Protestant thought.

As a result, the story we normally tell about modern theological history includes a crossroads, with Kant's influence veering off in the direction of constructive theological efforts to accommodate Christian faith and critical thinking. The other direction leads through Hegel to Feuerbach, Marx, and the abandonment of theism, with Kant's relevance to that part of the story presumed to be limited at best. The assumption is that Kant's natural dialogue partners are those who would sustain theism and seek avenues of continuity between theistic belief and the surrounding culture.

Such an account is a good example of what Alasdair MacIntyre once called "an important half-truth."[8] The part that is true concerns the powerful and undeniable role played by a Kantian conceptuality in the pursuit of progressive theology. Yet the specific content of Kant's philosophy, and the deepest principles emanating from it, suggest that this picture is also seriously misleading. For running powerfully through Kant's philosophy is what might be called a "principle of immanence" that is finally incompatible with theistic belief and which implicitly leaves Kant's own effort at theological mediation in a shambles. The principle of immanence is embedded in Kant's theory of rationality itself, especially in the powerful element of autonomy associated with the Kantian account of rationality. Bluntly stated, autonomous rationality is imperialistic in relation to all that comes before it, including the very idea of God. As a result, despite the way Kant's name quickly drops out of the story about post-Hegelian atheism, he is very much relevant to it. The teleological drive governing rationality's quest for satisfaction is simultaneously a drive to overcome otherworldliness in the portrayal of human destiny. Closely related is the fact that confusion about the true referent of language about God is already well developed in Kant's philosophy and is not simply introduced by Hegel's philosophical complexities. While it may not finally be the case that the secret of Kant's theology is anthropology, as it is for Feuerbach, I believe it can be shown that his own effort to ameliorate the theologically destructive effects of the *Critique of Pure Reason* implicitly makes things worse for traditional theism, not better. To the extent that this suggests his thought breaks through the boundaries set by his own stated intentions, we may be discovering yet another measure of Kant's stature as a great thinker.

My claim is not that Kant should have been saying something other than what he did, but that a theologically reductionistic aspect of his philosophy reveals him to be a more significant precursor to atheistic humanism than is typically supposed, and that the reasons for this connection go well beyond his criticism of the traditional theistic proofs. We have little or no trouble associating Hegel with atheism, even when we simultaneously acknowledge that Hegel can be appropriated by constructive theology as well – on this point as on others, Hegel's obscurity serves him well. I simply want to put forward a similar case regarding

Kant, while simultaneously raising questions about the project of mediating theology that he helped to legitimate. Beginning with chapter 2, I
attempt to argue my case by explaining and examining the several aspects
of what I am calling Kant's principle of immanence. The remainder of
this introductory chapter is devoted to establishing the wider context for
the narrower task of textual analysis and to explaining in preliminary
form what I mean by Kant's principle of immanence.

Two broad themes are particularly relevant to the issue of the wider
context surrounding this inquiry. The first of these is the general problem
of the relationship between human autonomy and theistic belief as it
took shape in the modern era. The specific sense in which *intellectual*
autonomy is at stake is of special relevance to Kant's own case and helps
us to see how his philosophy is part of a much broader historical development bearing on the general issue of "modernity." And second, there is
the important distinction between a Kantian conceptuality for theology
and the content of Kant's own philosophy, a distinction that differenti-
ates the unquestioned influence his thinking has had on modern theology
from the non-theistic direction in which his own philosophical claims are
moving. Clarifying this distinction will in some ways be emblematic of
this book as a whole, for it will suggest that, though there are many ways
in which to be Kantian, being a mediating theologian is probably not the
most authentic way.

THE CONTEXT: FROM DESCARTES TO FEUERBACH

Kant's effort to argue for the compatibility of the natural scientific outlook and religious faith is itself symptomatic of a complex set of historical developments. The very idea of discovering points or zones of
compatibility between faith and common human understanding suggests
the troubling possibility that emerging discoveries and ideas requiring
our respect might also put in question the claims associated with Christian faith. Only such a development could force Christian thinkers to
grapple with the wider culture's standards of belief and assent as a
necessary theological task, rather than simply dismissing them as a sign
of unbelief or heresy. That is, the very idea of theological mediation
presupposes a legitimate claim made on the intellect by forms of critical
inquiry potentially incompatible with Christian faith. The only way to
avoid the mediating task would be to reject critical inquiry itself.

As a result, the mediating sensibility invariably involves a vaguely
agonized balancing act. Balanced on the one side is the traditional
biblical commitment to divine transcendence, with associated claims

concerning God's reality and activity, the meaning of revelation, and the promise of salvation framed in the narrative terms associated with providence. Balanced on the other side, however, is an emerging sense of human autonomy, including an increasingly self-conscious sense of intellectual autonomy that finds puzzling or simply rejects most of the terms in which divine transcendence has traditionally been portrayed. The assumption is that any theology warranting thoughtful consideration by the surrounding culture – in contrast to the intellectual isolation of fundamentalism – must bear the burdens associated with such a balancing act. Kant's own philosophical project, and the consequences emerging from it that I wish to trace, are best appreciated in the context of this effort to reconcile the modern sense of intellectual autonomy with traditional appeals to God's transcendence or "otherness."

John Locke was among the first to understand and confront in sophisticated terms the discrepancy between what we naturally know or believe and what biblical faith would have us believe. When, in 1690, Locke distinguished among truths "according to reason," truths "above reason," and truths "contrary to reason," he both captured the tension between transcendence and intellectual autonomy and helped to inaugurate the now-familiar project of fashioning a spectrum of believability to help sort out the articles of faith.[9] The point of such a spectrum, embedded in Locke's set of distinctions, is that it indicates what a reasonable person could be expected to swallow in the course of leading the Christian life. Driven mainly by the growing emphasis on intellectual autonomy, mediating theology since Locke's time has implicitly involved such spectrums of believability, partly to assure the believer that traditional beliefs that had become especially difficult to reconcile with modern standards of judgment were in fact not intrinsic to Christianity. A good example is the loss of a genuinely theological interest in the miracles of Jesus within those circles of nineteenth-century Protestantism most influenced by the results of the historical criticism of the Bible. For those who had decided that the "Christ of faith" rather than the "Jesus of history" was decisive for the believer, the rapidly accumulating critical results undermining the literal accuracy of scripture simply posed no real threat. But just such an example amply demonstrates that the crucial maneuver in the construction of a spectrum of believability would be to design the spectrum in such a way that the things falling entirely off the end turn out not to be central to Christian faith.

The obvious difficulty facing mediating theologians is that the spectrum of believability changes from age to age, with many of the changes engineered precisely in the name of faith. Thus, in one context authentic Christian faith without belief in the resurrection of Jesus might be literally unthinkable, while, in another setting, such an account of faith may seem entirely natural and appropriate. Similarly, the notion that God is a "father" informs the Christian heritage in long-standing and powerful ways yet is now for some as unthinkable and intellectually repugnant as belief in demons or in a three-tiered universe. At work in these and similar instances is an extraordinary slippage between the form and the content of Christianity, indicative of the tradition's tremendous elasticity. Such examples further suggest that, not only does the spectrum of believability change from one historical period to another, but the criterion of what is central to Christian faith changes as well. The complex interplay between these two sorts of changes is both difficult to chart and the source of the polemical tone of much modern theological debate. The general situation facing the mediating theologian is hardly made simpler by the fact that vastly different spectrums of believability are not only separated by historical eras but may co-exist virtually side-by-side during the same historical period.

One way to summarize this broad development within Western theology is to suggest that the modern sense of intellectual autonomy is the reason that certain religious beliefs that once brought comfort now bring only uneasiness and embarrassment. The source of this troubling uneasiness resides in the way a traditional religious belief may not cohabit peacefully or naturally with countless deep-seated and unquestioned beliefs that are indispensable for one's living and acting in the world. A clear and striking statement of what is at stake here is conveyed by one leading twentieth-century Protestant theologian who remarks that, if "to be a Christian means to say yes where I otherwise say no, or where I do not have the right to say anything at all, then my only choice is to refuse to be a Christian."[10] No small degree of what we might candidly call the bizarrely technical nature of much modern theology is due to the immense difficulty of attending conscientiously to such an insistence on intelligibility while simultaneously retaining the traits of transcendence in the account of Christian faith. Although Nietzsche no doubt over-simplified a complicated matter when he claimed that human freedom is incompatible in principle with religious belief, his basic terms are emblematic of the underlying problem.

Since Kant is himself so closely associated with the development of modern thought, it is hardly by chance that the theme of autonomy looms in such dramatic fashion in his own philosophy. However, with respect to the specific issue of intellectual autonomy, Kant is perhaps best viewed as a particularly special moment in the tradition developing out of the new departures for thought and culture associated with Descartes. This is chiefly because modern debates over autonomy – whether or not a theological issue is at stake – presuppose a capacity for self-relatedness that only becomes fully present in the reflexive style of philosophy articulated by the Cartesian tradition. Very roughly speaking, modern notions of autonomy are typically parasitic on a more general account of how an individual self relates to itself, which then enables modern thinkers to explain what exactly is at stake in discussions of autonomy. Descartes' *cogito* is the chief source of that general account.

In retrospect, we associate the Cartesian starting point with the modern quest for certainty, the securing of philosophical foundations, and the rise to prominence of systematic doubt as a method of intellectual inquiry. Descartes' own mathematical genius would insure the highly abstract, universalizing quality of this undertaking. As Stephen Toulmin reminds us, Cartesianism produces a "devaluation of the oral, the particular, the local, the timely, and the concrete" in the search for what is indubitable.[11] At the same time, the Cartesian *cogito* signals the capacity to be conscious *that* one is conscious, which is in fact the capacity to be related or present to oneself in a special way. To assume the Cartesian starting point is not only to make the subject–object dichotomy decisive for thought and culture, but it is also to guarantee that the thinking self's relationship to *everything* else (beginning with its own body, or *res extensa*) will be mediated through this prior relationship to itself (understood as *res cogitans*).[12] My capacity to be aware that I am aware – to "think" that I am thinking – establishes both the intrinsic importance of self-relatedness and its priority to other-relatedness, in the sense that any possible "other" must first pass through a moment of self-consciousness in order even to be apprehended *as* other. In short, Descartes' position culminates in the claim that the capacity to think that I am thinking precedes and is always presupposed by my capacity to think or to be related to anything else. The entire external world is thereby mediated to me through my own capacity for reflexivity. There is thus something deeply and profoundly privileged about my relationship to myself, over against my relationship to anything "outside" myself.

It is this Cartesian priority of self-relatedness to other-relatedness that sets the terms for our modern notions of autonomy, including the kind of intellectual autonomy at stake in the progressive theologian's uneasiness with an unbelievable religious message. For on the terms of the reflexive Cartesian scheme there can be no autonomy when some "other" (understood now as anything distinct from my own subjectivity) relates to the self in a way that is prior to or disruptive of the self's natural relationship to itself. The very possibility of autonomy lies in just this self-relatedness, defined in terms of the capacity to be conscious that one is conscious. Nothing can justifiably disrupt, override, or undermine this reflexivity, for it is the reflexivity itself that is foundational, just as the certainty that he is thinking is foundational for Descartes in the elaboration of subsequent knowledge-claims. Descartes' own treatment of belief in God *subsequent* to his grounding of certainty in the consciousness of the thinking self exemplifies how everything else, including religious beliefs, will be mediated through this reflexivity in a way that preserves the self's autonomous activity. It is with just this sort of sequence in mind that Helmut Thielicke has spoken of a "Cartesian vestibule" that serves as a kind of anteroom for consciousness, where potential beliefs and knowledge-claims from the "outside" are greeted and regulated in terms of a self-relatedness that is already "inside" and possesses an integrity that cannot be forfeited.[13] It is because of this Cartesian vestibule – because, that is, of the priority of self-relatedness to other-relatedness – that it would even *occur* to the self to find a religious belief puzzling, unbelievable, or repugnant.[14] Freedom of thought has its locus in the process by which what is originally "outside" the self is brought "inside" and made part of the self's intellectual furnishings. Cartesian reflexivity thereby engenders new standards of cognitive assent which, in turn, inform emerging notions of autonomy, beginning with autonomy of thought, knowledge, and belief.[15]

This prioritizing of a moment of self-relatedness in the adjudication of beliefs and knowledge-claims is considerably buttressed by Kant's philosophical achievement. This is because Kant radicalizes the element of reflexivity introduced by the Cartesian theory of consciousness while also constructing a far more robust theory of autonomy than anything Descartes ever proposed. Kant achieves the former through his emphasis on the active nature of the mind, which so enhances the constructive role of consciousness in the production of experience as to put into question our ability ever to know reality as it is in itself. Whereas Descartes' position simply guarantees that our relationship to the external world will be mediated through a moment of self-relatedness, Kant's position turns epistemology almost exclusively into a kind of inventory of what consciousness brings *to* the encounter with the external world. There is no obvious exit outward, through the Cartesian vestibule, to a world not already entangled in the shaping activities of a synthesizing subjectivity. This, after all, is the cardinal lesson conveyed by Kant's central – if unhelpfully named – doctrine of the "transcendental unity of apperception," which is his most technical way of addressing the unified consciousness that undercuts Hume's skepticism about the "self." With this complex doctrine, Kant conveys the general point that the conditions of self-consciousness are coincident with the conditions making possible an objective world. In other words, Kant is attempting to show that the very unity of self-consciousness, permitting the ascription of multiple experiences to a single subject, cannot "even be conceived unless that very unity functions as the point of departure for constituting a world of objects."[16] But if the very notion of an objective world is thus so fully intertwined with subjective activity, access to that world apart from rationality's framing devices is impossible. Consequently, "critical" activity ceases to be viewed on the model of an external discussion between two separate partners – self and world – and becomes internalized instead: in the analysis of thought and knowledge, an inter-subjective conception is for Kant superseded by an inner-subjective one.[17] The very activity of "critique" becomes reflexive, without remainder.

In his own complicated way, Kant thus underscores the fundamental puzzle brought to light by Descartes. The Cartesian insight into the importance of consciousness leaves the European philosophical tradition struggling to find a means of understanding consciousness itself. However, simply to treat consciousness as just one more "object" of which we are aware will obviously not do, since "that which understands objects cannot have the same cognitive status as what it understands."[18] Kant attempts to resolve the problem through his bold claim that the transcendental unity of apperception, exemplified by the ability to posit "I think" in relation to all my representations, is simply a "fact," though certainly not an empirical one.[19] The degree to which this strategy truly settled the matter is readily evident in the extraordinary burst of creative activity associated with the efforts of later German idealists who took this claim as the point of departure for moving beyond Kant.[20] At the same time, what we might call the "self-grounding" quality of Kant's theory of human subjectivity turns out to be highly suggestive of the very themes associated with the problematic status of his conception of God.

As we shall eventually see in considerably more detail, this radicalizing of reflexivity is only reinforced by Kant's understanding of autonomy as the capacity to legislate laws to oneself. "Autonomy of the will," he tells us in his classic definition, "is that property of it by which it is a law to itself independently of any property of objects of volition."[21] Self-legislation compounds the motif of self-relatedness in a sobering way, while simultaneously exemplifying Albert Levi's remark that "the fundamental importance of *rules*" is "the profoundest and most unique intuition of Kant's whole existence."[22] The rule-making associated with the exercise of an authentic autonomy is the parallel in the practical sphere to the rule-making characteristic of Kant's model of an active, spontaneous intellect shaping the world of experience. Moreover, as Kant tries to make clear, self-legislation as the mark of autonomy is synonymous with the rejection of heteronomy, whether in matters of religious belief or in any other domain. When Kant offers his famous definition of "enlightenment" as "daring to know, daring to use one's own reason," he underscores his definition with the admonition to seek release from "self-incurred tutelage." Tutelage, he explains, is the inability to make use of one's intellect "without direction from another." Through an implicit association of "enlightenment" with maturity or adulthood, Kant argues that this tutelage is "self-incurred" when its "cause lies not in the lack of reason but in lack of resolution to use it without direction from another."[23] Kant can of course proceed with full confidence in what is already "inside" the autonomous subject because of the accompanying conviction that every rational being has immediate access, through reason alone, to the moral law. The democratizing of our opportunity for ethical fulfillment goes hand in hand with the reflexive style of philosophy. The theory of subjectivity underwriting Kant's account of autonomy knows no hierarchy of class or station.

Among other things, this link between a conception of autonomy and a quintessentially "modern" approach to subjectivity sheds valuable light on our own current preoccupations with the fate of the "subject." Even a deeply flawed Cartesian–Kantian theory of subjectivity, with its provision of the capacity for self-relatedness, provides the conceptual terms in which an account of human freedom can be rendered.[24] For any number of reasons, the theory may not be convincing, but one can at least understand what is at stake in the associated efforts to describe personal agency or self-determination. Alternatively, various contemporary efforts to deconstruct or otherwise undermine the Cartesian–Kantian view of the subject are often coupled with motifs of coercion and contingency that displace the vocabulary of autonomy.[25] The classically "liberal" political agenda is thus implicitly put in question as the characteristic traits of modern selfhood are demythologized. Consequently, the current suspicion of the subject has momentous consequences for a wide range of social, political, and cultural projects and not simply for theology.[26]

As we know, the intricate set of developments stemming from Descartes would help to define the key terms for the balancing of transcendence and autonomy that became the hallmark of serious religious thought in the modern period. In particular, the motifs of "inside" and "outside" the believer, though not always so starkly depicted, would often shape the discussion in subtle but important ways obviously dependent on the Cartesian turn.[27] In principle, for example, no religious news from the "outside" is necessary if the true test of an authentic religious belief is its natural fit with something "inside" reason or common human consciousness, a tenet crucial for the advent of natural religion. The human reach for transcendence may not need to extend beyond the grasp of natural consciousness itself. Without the emergence of some such human potential, it would be difficult to account for G. E. Lessing's famous remark that "religion is not true because the evangelists and apostles taught it; they taught it because it is true."[28]

In a certain sense, the metaphors of "outer" and "inner" exhaust themselves in the philosophical odyssey of Hegel. Hegel plays out the Cartesian–Kantian tradition of reflexivity by so apotheosizing the ideals of unity and totality as reason's proper aspirations that the conditions of the initial reflexivity are overcome: subject and object become transparent to one another to the point where the need for the very distinction is absorbed by a higher philosophical standpoint.[29] The dialectical movement produced by the conscious apprehension of consciousness in history is indeed the clue to the absolute truth, but the absolute is only reached when the terms of the initial reflexivity are surpassed by conceptual insight. Cartesian–Kantian dualism is a stage on the way to a unifying insight, not the conceptual framework that is requisite for any age. "Good" philosophy, for Hegel, does not allow stand-offs between subject and object, the "inner" and the "outer," or even between God and humanity to dictate our freedom of philosophical and cultural movement. Instead, good philosophy resolves all such stand-offs in terms of a higher perspective. Reason itself discovers its proper vocation in the very unity of thought and reality, a result that solves the problem of dualism in the most ambitious way.[30] In effect, Hegel elects to "overtrump the subjectivism of modern philosophy with a notion of Absolute Knowledge."[31]

But before Hegel had worked all of this out in his mature philosophy, he rummaged through the language of the "inner" and the "outer" in the religious life in a way that is particularly instructive. We see this especially in the young Hegel's struggles with the so-called problem of "positivity." A "positive religion," Hegel wrote in the mid-1790s, contains "concepts and information transcending understanding and reason and requiring feelings and actions which would not come naturally to men."[32] Far from involving truths that enjoy a natural fit with human consciousness, a positive faith "implies a system of religious propositions or truths which must be held independently of our own opinions." In other words, Hegel is here pitting positivity against moral and intellectual autonomy: positive religion is for him associated with "commandments" and "laws," as reflected both in the Hegelian term we translate as "positivity" (*Gesetzheit*) and in Hegel's derivation of the concept from his analysis of Hebrew religion.[33] Consequently, the only way to enforce a positive faith is through an authority external to the believer. Within a positive religious system – based, say, on appeals to miraculous and revelatory historical events that require belief despite their inherent unbelievability – the element of self-legislation central to a Kantian theory of autonomy simply disappears.

In the wake of this Cartesian narrative, it is perhaps not mere Whiggishness that gives Feuerbach's *The Essence of Christianity* the appearance of sheer inevitability.[34] The prioritizing of self-consciousness over God-consciousness that we see in Descartes has now passed through transformations in Kant and Hegel that lead finally to the genuine coincidence of humanity and God. Such, of course, is the force of Feuerbach's famous remark that "the secret of theology is anthropology."[35] With this claim, Feuerbach displays his knack for making accessible an insight left impenetrably obscure in its Hegelian breeding ground. In speaking of God, we have all along in fact been projecting humanity's own highest ideals and best potential onto a heavenly "other." Now that a post-Hegelian humanity has achieved consciousness of this standpoint, we stand under a genuinely moral obligation to recover predicates that are in fact our own. Authentic autonomy begins with recognizing humanity's own transcendence rather than continuing to forfeit our highest potential through a projection process that has seen its appropriate historical moment surpassed by a new era of conceptual insight. Feuerbach grasps that, in a truly profound sense, self-knowledge – which has always been at the center of the Cartesian project – really does constitute self-realization, and that epistemological states can actually trigger ontological change. The complex interplay between the autonomy–transcendence relation on the one hand, and the subject–object dichotomy on the other, has resulted in a deeper humanism toward which traditional belief in God has simply been instrumental. In short, the full realization of humanity as it essentially is turns out to be incompatible with continued belief in divine transcendence.

KANT'S LEGACY: CONCEPTUALITY OR CONTENT?

By focusing on the problem of God in Kant, we stand not only to increase our understanding of his own position, but to shed further light on the much more general issue of autonomy and transcendence that has so haunted modern mediating theology. As I have already indicated, my effort to achieve this depends heavily on distinguishing between a Kantian conceptuality for pursuing the problems of modern theology, and the content of Kant's actual philosophy. The former is of unquestioned influence on modern theology yet, I think, a source of considerable misunderstanding of Kant's own position. As though by default, Kant himself becomes assimilated to and therefore identified with the constructive ends to which his thinking has been put. In fact, however, where his own theological speculations are not utterly subordinated to a prior concern for autonomous rationality, they are remarkably thin and can be difficult to specify.[36] While the bulk of this book will be devoted to making this case, it will prove helpful if this introductory chapter offers a fuller explanation of what is commonly meant by a Kantian conceptuality for theology. The transition to the discussion of Kant's actual views will follow in the form of a brief overview of four features of Kant's principle of immanence.

Several issues come immediately to mind when we speak of the main forms Kant's legacy takes within modern theology. Most familiar, no doubt, is Kant's powerful criticism of speculative metaphysics that traditionally served as a supporting context for theology and which was highly influential in his own day. Generated by his notion of a "critique" of reason's powers, and exemplified by his criticism of the traditional proofs for the existence of God, this aspect of Kant's philosophy effectively eliminates our ability to make cognitive claims regarding anything transcending the conditions of human experience. Since "existence" is itself a pure concept or category of the understanding, its application apart from possible objects of experience is fundamentally problematic. The results for efforts to speak of "God's existence" are obviously devastating. While Kant is of course quick to locate flaws in the several arguments themselves, it "is not the steps in the various proofs but the titular concept 'existence of God' which ensnares speculative theology in dialectical illusion." In other words, Kant's "most radical claim in connection with natural theology is not that the existence of God cannot be proved theoretically but that theoretical reason cannot even legitimately *ask* whether or not God exists."[37]

Those who have felt the power of Kant's criticism of speculative metaphysics have, ever since, sought ways to maintain a cognitive element for theology without falling prey to Kant's attack. Alternatively, those attempting to promote a metaphysical context for doing theology, such as process theologians influenced by Whitehead or Roman Catholics working out of the Thomistic tradition, often take pains to establish their non-Kantian credentials or otherwise argue that Kantianism moves in an illicit, subjectivist direction that can be countered with superior philosophical wisdom. The implicit message is that Kant's impact is such that he deserves a reply. Even Karl Barth, operating with his own very different concerns in mind and eschewing both Kantian subjectivism and a metaphysical prop for theology, acknowledges that Kant "stands by himself" as "a stumbling-block and rock of offense . . . a prophet whom almost everyone, even among those who wanted to go forward with him, had first to re-interpret before they could do anything with him."[38] In their own way, these expressions of concern for Kant's impact on the prospects for theology are as telling as the strategies of those theologians who avoid metaphysics for openly Kantian reasons. We thus have a kind of Kantian variation on the plausible notion that "existing analyses of the relationship between subjectivity and modernity accept the Cartesian model of self-consciousness as the dominant one even where they argue against it...."[39] Kant remains a dominant force among his opponents to the extent that they feel the need to repudiate him.

A second and similarly important broad theme connecting Kant with modern theology stems from his epistemology or, more specifically, from his tendency to think dualistically when charting out the competence of human reason. In his effort to accommodate both a deterministic Newtonian science, on the one hand, and human freedom, on the other, Kant develops the philosophical habit of generating dualisms that help him assert the rightful claims of both. Thus, although the world of appearances operates according to strict Newtonian regularity, the world as it is in itself – which we can posit but never know – provides the sheer logical possibility for human freedom. Pairing this dualism between phenomena and noumena with the dualism of theoretical and practical reason, Kant can then "postulate" on practical grounds what theoretical reason can never claim to know. Moreover, he can do so with the full confidence that at least the sheer logical possibility of what has been postulated has been established at the outset. One might say – very crudely – that by the time Kant gets around to postulating the reality of immortality and God in the second *Critique*, they still have a "place" to enjoy their metaphysical reality, because the first *Critique* has not made their reality unthinkable, only our theoretical knowledge of them impossible.

This dualistic strategy has been immensely influential within post-Kantian theology for reasons similar to those influencing Kant himself. In particular, this dualistic epistemology makes it possible to embrace the most recent advances in human inquiry, exemplified by the natural sciences and by historical criticism, without serious concern for the potentially corrosive effects such inquiry might have on religious faith. Highly influential works of mid-century, such as H. Richard Niebuhr's *The Meaning of Revelation* or Rudolf Bultmann's "New Testament and Mythology," are impossible to discuss without detailed consideration of their dualistic Kantian epistemology.[40] Kantian epistemology effectively compartmentalizes our thinking, with the "fires" ignited by scholarly criticism, as Bultmann referred to them,[41] burning freely in the phenomenal zone, leaving faith's own noumenal zone unscathed. Likewise, faith itself is construed as a variation on practical reason, different in kind from the fundamentally instrumental nature of theoretical reason, thus insuring two modes of human apprehension appropriate to two different zones, such as Niebuhr's "internal" and "external" history.[42] Faith turns out to be something more like "doing" than "believing," leaving it less vulnerable to the results of scholarly inquiry, including the effects the study of "external" history might have on the integrity of the Christian community's experience of its own "internal" history.

However diverse the broadly liberal mediating tradition in modern theology has been, it has been fundamentally Kantian in its tendency to compartmentalize in this way when confronting, say, the implications of natural science for our understanding of revelation, or when relating the results of historical criticism to biblical faith. In an important sense, Paul Tillich's pronouncement of the "great achievement" of Protestant thought in boldly undertaking the free and unhindered criticism of its own scriptural sources[43] is a camouflaged ode to Kant and to the protective shield his influence offers. In effect, Kantian epistemology made the theological world safe for the reconciliation of tradition and modernity. This aspect of the Kantian legacy provides what amounts to an epistemological "fire wall" enabling theologians eager for reconciliation with the modern world to embrace scholarly results and cognitive advances apparently antithetical to Christian faith. Such a cross-over connection between theological method and an often skeptical academic culture underscores the complexity of Kant's influence.

A third broad theme emerging out of Kant's legacy concerns the way he radicalizes the Cartesian turn to the self, redirecting us from what is "outside" the believer to what is "inside." As we have already seen, by maximizing philosophical attention on the structure of reason itself, Kant elevates the original Cartesian interest in human subjectivity to a new level. With Kant, philosophy's concern for the "conditions of the possibility" of experience yields a preoccupation with human interiority as the locus of interest and, indeed, the very source of the intelligibility of an otherwise formless universe. The individual self – subjectivity, as codified in Kant's notion of the unity of apperception – "grounds" the world and, in doing so, assumes both an ontological and epistemological privilege in the philosophical ordering of things. For Kant himself, the truly crucial dimension of the emphasis on subjectivity emerges only as he refines his theory of autonomy, a refinement involving our ability to impose ends on ourselves that are not imposed on us by nature – authentic selfhood is a kind of antidote to nature's arbitrariness.[44] The capacity to respect a universalizing moral law that is intimately connected with this special conception of autonomy gives a unique dignity to this interior dimension of the self, underwriting Kant's remarkable claim that the moral law "infinitely raises my worth" at the very moment I recognize my otherwise puny status in the face of a limitless and indifferent universe.[45] Such a concept of human dignity is utterly impervious to theoretical inquiry. When Kant says that the only thing that can be said to be good without qualification is a good will,[46] he is simultaneously remarking on the supremacy of what is hidden from public view when assessing the central values of life. Within a philosophical perspective such as this, the characteristically modern break with the natural world in the construction of human meaning becomes complete. The "disenchantment" of the external world is correlative with an infusion of actualizing possibilities in the inner self.

The Kantian emphasis on the integrity of the hidden, inner recesses of the moral/religious self has enjoyed countless variations in religious thought since Kant's time. Somewhat ironically, this inner zone of integrity has been more evident in non-moral forms than in the expressly moral form fashioned by Kant himself, perhaps suggesting another sense in which a Kantian "conceptuality" as opposed to Kantian content has flourished more successfully since Kant's own time. Exemplified perhaps by Kierkegaard's idea of the "knight of faith" – whose status as such could never be detected from the "outside"[47] – Kant's influence is evident in the motifs of "authenticity," "ultimacy," the "whole self," and "personal decision" that typically signal a linkage between faith and "true selfhood." Even as post-Kantian theologians drop Kant's own interest in the specifically moral aspect of authentic religious faith, they maintain the telltale Kantian appeal to the inviolable interior of the self as the zone of religious action. Moreover, as in the case of Kierkegaard's knight of faith, the fact that there can be no theoretical penetration of this interior religious self from the outside suggests the snug fit between the third of these broad Kantian themes and the second: a dualistic epistemology is the natural counterpart to a radicalized conception of human interiority, or of a theory of selfhood immune to theoretical scrutiny and control.

In partnership with the dualistic epistemology, this Kantian emphasis on the interior self has been the source of considerable controversy even as it has been an aid to theological reflection. For example, the significance of the religious self's interior or hidden dimension can become so inflated and all-embracing that the reference to some transcendent "other" is potentially lost from view. In such cases, the perfectly understandable modern search for meaningful "non-objectifying" language about God gradually substitutes for all efforts to speak of God apart from ourselves. Bultmann's existentialist theology perhaps exemplified this tendency, generating in some quarters a deep suspicion about its ability to speak of God at all in the course of reinterpreting Christian faith as a kind of life stance.[48] Similarly, Kantian interiority is coupled in potentially disturbing ways with the self's apparent inability ever to alter the "real" or noumenal world, since the rules enforcing the dualistic perspective operate from the "inside out" as well as from the "outside in." The successful concealment of the authentic self from prying, theoretical eyes betrays its high cost in the impossibility of ever accounting for how free action might relate intelligibly to the wider human condition. Freedom has been "exiled into interiority" and evidently cannot shape the world around it,[49] raising profound questions for Christian ethics. The perennial difficulty of explaining how Kierkegaard's knight of faith relates to his wider community – or even recognizes other knights of faith – exemplifies the problem without by any means exhausting the possible examples. Criticisms by liberation theologians and others of the "privatizing" of faith in much modern theology often turn out to be covert criticisms of Kant and his influence, even when his name goes unmentioned. In their own odd way, then, even problems such as these reflect the penetration of Kantian themes into significant segments of modern Christian thought.

KANT'S PRINCIPLE OF IMMANENCE

In summarizing this general overview, we might say that Kantianism makes the world safe for Christian faith by compartmentalizing faith and theoretical inquiry in a manner that is respectful of both. Such, after all, is the chief aim of mediating theology. Yet two things are worth pointing out in connection with this legacy. Particularly striking is the absence of any real impact on constructive ideas or commentary about God as a result of Kant's influence. Indeed, with the exception of the basically negative implications of Kant's criticism of the traditional proofs for the existence of God, the issue of God hardly arises, even as we can think up numerous cases in which Kant's influence is otherwise evident. Kant provides a framework for thinking theistically while also embracing the modern world, but such a contribution is different in kind from providing a way of thinking about God as such. In fact, it can be difficult to elaborate at much length on Kant's *actual* view of God as accounted for in his moral argument in the *Critique of Practical Reason* and its reformulation in the third *Critique*, as opposed to his views concerning proofs for the existence of God or concerning the God of his received Leibnizian–Wolffian tradition.

This point in turn suggests the significant difference between a Kantian conceptuality and the content of Kant's own position. Those adopting the conceptuality assume that Kant has fashioned a safe region for faith by demonstrating its independence from theoretical and speculative inquiry. Faith is not tied to theoretical claims that could in principle be refuted, but flourishes instead in a personal moment of consciousness or a special form of apprehension. Yet it is precisely Kant's own way of rendering this personal feature of faith that turns out to be theologically subversive, for his account is driven by a radical conception of autonomous rationality that undermines the integrity of theological statements. In contrast to the endless adaptability of a Kantian conceptuality for theological purposes, Kant's own thinking is thus moving in a non-theistic direction. This is the point so easily missed when his name is invoked on behalf of the reconciliation of theism and modern culture. To be sure, there is a long-standing tradition of philosophical criticism that maintains the possibility of moral action on Kantian grounds *without* belief in God, but this criticism is typically pressed as though Kant's project simply needs certain argumentative refinements in order to achieve greater consistency.[50] But my interest is not in rehabilitating Kant's arguments to give consistency to his moral philosophy; rather, my interest is in framing the deeper historical point regarding the innermost tendencies of Kant's thinking that place him in continuity with non-theological resolutions of the modern tension between intellectual autonomy and theism. Once again, I believe that Kant's way of handling the specific issue of divine transcendence leads, finally, to the same kind of transposition of references to God to references to ourselves that we associate with Feuerbach. At a minimum, we surely possess too thin an account of Kant as precursor to this particular solution to the problem of intellectual autonomy in the modern world, while, at a maximum, we may miss the connection altogether.

Let me suggest that the Kant most evident in our re-telling of modern theological history is the "mainstream" Kant, who provides the conceptuality for theology that has proven to be so useful and flexible. This Kant leaves theologians suspicious about relying on metaphysics, happy to engage in double-entry bookkeeping when discussing faith and historical criticism, and eager to promote arresting conceptions of the hidden, interior self when explaining the "ultimacy," "resolve," or new "self-understanding" associated with Christian faith. But shadowing this familiar mainstream Kant is a "subversive" Kant whose influence resides in what I have called his principle of immanence. The force of this principle is to appropriate to the immanent domain of rational activity those prerogatives, traits, and characteristics traditionally associated with divine transcendence – roughly speaking, the same transposition process we associate with *The Essence of Christianity*. This dynamic is what I mainly have in mind when I refer to the "innermost tendencies" or "direction" of Kant's philosophy. His is not a moral theism struggling to reconcile itself with modernity and a new-found conception of human autonomy, but a radical vision of autonomy coping, at times rather clumsily, with the remnants of an inherited tradition and received vocabulary.[51] The principle of immanence reveals this emphasis and is itself disclosed in at least four aspects, all of which touch on major themes in Kant's philosophy.

There is, first of all, a subtle but significant diminishing of theistic content in the course of Kant's own moral argument for the existence of God. Designed to rectify the theological difficulties associated with the speculative metaphysics of the day, Kant's moral argument in fact induces what we might characterize as "theistic shrinkage," generated by the requirements of practical reason. The God of the moral argument is chiefly an instrument in the realization of a rational goal and little more, notwithstanding Kant's rather self-conscious effort to argue that God is also the metaphysical "ground" of the highest good itself. Certainly Kant's argument does not account for the full roster of divine predicates at stake in the proofs that Kant has previously destroyed, and there is no obvious way Kant can reintroduce all of these predicates without trading on the sheer "concept" of God in the very manner he criticizes in his arguments against the school metaphysicians. The presumed recovery operation constituting the moral argument is thus less than it appears to be, as immanent rational activity intrudes on traditional zones of divine privilege.

Moreover, commentary on Kant typically focuses on the way practical reason has a compelling "interest" that overrides the theologically negative results of theoretical reason's best efforts. What goes largely unnoticed is the way practical reason's interest becomes so paramount in the course of the argument that it dictates even the terms of divine willing. The moral argument may be designed to recover the positive cognitive relationship with God jeopardized by the *Critique of Pure Reason*, but the result is the subordination of the divine will to the dictates of reason's own conception of, and interest in, the highest good. The rational necessity that God proportion happiness and virtue in a just way is simultaneously the disclosure that God apparently has no free decision to make in the salvation process, a possibility that parallels in striking ways the more familiar point that Kant's God could never "break" the moral law. As we shall see in the following chapter, Kant's efforts to suggest why such insights are not a diminution of divine transcendence either beg the central question at stake or increase the suspicion that an imperialistic, universalizing rational principle has displaced the divine prerogative. Indeed, we might loosely say that the terms of Kant's argument create a subtle but dramatic transfer of the Lutheran image of the "bondage of the will" from humanity to God, a particularly telling alteration in "index symbols"[52] within a cultural setting that is identified in part by a pathway from Luther to Marx. Such a shift in perspective follows inexorably from an indisputable feature of Kant's moral argument: instead of moving from the reality of God to judgments about human freedom, the argument must account for God and the divine will subsequent to our apodictic certainty of the reality of human freedom. Kant's position never really modifies the important reversals that are at stake in this ordering of thought.

In this initial aspect, then, the principle of immanence becomes apparent in the very terms by which Kant tries to overcome the negative results of his own criticism of the traditional, metaphysically based theology associated with the school of Leibniz and Wolff. An even more powerful indicator of the principle of immanence is conveyed by Kant's conception of autonomy in terms of the will's ability to provide itself with ends not provided by nature. In response to a set of problems made clear to him largely through the influence of Rousseau, Kant promotes the unhooking of the rational will from all external constraints, reconceiving it as a capacity to generate its *own* constraints. Something such as this image of self-invention is what is central to Kant's definition of autonomy as the will's capacity to legislate laws to itself. Constraints that inform us morally are no longer associated with a preconceived arena of metaphysical or theological truths, much less biblical claims. Instead, Kant defines the will's constraints in the form of a universalizability principle that reflects the will's own structure, hinting at the kind of "transparency" between self and ethical requirement that so mesmerized the young Hegel.

As potential sources of moral motivation, divine commands of the traditional sort thus end up in the same dustbin of heteronomy as do sensuous inclinations. The emerging specter of human autonomy's self-sufficiency is evident in the Kantian insight that "religion is the recognition of all duties *as* divine commands":[53] they do not become "duties" because they are divinely commanded; rather, we understand them *as* divine only subsequent to recognizing them as moral duties, reflective of the good will's own structure. In this aspect, Kant's principle of immanence effectively domesticates the divine will in terms of a prior rational principle that is not only immediately accessible to rational beings, but self-given as well. The characteristically modern note of human independence from an outmoded conception of divine sovereignty or metaphysical necessity is particularly evident in the fully rendered Kantian conception of autonomy, which is compatible with God's "holiness" only because the latter has been reconstrued in Kant's universalizing terms. On this view, the very idea of a divine command as the source of moral obligation suffers the potential irrelevance spawned by redundancy.

A third indicator of Kant's principle of immanence is more subtle but similarly powerful. This indicator resides in the metaphors Kant attaches to reason's activities and in the argumentatively important ways he exploits these metaphors. In effect, by devising what Yirmiahu Yovel has provocatively called an "erotic glossary of reason" involving not only "ends," "tasks," and "interests" but also "needs," "satisfactions," "aspirations," "strivings," and "affection,"[54] Kant accelerates through metaphor the transfer of divine prerogatives to the immanent zone of rational activity. Reason for Kant is both active and restless, exhibiting the momentum that presses irresistibly toward the conclusion of a logical progression. Its activity manifests itself in totalizing tendencies that, so often in the past, have led to dialectical impasse and transcendent illusion: reason is forever reaching for an absolute closure that it can never truly grasp. Kantian metaphors of "activity," "interest," and "need" are not simply striking in themselves but drive much of the argumentation in Kant's philosophy. For at decisive turns in Kant's thinking, the argument moves forward thanks to explicit appeals to a need or interest of reason requiring satisfaction. These instances include such key issues as the generation of the concept of the highest good, the depiction of the primacy of reason in its practical aspect over its theoretical aspect, and the demonstration of divine existence through the necessity to proportion happiness to virtue. Hardly incidental to the critical philosophy, themes such as these suggest that the transfer of transcendence to the immanent human domain is itself an activity implicitly structuring Kant's thinking, as it is structuring reason itself. Indeed, the aspects of the principle of immanence identifiable in the details of the moral argument and in Kant's aggressive theory of autonomy are considerably reinforced here by the virtual personification of reason. In assuming the very characteristics of divine agency, reason becomes providential in both its restless quest for the satisfaction of its aim and the definition of the aim itself. In light of the effects of the other aspects of the principle of immanence, this personification of reason occurs against the backdrop of the increasingly faceless nature of God, for God now has less and less to do.

Reason's final aim coincides with autonomy's vocation. Autonomy achieves its ultimate vocation in the establishment of the ethical commonwealth, an ideal moral community in which all moral agents treat one another as ends in themselves and never as a means only. As the fourth indicator of Kant's principle of immanence, the ethical commonwealth represents a fuller, more thematized version of what Kant introduced as the "kingdom" or "realm of ends" in the *Foundations of the Metaphysics of Morals*. In the movement from this initial point of departure to Kant's account of the ethical commonwealth in *Religion within the Limits of Reason Alone*, we can discern a significant tendency toward the worldly realization of idealized ethical life. Shadowing this trajectory is an increasingly articulate Kantian vision of the political ends of reason's expression, which is perhaps another way of drawing attention to the powerful secularizing tendencies in Kant's thought. This worldly and political direction in Kant's thinking is in turn intimately connected with his metaphors of reason's activity, for it is the depiction of reason as "active" that makes reflection on the ethical goal unavoidable.

There is in fact a particularly telling progression in Kant's thought from the postulate of the immortality of the soul to the ethical commonwealth, displaying his principle of immanence in a clear and succinct way. The rationale generating both the postulate and the idea of the ethical commonwealth is reason's demand for the perfection of virtue, but the terms and implications of these two loci of moral perfection are so different as to suggest important developments within Kant's overall authorship between the second *Critique* and the *Religion*. At a minimum, any effort to reconcile these two issues in a coherent way requires something like one commentator's suggestion of a narrower view of the highest good, "which focuses on the relation of the highest good to the moral law and the good will," and a wider view which emphasizes "the social and historical nature of this good and the role of culture in its possible realization."[55] Interpretive difficulties aside, what is striking in a broader sense is the way the movement from the postulate of the immortality of the soul to the later comments on the ethical commonwealth track almost exactly the movements revealed by the other aspects of the principle of immanence. As this change in venue for humanity's moral striving redirects our attention from the noumenal world of a projected afterlife to the actual historical circumstances of rational beings aiding in one another's moral progress, we truly are shifted from heaven to earth.

Just as significant is the fact that the altered argumentative terms introduced by this change in venue put into question Kant's ability to postulate the existence of God. By the terms of the moral argument, God's reality is established only subsequent to Kant's depiction of the requirements set by the postulate of immortality. By itself, the postulate of immortality necessitates a noumenal agency with the capacity to proportion happiness to virtue, but it does not fill this rational requirement. This unmet need of reason thus drives the subsequent postulation of God's existence. But if the original rationale for the postulate of immortality is now taken over by the ethical commonwealth, Kant's ability to rebound from the theologically negative consequences of the *Critique of Pure Reason* would appear to be seriously compromised. While Kant retains references to God as a kind of moral partner in the creation of the ethical commonwealth, the shift of interest from the noumenal realm of immortality to the historical realm of social and political practice certainly compounds the problems for a conception of divine transcendence already exposed by the other aspects of the principle of immanence.

Taken together, these four indicators of Kant's principle of immanence are suggestive in themselves and form the basis of a powerful case for deepening our standard account of Kant's relationship to nineteenth-century atheism as well as our understanding of his relation to modern mediating theologies. The aim of the chapters that follow is to shed light on these connected interpretive lessons through more detailed examination of each of these aspects of immanence, framing moments of analysis of Kantian texts within the broader context provided by the interplay between an autonomous rationality and divine transcendence. Again, one of my main points regarding Kant's own position is that the topics and themes suggestive of a principle of immanence – such as his definition of autonomy – are clearly central to his philosophical vision, rather than marginal or accidental features that leave the core of his position untouched. At stake, finally, is an expansion of Yovel's claim that the "critique of reason is also, for Kant, a declaration of its independence. Despite its finitude – and also because of it – human reason takes over the role of God as legislator for both nature and morality."[56] By viewing and developing this claim in the context of the broader interests of modern mediating theologies, we stand to gain insight into a range of issues going well beyond the narrow boundaries of Kant interpretation.

Finally, it is worth emphasizing that the themes connected with the principle of immanence hint at an inner direction of Kant's philosophy that is systematic and not merely incidental in nature. This point is important, because the integrated collusion of the several aspects of the principle of immanence stands in a telling contrast to some of the ways that Kant continues to refer to God following the publication of the first edition of the *Critique of Pure Reason* in 1781. Often, these references fit together only awkwardly with the main principles governing his thinking. Obviously, the relationship between God and the self-legislating quality of the free will is a case in point, which is perhaps a specific instance of the more generic problem of the exact relation between God and the moral law. Perhaps surprisingly, we thus find Kant deeply involved in a debate concerning free will and divine power that has its roots many centuries in the past. We confront similar difficulties in Kant's awkward appeal to "divine aid" in our recovery from radical evil in *Religion within the Limits of Reason Alone*.[57] Although reliance on something very much like divine grace fits quite naturally with the broader Protestant tradition out of which Kant emerges, it is not easily reconciled with the characteristic Kantian principle that:

> [m]an *himself* must make or have made himself into whatever, in a moral sense, whether good or evil, he is or is to become. Either condition must be an effect of his free choice; for otherwise he could not be held responsible for it and could therefore be *morally* neither good nor evil.[58]

While it may be possible in principle to integrate such a claim with an appeal to divine grace – as Kant, in fact, attempts to do – the result can only appear strained rather than systematic. As we shall see in chapter 5, Kant compounds this problem in his account of God's relation to the collective mode of moral agency involved in the formation of the ethical commonwealth. The awkwardness of his attempt creates philosophically odd results. By contrast, there is no awkwardness whatsoever in the snug fit between the principle of immanence and the governing features of Kant's overall viewpoint. Indeed, the role that Kant's concept of autonomy plays in this investigation suggests that the principle of immanence *is* the governing feature of his overall viewpoint. In thus discovering an emerging and highly systematic transfer of divine prerogatives and predicates into the sphere of rational activity, we perhaps find that the inner momentum of Kant's deepest philosophical claims is gradually overriding his inbred pietism. A thread of continuity is easier to trace in things Kant himself may not have been prepared to admit. Shifting metaphors, we might say that, with his aggressive account of autonomous rationality, Kant has cut off the head of the traditionally religious body, yet the corpse continues for a time to twitch and move, as though life is still in it when it is not. Only the developments of the succeeding century could show this to be the case, yet by then, the Kantian conceptuality for constructive theology had picked up sufficient steam to confuse us about Kant's true legacy.

Overall, then, my chief aim in what follows is not to uncover flaws or gaps in Kant's argumentation but to build historical perspective. If, as Jerome Schneewind has recently and convincingly argued, something genuinely "new" regarding humanity's standing in the world comes to expression in Kant's theory of autonomy even as he maintains much of the vocabulary of his own biblical heritage,[59] flaws in argumentation would seem to be the least of Kant's problems. For here we perhaps see late Enlightenment Europe at odds with itself, as its great capstone thinker attempts to chart out the destiny of autonomous rationality while still saddled with the motifs and deep structure of a heritage incapable in principle of grasping what it would mean for the will to legislate its own ends. As the ironic reversal of the theme of the "bondage of the will" suggests, we may in large part be discovering what it means to think of Kant as a way station between Luther and Marx. If such is the case, the specifically national idiom that is at work here is no hindrance to wider interpretive lessons, any more than the vexed fate of Kant's ideal of autonomy discredits his effort. In short, this thinker who so readily brings to mind the very idea of "modernity" – with his trust in science, his emphasis on the human subject, and his preoccupation with freedom – may be particularly well placed to help us gain needed perspective on our own theological and cultural confusions.

CHAPTER TWO

Kant's Moral Argument: Diminishing the Divine

KANT AND THE TRADITIONAL PROOFS

Beginning with the publication of the *Critique of Pure Reason* in 1781, Kant's approach to philosophical proofs for the existence of God appears to pass through two strikingly different moments. The initial moment is fundamentally negative in character, consisting of an extended polemic against the view, dominant in Kant's day, that we are on comfortable cognitive terms with God in ways that are exemplified by the traditional proofs for God's existence. In many respects, in fact, Kant's famous dismantling of the ontological, cosmological, and teleological proofs for the existence of God in the first *Critique* has the appearance of an opening salvo in an atheist manifesto. Despite the element of hyperbole, Heine's depiction of this Kant as a kind of "theological Robespierre" – methodically and ruthlessly slicing his way through all forms of speculation that presume to offer knowledge of the transcendent – accurately conveys the destructive implications of this moment in Kant's reasoning about God.[1] Certainly the position developed in the *Critique* is highly subversive in relation to the reigning philosophical systems of the day, which tended to embrace something like a continuum connecting scientific, metaphysical, and theological knowledge in a presumably rational and secure way.[2] Although the *Critique of Pure Reason* also offers a preliminary and skeletal version of moral theology, the chief theological impact is to sabotage the interconnections forming this continuum.

As we know, however, this initially negative moment is followed in the *Critique of Practical Reason* by an apparent recovery. This recovery takes the form of Kant's moral argument for the existence of God, sometimes referred to as the "moral proof." Kant himself remarks that the "moral proof is not in any sense a newly discovered argument, but at the most only an old one in a new form."[3] Certainly one thing that is new about Kant's moral argument is its emphasis on the practical, or self-involving, character of theistic belief. While God cannot be said to be an object of theoretical knowledge in the form embraced by the school metaphysicians associated especially with Leibniz and Wolff, it is altogether legitimate to "postulate" the existence of God as rationally necessitated by the indubitable experience of moral obligation. Along with freedom of the will and the immortality of the soul, the existence of God is an indispensable component in a delicately balanced rational mosaic emanating from sustained reflection on the idea of the "highest good." Indeed, the neat fit among the postulates of God, freedom, and immortality is for Kant suggestive of the rational structure of the moral life itself. Despite the uncertainties regarding our cognitive access to God produced by the first *Critique*, the Kant of the second *Critique* is adamant that rational faith provides objective certainty of God's existence, and not simply subjective satisfaction.[4] This claim, in turn, is dependent on Kant's more foundational claim that practical reason ultimately enjoys priority over reason in its theoretical employment, thus trumping on practical grounds the apparently negative theological results of the first *Critique*. Heine's commentary is once again apt, for his famous joke about Kant needing to restore a proof of God's existence for the sake of his troubled aging servant at least conveys the element of reversal in Kant's thinking.[5]

In rough terms, this general picture captures the relationship between the first two *Critiques*, at least with respect to the specific issue of Kant's attitude toward our ability to reason our way to divine existence. However, this typical way of tracing the shift in perspective between the *Critique of Pure Reason* and the *Critique of Practical Reason* tends to mask a deeply subversive element in Kant's thinking. Specifically, the motif of a positive recovery from the theological damage of the first *Critique* overlooks the fact that Kant's moral argument leaves God diminished in ways that are considerably more damaging than anything left behind by the earlier work. Not only do the actual terms of the moral argument account for a reduced roster of divine attributes, but the argument also marks the introduction of severe limitations on God's will that seriously compromise the very idea of divine transcendence. In important respects, natural theology is worse and not better off subsequent to Kant's moral argument.

The aim of this chapter is to clarify and amplify these interpretive claims and to set the stage for a more detailed account of Kant's view of autonomy and of rationality itself.

The moral argument emerges not simply within the context established by the stringent metaphysical and theological results of the *Critique of Pure Reason*, but in the context as well of nearly three decades of efforts by Kant to address the problem of God, including the issue of theodicy. In short, Kant's thinking about the issue of theistic proofs did not appear out of a vacuum at the time of the writing of the first *Critique*. Naturally, his earlier writings touching on theological matters were not informed by the transcendental turn we associate with Kant's philosophy from 1781 on, but these works sometimes betray tendencies that illuminate or clarify the later and more famous writings. A brief overview of Kant's forays into natural theology prior to 1781 will perhaps make this point clear and provide a frame of reference for an account of the moral argument itself.

As early as 1755, in a lengthy essay entitled "Universal Natural History and Theory of the Heavens," Kant discusses the existence of God in relation to the interplay between Newtonian mechanics and the evidence of design and order in the physical world.[6] This anticipation of important themes that would be central to his later work is repeated in the so-called *Beweisgrund* of 1763, which has been translated as *The One Possible Basis for a Demonstration of the Existence of God* and is an object of continuing interest among Kant scholars.[7] The importance of this work at one level is suggested by the fact that Kant himself believed that a respectful review of it by Moses Mendelssohn is what first brought his philosophical efforts to public attention and helped propel him toward the development of a full system.[8] The *Beweisgrund* can perhaps be viewed as a way station between Descartes' version of the ontological proof and Kant's subsequent criticism of the proof in the first *Critique*. Certainly the work is striking for the way it foreshadows the *Critique*'s claim that existence is not a predicate, an insight that both dooms any effort to establish the existence of "the most perfect being" simply through an analysis of terms and is a key component in Kant's eventual dismantling of the pretensions of natural theology.[9] Instructive here, perhaps, is the growing tendency toward softening the traditionally hard line between Kant's pre-critical and critical writings that is evident especially in the recent work of leading commentators on Kant's moral philosophy.[10] Interestingly, Kant agreed to the publication of new editions of the *Beweisgrund* in 1770 and, more significantly, in 1790 as well, suggesting that he did not view its standpoint to be radically discontinuous with his later thought.[11]

By electing to write an "Inquiry Concerning the Distinctness of the Principles of Natural Theology and Morality" in response to the Berlin Academy's essay competition of 1763, Kant continued his rise from

KANT'S MORAL ARGUMENT 31

obscurity through the vehicle of theological topics.[12] This so-called "Prize Essay" was published the following year, though it came in second in the competition to an essay submitted by, of all people, Kant's friend Mendelssohn. The Prize Essay is better known for its flirtation with Francis Hutcheson's moral sense theory of ethics – and the light thereby shed on the development of Kant's ethical theory – than for any groundbreaking insights into natural theology itself.[13] Nonetheless, Kant's effort underscores both the consistency and the persistence of his theological interests. Rather oddly, in light of his growing reputation as a serious thinker, Kant seemingly jeopardized his philosophical stature with the publication in 1766 of the work translated as *Dreams of a Spirit-Seer, Elucidated by Dreams of Metaphysics*, a work that, Ernst Cassirer tells us, "in its literary form and its stylistic dress alike upset all the traditions of the literature of scientific philosophy."[14] Cassirer has partly in mind the satirical, tongue-in-cheek manner of the work, and partly the work's engagement with the odd spiritualism and psychic visions of Emanuel Swedenborg. Yet *Dreams* is relevant to any overview of Kant's precritical theological efforts because – whatever Kant's actual motivation in producing it[15] – the work is implicitly a clever polemic against direct, unmediated knowledge of metaphysical or theological truths, as might be found in special intuitions or mystical experiences. As such, *Dreams* anticipates in unsystematic form Kant's eventual rejection of the idea that the human intellect possesses an "intellectual intuition," enjoying the capacity to generate knowledge of things in themselves. In rejecting this option, Kant ultimately develops instead his theory of an essentially passive "sensible intuition" that would effectively necessitate experiential conditions for all claims to theoretical knowledge. Such a move would of course be fateful for the eventual character of the critical philosophy, especially regarding the possibility of speculative metaphysics and knowledge of transcendent truths. Moreover, according to Richard Velkley, *Dreams* is the first of Kant's works "to display the consequences of the absorption of Rousseau's revolution,"[16] which simply underscores the significance of this otherwise odd interlude in Kant's authorship.

There is thus a series of significant developments and fresh departures in Kant's thinking about natural theology prior to the appearance of the *Critique of Pure Reason*. Adding further complexity to this overview is the fact that, in certain years following the publication of the first *Critique*, Kant's duties at the university in Königsberg included lecture courses on philosophical theology, involving prescribed texts in accordance with the regulations of the day. But these set texts, by metaphysicians of the Leibniz–Wolff school such as Eberhard and Baumgarten, espoused positions that the *Critique* clearly repudiated; indeed, the positions of these texts are precisely Kant's target as he criticizes the proofs.[17] In effect, then, the standard university practices of his time required Kant to have his students read and take seriously works which his own publications had called into question. "Here as elsewhere," one commentator drily remarks, Kant "followed bureaucratic instructions imperturbably."[18] Since the version of Kant's lectures subsequently edited and published in 1817 offers what their English translator characterizes as "surprisingly sympathetic treatments of physicotheology and of Kant's own 1763 proof for God's existence"[19] (i.e., the *Beweisgrund*), the "layering" of Kant's thinking about God over many years assumes an increasingly subtle and complicated appearance.

These interpretive matters only acquire deepened complexity in the course of Kant's renewed visit to the theistic proofs (including his own) in the *Critique of Judgement* (1790), as well as in light of his account of divine action and, especially, divine aid in our recovery from "radical evil" in *Religion within the Limits of Reason Alone* (1793). The references to God scattered throughout Kant's additional writings on history, ethics, anthropology, and other topics, though less fully developed, are often provocative or otherwise striking, in part because they do not always seem consistent with views he expresses more systematically elsewhere. In due course, I shall return to a key instance of this inconsistency, involving the relationship between God and the creation of the "ethical commonwealth," as discussed by Kant in the *Religion*. This instance is crucial for the full clarification of Kant's principle of immanence, since it raises in concentrated form the question of the relation between God and humanity in the totalization of virtue.

The nearly half-century-long trajectory of Kant's writings about God and theistic proofs finally concludes on a vexing and ambiguous note, for these final comments are in the unpublished form eventually edited and published as the *Opus Postumum*. In a series of extended notes and outlines involving trains of thought of varying degrees of completeness, the aging Kant is obviously rethinking the interconnections among self, world, and God, often leaving it unclear if he is developing his own position or entertaining views that he will dispute.[20] Whether or not Kant was still in complete control of his faculties as he grappled with these enormously complex issues remains an open and debated question. What we do know is that Kant originally intended this work to be a major culminating statement, dealing primarily with what he characterized as the "transition from the metaphysical foundations of natural science to physics," thus filling a "gap that now stands open" in the critical philosophy.[21] The potential importance of this project for any consideration of Kant's philosophical theology is rather dramatically conveyed by his suggestion at several points in the work that God is not "a being" that exists "outside me," but is somehow coincident with my own experience of moral obligation. "There is a God in moral-practical reason, that is, in the idea of the relation of man to right and duty," Kant writes. "But not as a being outside man."[22] Anyone who has struggled to grasp Kant's understanding of the exact relationship between God and the moral law will find such remarks richly suggestive and, no doubt, more than a little frustrating. In his commentary on Kant, Father Copleston has suggested that in the *Opus Postumum* Kant "appears to be concerned with finding a more immediate transition from consciousness of the moral law to belief in God," but this may be a polite way of saying that Kant is here blurring the line between the two altogether.[23] Moreover, the fact that the *Opus Postumum* includes numerous references to Spinoza, in an era when Spinozism was virtually synonymous with atheism,[24] simply underscores the provocative, if inconclusive, nature of this piece of writing.

Kant's sustained interest in the problem of God over many decades is thus telling but, in the end, not altogether revealing. In contrast to his treatment, say, of Newtonian science or the concept of freedom, Kant does not address the issue of God as a central feature of his philosophy from which he then works outward, but always seems to be trying to make room for it within a philosophical vision that finds its animating principles elsewhere. The very notion of God appearing as a "postulate" of practical reason – in effect, a kind of residue, arising both subsequent to and parasitic upon the development of themes associated with our experience of freedom – is symptomatic of this situation. Clearly, this subordination of divine existence in the philosophical order insinuates revealing lessons, lessons that the full contours of the present work may illuminate. My point for now is simply that Kant's thinking about God is hardly exhausted by the dynamic between a negative and positive moment conveyed by the first two *Critiques*, and a genuinely complete account of Kant's philosophical theology as a whole would have to be rendered in terms of this wider context, including the issues associated with any development of his views over time. As one commentator has remarked, "a comprehensive account of the entirety of Kant's view of God...is still awaited."[25]

This study will hardly fill that very large gap, for however important such a wider perspective may be for a full rendering of Kant's position, my focus is considerably narrower. Again, my specific concern is to identify and trace the effects of the dynamic I have characterized as Kant's principle of immanence, which systematically transforms certain characteristic traits of divine transcendence into fresh terms associated with an autonomous rationality. In this respect, it is the principle of immanence that makes God a "problem" for Kant, in the straightforward sense that there is less and less for Kant's God to "do." My aim, then, is to show how this principle picks up momentum through the period of the critical philosophy and lays down tracks of continuity with nineteenth-century atheism. I might add that, just as historians of existentialism have no need to reconcile the obvious link between existentialism and the Kantian theory of freedom with Kant's own ethical sensibilities, I face no particular need to relate the principle of immanence to Kant's own intentions or personal religious convictions. Instead, as in the case of the rise of existentialism, we are dealing here with a theme that effectively takes on a life of its own in the work of later thinkers, becoming associated with developments that might well leave the earlier thinker puzzled at the very least, and perhaps deeply chagrined to boot. It is just possible that the degree to which this might happen in a given case is a fair measure of a thinker's stature.

KANT'S MORAL ARGUMENT

The train of thought extending from Kant's criticism of the traditional proofs to his own moral argument for God's existence actually functions in a context marked by a pair of equivocations. In this regard, the appearance of a smooth transition from the standpoint of the first *Critique* to that of the second is somewhat deceptive. In the first place, the most common way of depicting Kant's theological recovery from the damage done by the *Critique of Pure Reason* implies that he has salvaged the same God who had previously been put in question. The easily unnoticed fact is that the traits or attributes of the deity who is at issue in the first *Critique* are considerably more numerous than those of the God produced by the moral argument. The God of the metaphysics handbooks that is at issue in the prior instance possesses all of the attributes conveyed collectively by the traditional theistic proofs: God is the most perfect being (the ontological proof), the uncaused first cause and creator of the world (the cosmological proof), and the designer-architect of the universe who possesses goals, aims, and purposes that are reflected in the natural order of things (the teleological proof, or what Kant calls the "physico-theological" proof). As we shall see momentarily, it is far from clear that the stringent terms of Kant's moral argument in the *Critique of Practical Reason* provide or account for this full roster of traditional divine predicates. Instead, the results of the moral argument are stripped down and rather limited, specified by the austere terms and limited maneuvering room stipulated by the argument itself. This is not to say that this limited theological result is Kant's actual intention, for Allen Wood is no doubt correct when he states that Kant's own "conception of God belongs squarely in the scholastic-rationalist tradition," possessing all the attributes that are at stake in the traditional proofs.[26] The issue, rather, concerns whether or not Kant's moral argument in fact accounts for this traditionally robust conception of God.

There thus arises the confusing possibility that a different God may be at stake subsequent to the shift of context from the negative effort of the first *Critique* to the constructive effort of the second. What we might speak of as the "theistic shrinkage" resulting from this shift is indicative, I think, of the general direction Kant's reflections on divine transcendence are actually taking. Kant does not so much retrieve a God he had earlier put into question as he subtly alters the object of the debate, considerably enfranchising an autonomous rationality in the process.

In addition, there is an elusive but very important difference between arguing over the possibility and nature of divine existence, and arguing over the question of our cognitive or intellectual relationship to God. This difference, too, is easily missed in the rough-hewn manner in which we often depict Kant's views. To be sure, something like this equivocation runs widely through eighteenth-century philosophical literature, exemplified – probably intentionally – by the argumentative ironies David Hume packed into his *Dialogues Concerning Natural Religion* (a German translation of which Kant evidently had access to by the early 1780s).[27] My point for now is simply that, in accounts of the movement from the first to the second *Critique* and in the accompanying portrayals of Kant's attitude toward God, quite a bit hangs on whether we are charting changes in Kant's view of divine being and nature, or changes in his view of our cognitive relationship to God. Again, certain implications of this form of potential confusion will be highlighted in due course.

The moral argument for God's existence is triggered by Kant's general effort in the second *Critique* to show how it is that reason can be practical. Kant is not bifurcating reason between the practical and theoretical so much as he is attempting to disclose the different aspects of a fundamentally unified rational capacity, a point that takes on crucial dimensions when Kant finally argues for the primacy of practical over theoretical reason.[28] The force of the moral argument resides in Kant's demonstration that the element of "willing" intrinsic to reason in its practical aspect necessarily entails belief in the existence of God. The moral agent does not ponder the possibility of God's existence as one metaphysical option among others, deciding for or against it. Rather, the agent discovers through an examination of practical reason itself that the existence of God is presupposed in the very activity of moral agency. Of course, it is unlikely that most moral agents will ever initiate such an examination of the exercise of practical reason and its entailments. One could say that Kant's moral argument is this very examination undertaken in a deliberate and self-conscious way. In the course of this undertaking, Kant rounds out his own famous comment offered in the Preface to the second edition of *Critique of Pure Reason*, where he states he had "found it necessary to deny *knowledge* in order to make room for *faith*."[29] In his brief account of the difference between what he calls "moral theology" and "speculative theology" in the "Canon of Pure Reason" at the very end of the first *Critique*, Kant provides a preview of his strategy. More importantly, he provides in that earlier context the guiding principle that insures the priority of the moral law to claims about God: to the extent that "practical reason has the right to serve as our guide," he tells us, "we shall not look upon actions as obligatory because they are the commands of God, but shall regard them as divine commands because we have an inward obligation to them."[30] Here we have in skeletal form Kant's response to Plato's rhetorical question: "Do the gods love holiness because it is holy, or is it holy because they love it?"[31]

Kant injects argumentative momentum into the move from theoretical agnosticism to practical certainty by introducing the crucial concept of the "highest good." In an adaptation of a basically Leibnizian formula,[32] he defines the highest good as the proper proportioning of happiness and worthiness to be happy, on the understanding that the latter is synonymous with virtue.[33] The occasion for the appearance of the idea of the highest good is Kant's account of practical reason's irrepressible search or drive for the "unconditioned totality" of its object.[34] Earlier, the *Critique of Pure Reason* had shown that reason in its theoretical aspect possesses an "interest" to seek out the "unconditioned" or "absolute" end product of its exercise. Reason, Kant tells us in that previous context, "is directed always solely towards absolute totality in the synthesis of conditions, and never terminates save in what is absolutely, that is, in all relations, unconditioned."[35] In effect, reason cannot rest until it has achieved this unconditioned object; its search for the unconditioned member of a series of conditions is the correlate on the theoretical side of the unconditioned command of the categorical imperative on reason's practical side. Although this characteristic of reason can lead all too easily to metaphysical illusion, it is a natural and unavoidable tendency that, correctly understood and channeled, can be a valuable aid to philosophical discovery. Kant's exploitation of this feature of reason enables him to reintroduce a strong teleological element into his thinking even as he is endorsing the profoundly non-teleological character of Newtonianism. In the specific case of practical reason, the unavoidable drive toward an unconditioned totality yields the idea of the highest good, involving both the "supreme" and the "perfect" product of the exercise of reason in its practical aspect. The result is a synthesis of the totalization of the intentions and the consequences of moral endeavor.[36] To say that there can be no "higher" good than the "highest" good is simultaneously to say that practical reason has reached a result that has no further "conditions."

Kant's introduction of the idea of happiness at this point in his moral philosophy has of course been a topic of enormous debate. However happiness might be defined,[37] the very notion suggests a concern for the consequences of the moral agent's actions that seems on the face of it to be utterly incompatible with Kant's characteristic emphasis on motivation derived from a sense of duty. In fact, as Kant attempts to clarify several years following the publication of the *Critique of Practical Reason*, it was never his intention in his moral philosophy to dismiss consideration of the ends of moral endeavor, but simply to stipulate that these ends are not the proper basis of motivation.[38] In the *Critique* itself, Kant argues that, while the highest good may be the final end of moral endeavor, none of its features – including happiness – is an appropriate determining ground of the will, for only the moral law can serve as such a ground.[39] That is, as an aspect of the highest good, happiness comes into view not as we consider the ways in which the will is motivated, but only when we reflect on the total product of moral action itself. In principle, the moral agent is capable at any time of reflecting on the highest good as the end product of moral endeavor, but for Kant this is not the same as saying the agent is then motivated by the hope for happiness. The truly moral agent is motivated solely by respect for the moral law.

Kant's depiction of the highest good through the connection between virtue and happiness is, in part, a reflection of the terms in which much eighteenth-century debate about the nature of ethics occurred. For Kant himself, "it is necessarily true that each of us desires his or her own happiness,"[40] an insight that captures the significant shift from an earlier cultural setting in which the same point would have been rendered in terms of "salvation" rather than "happiness." Already in the very terms of Kant's moral argument, the object of the human quest is less theologically freighted. By Kant's time, in fact, issues connected with the relation between virtue and one's own "interest" cut across several schools of thought with which he was clearly familiar.[41] Similarly, the link here to Aristotelian ethics is unspoken but significant.[42] Most explicit, however, is Kant's appeal to other classical sources, such as Stoic and Epicurean accounts of the highest good, as he works through definitional issues and poses alternative accounts of virtue and happiness.[43] Appearing at the very outset of the "Dialectic of Pure Practical Reason," this dialogue with classical sources provides Kant with the necessary terms for framing an antinomy regarding the relationship between happiness and virtue: it would seem as rational to argue that virtue must be the cause of happiness as to argue that it is not.[44] Kant is thus able to replicate the architectonic structure of the first *Critique* and claim that

> if the solution of this dialectic is attained, we may expect a result just as useful as that accruing from the dialectic of theoretical reason, since the self-contradictions of pure practical reason, if properly exposed and not concealed, impel us to an exhaustive critical examination of its capacities.[45]

In other words, Kant can demonstrate in the practical as well as in the theoretical realm the need for the critical philosophy, with its unique capacity to identify and untangle the conceptual nests produced by the unexamined use of reason.

Engagement with classical sources was hardly a fresh departure for Kant, since such references had been evident in his discussions of ethics and freedom as early as the mid-1760s. In part, at least, Kant's turning to such sources may suggest a growing dissatisfaction with the instrumental accounts of reason of his own day as a basis for a definition of virtue or for a full account of the moral life.[46] Here as elsewhere in Kant's attempt to provide a proper end for the free will, Rousseau is the key mediator, for "Kant sees himself as taking his cue from Rousseau in reviving the ancient controversy about the nature of the complete good that is the end of all human efforts at living well."[47] The question of the perfection or end of moral endeavor is not easily addressed in terms provided by other modern philosophers, at least not without dogmatically introducing a theological principle disruptive of reason's freedom of movement. Here, the totalizing tendencies associated with Kant's own theory of reason find surprising reinforcement in a return to ancient sources, where the question of perfection is clearly framed in terms of the concept of the "highest" good.

Implicitly, Kant's rendering of the highest good as the proper proportioning of virtue and happiness is also a covert theodicy. The issue of theodicy had shadowed all of Kant's theological ruminations from early on, as it had influenced eighteenth-century thought generally, especially following the Lisbon earthquake of 1755.[48] While we often think of Kant's theory of the highest good as a highly effective – if somewhat artificial – argumentative device that helps him to recover the immortality of the soul and the existence of God from a theoretical wasteland, it is at the same time an ingenious way of reconciling the goodness of God, human freedom, and our experience of evil in the world. We can see this implication as we trace out the postulation process that follows from Kant's initial definition of the highest good.

By requiring the perfection of virtue and its linkage with happiness, the concept of the highest good posits what is apparently an utterly unobtainable goal. But through an aggressive use of the two standpoints theory that his distinction between phenomena and noumena provides, Kant suggests that the notion that "a virtuous disposition necessarily produced happiness is not...*absolutely* false" but "is false only if I assume existence in this world to be the only mode of existence of a rational being."[49] Since the first *Critique* made it possible at least to "think" (though not to "know") myself as existing in an intelligible as well as the phenomenal world, there is at least a conceptual means of accommodating the idea of progress toward moral perfection if a powerful, rational case for such an idea can be made. Kant believes he has demonstrated both the rational necessity of the concept of the highest good and the "complete fitness of the will to the moral law" as one of its components.[50] Tellingly, it is precisely at this juncture that Kant adds his brief but crucial argument concerning the primacy of practical over theoretical reason. This move provides him with the rationale for positing claims required by reason in its practical aspect even when those claims "are beyond any possible insight" of theoretical reason, as long as theoretical reason has not definitively ruled out such claims in advance.[51] While insisting throughout that "it is only one and the same reason which judges a priori by principles, whether for theoretical or for practical purposes,"[52] Kant is effectively arguing that reason is dualistic in perspective, but that the two sides of reason are not antagonistic: "Which interest is superior? It is not a question of which must yield, for one does not necessarily conflict with the other."

> It is a question of whether speculative [i.e., theoretical] reason, which knows nothing of that which the practical reason offers for its acceptance, must take up these principles and seek to integrate them, even though they transcend it, with its own concepts, as a foreign possession handed over to it; or whether it is justified in stubbornly following its own isolated interest....[53]

The revealing personification of reason here – which I shall have occasion to examine in much greater detail in chapter 4 – suggests a reconciliation of potentially competing interests, with a view to an overriding good. In the present case, the overriding good is the full depiction of those features of the highest good that are required if the very idea of the highest good is not to be put in jeopardy. Kant's stake in preserving the rational necessity of the highest good and, thus, of all its constituent features is rather dramatically revealed by his remark that the "impossibility of the highest good must prove the falsity of the moral law" itself. "If, therefore, the highest good is impossible according to practical rules, then the moral law which commands that it be furthered must be fantastic, directed to imaginary ends, and consequently inherently false."[54] In effect, the assurance that practical reason has purchase on reality is dependent in part on demonstrating the rational necessity of the perfection of virtue and the proper proportioning of virtue and happiness. One might reflect that at no other point does Kant's ethical theory seem so subject to the problems of psychological reductionism. At the same time, however, Kant's striking way of underscoring his point clearly conveys the interlocking nature of the set of claims his theory of the highest good brings to light.

With the additional maneuvering room provided by the primacy of the practical, Kant concludes that the "infinite progress" toward moral perfection is possible "only under the presupposition of an infinitely enduring existence and personality of the same rational being; this is called the immortality of the soul."

> Thus the highest good is practically possible only on the supposition of the immortality of the soul, and the latter, as inseparably bound to the moral law, is a postulate of pure practical reason. By a postulate of pure practical reason, I understand a theoretical proposition which is not as such demonstrable, but which is an inseparable corollary of an a priori unconditionally valid practical law.[55]

At this point, the postulation of the existence of God follows naturally. Obviously, the required proportioning of happiness to virtue involves "the supposition of the existence of a cause adequate to this effect, i.e., it must postulate the existence of God as necessarily belonging to the possibility of the highest good. ... "[56] There must, that is, be an agency with the intellectual intuition capable of apprehending degrees of virtue as well as with the metaphysical weight to bring about the proper proportioning. Kant has little trouble in equating this required agency with the traditional idea of God.

Considered only as a theoretical claim, the existence of God is for Kant simply a "hypothesis," one possible explanation of the world among others. Considered in connection with the realization of the highest good, however, the existence of God is rationally required for all the reasons associated with the necessity to preserve the possibility of the highest good. In effect, then, Kant has managed to link together the existence of God with an antecedent moment in the moral agent's personal consciousness, giving God's reality the most immediate grounding even as he is dismantling theoretical and speculative routes to the same result. Moral theism "arrives at a conception of God which is rooted in an autonomous interior act," which means that, for Kant, "faith in God is religious only if it is a personal act."[57] There can be no question here of an intrusion on my intellectual autonomy, in part because my experience of autonomy precedes my conviction that God is real. We "have no direct consciousness of God and immortality. We experience our freedom" which is "inside us, and it is in part this inwardness which accounts for its fruitfulness," including the awareness of God.[58] The superiority of the moral argument to all speculative efforts to demonstrate God's existence is thus implicit in the conviction that God's reality is as close to me as my own apprehension of the moral law and the experience of freedom that goes with it.

The Kantian emphasis here on the subjective, interior dimensions of moral faith is the natural counterpart to his rejection of exterior, theoretical demonstrations in theological matters.[59] The profoundly personal nature of Kant's moral theism is also its epistemological strength, since the believer's incorrigible awareness of the moral law serves as the indispensable mediator between human autonomy and divine transcendence. Consequently, by the time Kant has fully deployed his moral argument, he has made it clear that the integrity of the moral law itself is implicated in the supposition of a divine being.[60] One could only deny God's existence by also denying the validity of the moral law.

DIMINISHING THE DIVINE

For some, Kant's moral argument is the very center of his philosophical vision, holding together all that is implicit in the notion of the "priority of the practical" and rescuing human life from the metaphysical impoverishment produced by the critique of theoretical reason.[61] For others, the moral argument is, at best, a weak and arbitrary appendage to an otherwise profound philosophy of freedom or, at worst, symptomatic of an "underhanded Christianity" reinforced by an odious slave mentality. Infamously, Nietzsche captures the spirit of the most polemical reaction to Kant's effort, claiming that the categorical imperative "crept stealthily into his heart and led him astray – back to 'God,' 'soul,' 'freedom,' and 'immortality,' like a fox who loses his way and goes astray back into his cage. Yet it had been *his* strength and cleverness that had *broken open* the cage!"[62] As an echo of Goethe's charge that Kant had forever "smeared his philosopher's cloak" with his doctrine of radical evil in order to win favor with Christians,[63] Nietzsche's reaction suggests the frustration of one who saw limitless and uncharted possibilities in Kant's theory of freedom if left uncompromised by theological backsliding.

For my immediate purposes, no such dramatic charge is necessary in order to indicate the ways in which Kant's moral argument intimates a principle of immanence, subtly undermining the traditional idea of divine transcendence. There is, first of all, the question of the specific predicates or attributes of God for which the moral argument actually accounts. As I suggested at the outset of this chapter, the notion that the second *Critique* simply retrieves the same God put in question by the first *Critique* does not altogether survive close inspection. Second and more importantly, however, there is the problem posed by the apparent yoking of the divine will to the requirements of the highest good – as though the preordaining God of Luther and Calvin had been given a script to follow by the philosophers. The implications of this linkage between God's will and the requirements of the highest good are not only important with respect to Kant's position, but indicative of major sea changes occurring in European thought at the close of the Enlightenment. Taken together, these two latent yet powerful features of the moral argument suggest that Kant's practical philosophy may be less successful at recovering lost theological ground than it is at pointing a way toward a more consistent humanism, underwritten in part by a philosophical procedure for transforming theistic content into an increasingly robust account of human action.

As we know, the God jeopardized by the initial stages of Kant's critical philosophy is the God of the traditional proofs. Kant himself depicts this God by extrapolating from what he terms the "ideas of pure reason" in the first *Critique*. The "ideas" or "pure concepts" of reason are parallel to, but distinguished from, the "pure concepts" of the understanding. The latter are the categories, such as substance and causality, which have a legitimate cognitive use, as depicted in the "Transcendental Analytic" of the *Critique*. The "ideas of pure reason," on the other hand, do not have a proper cognitive function but should be viewed as rationally generated organizing devices for depicting the absolute "whole" or "unity" of the concepts of the understanding. The ideas reflect reason's natural drive toward totality, as suggested by the restless quest for the conclusion of any instance of inferential reasoning. Indeed, the ideas of reason are for Kant associated with the basic forms of inferential reasoning, just as the categories correspond to the basic forms of judgment.[64] At work here, in other words, is the same totalizing activity reflected in Kant's depiction of the highest good. Whereas the pure concepts of the understanding (the categories) relate to possible objects of experience, "no corresponding object can be given in sense-experience" for an idea of pure reason; the ideas "contain a certain completeness to which no possible empirical knowledge ever attains."[65] The only legitimate use of ideas of reason is as regulative devices, guiding and shaping inquiry without themselves being passed off as objects of theoretical knowledge. Developing this insight and charting out the difference between a constitutive and a regulative employment of the ideas of reason is a central theme of the "Transcendental Dialectic" of the *Critique of Pure Reason*, just as distinguishing between categories and ideas is a major purpose of the *Critique* as a whole.

Kant explains that "God" is a special kind of idea of reason, which he terms the "ideal of pure reason." The notion of God does not simply help us depict the totalized product or result of this or that concept of the understanding but is, instead, uniquely comprehensive.

> This ideal is the supreme and complete material condition of the possibility of all that exists – the condition to which all thought of objects, so far as their content is concerned, has to be traced back. It is also the only true ideal of which human reason is capable. For only in this one case is a concept of a thing – a concept which is in itself universal – completely determined in and through itself, and known as the representation of an individual.[66]

In keeping with the epistemological stringency that informs the "Transcendental Dialectic," Kant goes on to warn that reason "does not presuppose the existence of a being that corresponds to this ideal, but only the idea of such a being...."[67] Rather ingeniously – if not somewhat perversely – Kant is here explaining how reason achieves the very idea of God in the course of an argument designed to demonstrate the illegitimacy of all claims to theoretical knowledge of God's existence.[68]

By this route Kant arrives at the essential concept of divine being that is at stake in the traditional proofs. In effect, Kant is agreeing with the scholastic–rationalist tradition's conception of what or who God is but simply attempting to chart a more respectable epistemological route to claims about God's existence. Thus, in the fitting characterization offered by one commentator, Kant's God "is the supremely perfect being, extramundane, immutable, timelessly eternal. He is also living, knowing, and willing: omniscient, omnipotent, supremely holy, just, and beneficent."[69] In short, this is the God arrived at if we pool the varied implications of the ontological, cosmological, and teleological proofs: the most perfect and self-subsistent being on whose intentions and activity the entire created order depends. Kant's presumably destructive tendencies regarding the possibility of natural theology never turn on the criticism of this view of God but turn instead on his account of the proper and legitimate grounds for holding such a view. The moral argument is designed to provide these grounds as a needed antidote to the weak grounds offered by the more traditional proofs.

Kant's intentions notwithstanding, it is simply not clear that the moral argument justifies maintaining this full roster of divine predicates. The much more austere product of the moral argument is fundamentally instrumental in nature, a "cause" that is "adequate" to the rationally necessitated effect of properly proportioning happiness and virtue. This instrumental conception of providing a fitting end or result to virtuous activity is, after all, what gives the ring of plausibility to Beck's suggestion that the moral argument is really simply a watered down version of the teleological proof.[70] Moreover, any implication regarding the beneficent or wise "intentions" of God is always implicitly trumped in Kant's account by appeals to the "needs" or "interests" of reason as the authentic source of what is only incidentally portrayed as the divine intent. The paradigmatic instance of this is, of course, the satisfaction of the requirements of the highest good. While it may be theologically comforting to claim that God "wills" or "intends" the rewarding of the virtuous with happiness, the rewarding process itself is, as we have seen, driven by rational mandates. By Kant's terms, God's activity in connection with the satisfaction of the highest good is secondary, in the sense that any instrumental activity is secondary to some larger purpose or aim. In this case, the purpose or aim is defined by a need of reason.

Alongside this problem is the conundrum generated by Kant's own insistence that "existence" itself is one of the pure concepts of the understanding – a category of modality.[71] This of course means that the concept of existence should be viewed in relation to the unifying or synthesizing activity of the mind rather than in relation to reality as it may be apart from our apprehension of it. But this commonplace of Kantian philosophy suggests that, even if Kant endorses the scholastic notion of God as the *ens realissimum*, it is not clear what sense he can give to its reality by the terms of his own viewpoint: there is no unproblematic way in which Kant can refer to "God's existence." Something such as this problem presumably stands behind Kant's own conception of God as the transcendental "ideal."[72] The puzzle associated with the connection – or lack thereof – between Kant's God and the category of existence no doubt draws us into the subtle and profound matters at stake in the transition from a speculative to a practical view of God. That is, God is real "for us" in the course of a life of moral earnestness rather than as the theoretical object of a proof. Yet in so far as the practical interest takes over in this way, it would appear to assimilate to the prior interests of our moral agency even the classic conception of God's onto-logical integrity. As a result, it becomes less and less clear what Kant's moral argument is an argument *for*.[73]

Most significantly, perhaps, the clear subordination of interest in establishing God's existence to a prior concern for rational autonomy is difficult to reconcile with the themes of the "most real" and the "most perfect" – that is, the "most important" – conveyed by Kant's notion of the "ideal of pure reason." By Kant's own account, God's existence is not demonstrated as a theoretical claim involving all the attributes associated with the God of the more traditional proofs but is instead a postulate of practical reason that is necessitated by sustained reflection on the total design of the moral life. Moreover, by the strict terms of the argument, the "willing" that God does in connection with realizing the highest good seems to be exhaustive with respect to God's mode of "being." The issue is not theoretical knowledge of God's existence in any case, for not only has Kant already ruled out that possibility, but he has at no point made establishing God's existence the explicit priority of his practical philo-sophy. Instead, the decisive and driving priority is the intelligibility of the insight that moral earnestness ultimately leads to a rational result, within the context of showing how it is that reason can be practical. God's existence is both instrumental toward, and secondary to, this end. Yet since, as Ralph Walker observes, "one can perfectly well be a serious moral agent while remaining altogether pessimistic about whether virtu-ous acts achieve anything or will ever be rewarded,"[74] it is certainly not clear that God's existence is finally necessary for moral earnestness itself. Even Kant seems to suggest as much toward the end of the *Critique of Judgement*, where he conjures up a morally worthy person (apparently modeled on Spinoza) who "considers himself firmly persuaded that there is no God and . . . no future life either."[75] Kant's development of his own thought experiment never jeopardizes the moral worthiness of the ima-gined agent, but simply draws attention to the "aimless chaos of mat-ter"[76] that would surround such a figure in the absence of a moral governor of the world – a kind of Kantian precursor to Camus' effort to imagine saints in a godless universe. By Kant's own terms, there is certainly something poignant and even tragic about a morally righteous person in the absence of God, but there is nothing incoherent or imposs-ible about it.

We might characterize the resulting situation by saying that the postu-late of God's existence is part of the larger plot concerning the intelligi-bility of the moral life and not itself the point of the plot. This aspect of Kant's reasoning is made clear by his insistence that the "moral necessity" to "assume the existence of God" is "subjective, i.e., a need, and not objective, i.e., duty itself."

> For there cannot be any duty to assume the existence of a thing, because such a supposition concerns only the theoretical use of reason. *It is also not to be understood that the assumption of the existence of God is necessary as a ground of all obligation in general (for this rests, as has been fully shown, solely on the autonomy of reason itself).*[77]

Evidently, God is not only instrumental with respect to proportioning happiness and virtue, but instrumental as well with respect to maintaining the integrity of a rationally necessitated idea. The postulate of God's existence is in fact "only usable for the purpose of a conception of the world that supports the rationality of adopting the highest good as our end."[78] In effect, the overall argument is primarily a *negative* argument against the futility of moral seriousness and only secondarily a positive argument concerning a major metaphysical claim: Kant's main concern is not a theological content but moral encouragement.

Consequently, the manner in which Kant moves from theoretical agnosticism to practical certainty so inflates the importance of the moral life that the specifically theological result assumes the secondary status characteristic of a supporting role. We see this especially clearly in Kant's clarification of the moral argument in the *Critique of Judgement*, where he acknowledges that the very attributes of God following from the argument may "involve a latent anthropomorphism." Indeed, he goes on, "the object which we have in view in employing" the divine attributes "is not that we wish to determine the nature of that Being by reference to them – a nature which is inaccessible to us – but rather that we seek to use them for determining our own selves and our will."[79] He echoes his own point in *Religion within the Limits of Reason Alone*, where he remarks that it "concerns us not so much to know what God is in Himself (His nature) as what He is for us as moral Beings."[80] The prioritizing that is at work in such a train of thought is helpfully captured in a comment by Wood: the "postulate of God's existence is the postulate of a systematic moral purposiveness in the world."[81] Indeed, in his own preview of the moral argument in the "Canon of Pure Reason" at the conclusion of the first *Critique*, Kant himself frames the issue in the most revealing way: "reason finds itself constrained to assume the existence of God," he says, for "otherwise it would have to regard the moral laws as empty figments of the brain...."[82]

The possibility of theistic shrinkage and the subordination of interest in God to an interest in autonomous rationality naturally reinforce one another in ways suggestive of Kant's principle of immanence. Lurking as a sub-text in the *Critique*'s argumentation is a surreptitious and ironic trading on the "concept" of God, subsequent to the deployment of the postulation process. By this I mean that, once Kant has established the existence of God as a necessary entailment of the reality of the highest good, he gradually reintroduces many of the traditional divine predicates *whether or not they have been accounted for by the terms of the postulation process*. In other words, Kant exploits his moral argument to reintroduce the idea or concept of God that he has otherwise held up to the most suspicious scrutiny. The irony, of course, is that it was this very trading on the *concept* of God in ways unrelated to any possible intuition that had originally informed Kant's criticism of traditional speculative metaphysics and natural theology in the first *Critique*. Kant is certainly not alone in offering a proof for God's existence that does not account for all of the divine predicates. But in Kant's case, the moral argument is not augmented by additional proofs or by appeals to scripture that might yield the full sum of divine attributes. Instead, Kant's argumentation is constrained on one side by explicit strictures on speculation and, on the other, by the overriding interest of practical reason.

Consequently, we begin to see an emerging asymmetry between the boldness and finality with which Kant banishes a certain sort of cognitive access to God, and the questionable nature of his attempt to smuggle God back in. The arguments animating the negative moment in Kant's account of God enjoy more obvious force than those sustaining the positive moment. The asymmetry becomes even worse if we reintroduce the questions raised by Kant's appeal to the idea of happiness, on which the very notion of the highest good – and thus the entire postulation process – depends. We might conclude, crudely but not misleadingly, that in the first *Critique* God is shown the way out by the front door, for all to see. In the *Critique of Practical Reason*, however, God returns almost furtively by the back door, just before day's end, after all the truly important matters concerning the integrity of the moral life have been addressed.

The fact that the context providing for the reappearance of God involves a "curious fluctuation in the distinction between *hypothesis* and *postulate*"[83] only makes matters worse. While explaining the epistemological status of a postulate at one point through reference to a "necessary hypothesis,"[84] Kant at other times distinguishes between a postulate and a hypothesis as well as between a postulate and a presupposition, creating ambiguity at just the point where his position can least afford additional stress – which is to say, precisely at the point where he is defining the cognitive status of our relationship to God.[85] We thus have a powerful note of ambiguity compounding the difficulties for Kant's

moral argument already inflicted by theistic shrinkage and the subordination of divine existence to autonomy's requirements. The result is hardly
reassuring as a strategy for bouncing back from the destructive results of
the *Critique of Pure Reason*.

The compromising of divine transcendence reaches a powerful climax
in the restrictions that are clearly placed on the divine will by the terms of
the moral argument. Just as the postulation of God's existence is subordinated to the requirements of the moral life in the sequencing of
Kant's argument, the divine will itself appears to be subordinated to the
dictates of the highest good. Simply expressed, God has no choice in the
matter of properly proportioning happiness and virtue. There is no
question here of the self-existence of God associated with the scholastic–rationalist tradition; instead, God's will is inextricably entangled with
the dictates of the highest good which, in turn, have been rationally
generated rather than divinely ordained. God's apparent lack of choice
in proportioning happiness and virtue underscores in yet another way
what I have been characterizing as the metaphysically thin and fundamentally instrumental character of the God of the second *Critique*. Not
only does the God of the moral argument function to produce a certain
result, but it is a result already prescribed by rationality. While it may be
true that a being with a truly holy will *needs* no law to determine itself,[86]
the determination of such a will in accordance with the moral law
suggests our capacity to describe the channels down which divine agency
inevitably flows. Rather oddly, this suggests that we could always "pre-
dict" what God would will in a given situation, which is perhaps another
way of assuming the divine prerogative. The absence of mystery here
goes together with the preeminence of rationality itself, and the net effect
is the hint of God's redundancy.

Consequently, unlike the God whose existence Kant has undermined in
the first *Critique*, the God Kant is now attempting to recover is, at each
step of the way, subordinate to a series of rational mandates that take
precedence over the idea of a self-existent and independent divine will.
Expressed in traditional theological terms, it is as though the distinction
between God's "absolute" and "ordained" power has been utterly erased.
God has no absolute power above and beyond the power to proportion
happiness and virtue, and this ordained power simply reflects the requirements of reason's totalizing tendencies. God's will courses through the
channels shaped by rationality's structure, as disclosed in this case by the
concept of the highest good. While Kant insists that it is "morally
necessary to assume the existence of God,"[87] it is necessary only to
complete or round off a train of thought that has its point of departure
in an autonomous rationality.

Now in one respect, Kant's position is simply a continuation of the varied but powerful tradition within Christian thought that conflates the rational and the divine in an integrated vision. This broadly "Greek" position, inspired by the Fourth Gospel and evident in a wide range of Christian thinkers, finds no tension but only harmony in God's freely choosing to act in a manner consistent with a theory of rationality that could be depicted apart from reference to God. Not surprisingly, some sort of natural law theory often informs the ethical views accompanying theological positions falling into this general category. Such outlooks, linking thinkers as otherwise diverse as Anselm and Aquinas, or Hooker and Clarke, may take shape as a reaction to views of the divine will that leave it appearing arbitrary and unreasonable. For example, in his particular context, Kant is continuing Leibniz's reaction against the "voluntaristic" theology of Pufendorf and others that holds that God creates morality more or less by fiat, making morality binding simply by virtue of being commanded by God. This extreme emphasis on divine sovereignty, exemplified in the Protestant Reformers as well as in Scotus and Occam, enjoins "an attitude of humble submission and obedience to God's commands, simply as his commands, [as] the only appropriate stance for us."[88] The resulting implication that God is a kind of despot would of course be impossible to hold alongside a Kantian theory of autonomy, while also making it "impossible for us to love God."[89] Moreover, the apparent arbitrariness of a morality created by divine fiat implies that the universe itself may not be naturally rational even though it is divinely created. Along with other antivoluntarists, then, Kant would join the effort of devising an alternative to voluntarism partly in order to defend the very reasonableness of the universe itself. In this respect, Kant's notion of the highest good as an expression of confidence that we live in a morally ordered universe is an explicit rejoinder to voluntarism as well as a reversion to classical ideas.[90]

The antivoluntarist program thus involves the search for a morality that is shared by God and humanity. Antivoluntarists thereby trade the problem of holding up a God who is an arbitrary despot for the problem arising out of the idea that God wills the good simply because it is good. For if this is what God does, then the good is in some sense independent of and anterior to God's will.[91] Kant's own position radically compounds this problem in a way that further attenuates the connection between rationality and divinity. For, as we shall see in more detail in the following chapter, Kant's transcendentalism, together with the capacity of the will to prescribe laws to itself in a manner requiring no wider metaphysical structure, leaves a gap rather than corridors of continuity between reason and God. The "autonomy of autonomy" in Kant jeopardizes the lingering religious quality of his brand of antivoluntarism, since there is for him no need to set the formal basis of morality in a theological context. Here we have yet another implication of Kant's consistent principle that morality *leads to* religion and does not arise from it: the religious aspect is a gloss on the moral aspect, offering the encouragement that moral earnestness is not in vain. For Kant, "the absolute rationality of the moral order bespeaks no direct communication between human and divine reason"[92] simply because human reason is self-sufficient. In effect, the links between the two in Kant's case are recognized and established *subsequent* to reason's satisfaction of its own needs in a manner that implicitly acknowledges reason's prerogative. Accordingly, the prioritizing of a train of thought that moves from an "interest of reason" to a "postulate" of divine existence makes it difficult to reconcile rationality and the divine will in the traditional manner. As we shall subsequently see, the several implications of Kant's theory of autonomy turn this difficulty into a virtual impossibility. In the Kantian case, the effort to reconcile the divine will with rational properties that guide even God's actions eventually leads, not to an integrated theological vision reminiscent of the Fourth Gospel, but to the secularization of ethics.

In a perhaps narrow but nonetheless important respect, the gap between divinity and rationality implicit in Kant's moral argument is the ultimate and inevitable consequence of his own definition of that which is good without qualification as the "good will."[93] Subsequent to the *Foundations of the Metaphysics of Morals*, where Kant provides this definition,[94] the second *Critique* does not then proceed to reveal a synthesizing coincidence between the good will and God's will but, instead, appeals to an instrumentalist conception of the divine will in order to maintain the integrity of autonomous moral action. In the process, the appeal to the divine will is rendered questionable by the introduction of a consideration of happiness. More seriously, the actual definition of the good will is embedded in a theory of autonomy for which divine commands are, in principle, as heteronomous as sensuous inclinations as a source of moral motivation.

As we have already seen, the depiction of the highest good is reason's way, not of providing a ground for moral endeavor, but of exhibiting the fact that moral endeavor is not ultimately futile. The postulation of God's existence in the course of Kant's reasoning about the highest good does not suddenly reverse the position announced in the *Foundations* but effectively buttresses the insight about the good will while broadening Kant's larger argument concerning the rational result of moral action. We see this plainly if we simply pose the question: "What if God refused in a given instance to proportion happiness and virtue?" In such a case, there would be no change in our conception of the good or of the nature of moral agency, but only the discouraged sense that reason's total aims had not been realized. Moral goodness itself would not collapse in the face of God's refusal to reward it. Once again, then, the priority of the self-legislating activity of the human will in the depiction of the good is reinforced rather than put in question by the moral argument for God's existence. One consequence is that God's will really is yoked to the demands of the highest good.

In view of the broadly Protestant tradition lying in Kant's religious and cultural background, the resulting transfer of the bondage of the will from humanity to God could not be more striking. In his polemic against Erasmus's humanist effort to relate freedom of the will to salvation, Luther depicts the desperate situation of a humanity wallowing in sin in terms that yield the worst sort of bondage: the utter impossibility of our participating in our own salvation apart from divine grace. Luther argues that, in fact, the will "without God's grace is not free at all, but is the permanent prisoner and bondslave of evil, since it cannot turn itself to good."[95] The implied connection here between our bondage and God's awesome freedom becomes explicit as Luther portrays God as the being "for whose will no cause or ground may be laid down as its rule and standard; for nothing is on a level with it or above it, but it is itself the rule for all things." From Luther's perspective, the "reasonable" conclusion for us to draw is that the divine will is beyond "human reckoning," for "inasmuch as He is the one true God, wholly incomprehensible and inaccessible to man's understanding, it is reasonable, indeed inevitable, that His justice should also be incomprehensible."[96] Roughly two hundred years before Luther staked out this position, William of Occam proposed that God's power is such that, if God had so chosen, we could have been commanded to hate rather than to love God.[97] Now, a little more than two hundred years after Luther's death, Kant demonstrates through rational human procedures that God cannot transgress the requirements of the highest good. For Kant, God's intentions, far from being beyond "human reckoning," are made transparent by the demands of rationality as disclosed to finite beings.

A long and complex tradition of reflection on human freedom and God's power runs through this historical trajectory, as voluntarist and antivoluntarist theories of divine commands struggle toward resolving long-standing and probably intractable difficulties. But there can be no question that, with Kant's position, we are confronting a significant moment in the process of the secularization of ethics in the West, involving the possibility that even God's actions can be guided by an independent conception of the good as an intermediate stage in the movement toward an altogether non-religious conception of ethics.[98] That the specific details of Kant's moral and religious philosophy would promote this trend should hardly come as a surprise, in light of his own overarching principle that morality does not rely on religion but the other way around.[99]

Viewed from this broader perspective, the relation of Kant's God to the rational requirements of the highest good should perhaps be understood as a variation on the more familiar idea that Kant's God is not free to break or disobey the moral law. The standard rejoinder to this claim by Kant's defenders is to argue that no limitation on God is therein implied for the simple reason that, being holy, God would never *want* to break the moral law. But the prior assumption of God's holiness no doubt begs the question at stake, which concerns the ground of the initial definition of the good. Kant himself addresses something very much like this issue of the underlying source of the good in a section of the *Critique of Practical Reason* portraying God as the metaphysical "ground" of what Kant calls the "highest original good."[100] The idea of the highest original good functions for Kant in much the way God's absolute (as opposed to ordained) power functions for someone such as Occam. In effect, Kant appeals to an original metaphysical unity, for which God is responsible through God's own free action, that will negate any attempt to drive a wedge between God's will and the needs of reason, including the need to achieve the highest good. Separate from nature, God is the very ground of "the agreement of nature not merely with a law of the will of rational beings but with the idea of this law so far as [rational beings] make it the supreme ground of determination of the will."[101] That is, God's own original nature is consistent with the goals of the highest good. Therefore, to postulate God's existence as a necessary condition of the realization of the highest good is not to demean God's transcendence but is, in fact, to disclose an important feature of the divine nature. Implicit in this argument, presumably, is the claim that, in not willing to transgress the moral law (or in not willing to refuse to proportion happiness and virtue), God is not submitting to rational necessity but revealing the divine will itself.

Such a defense appears to be another instance of Kant's trading on the "concept" of God subsequent to the postulation process, whether or not the postulation process has provided for the divine attributes to which he is now appealing. After all, the source of the relationship between God and the world that Kant is here exploiting would seem to be the cosmological proof rather than Kant's own moral argument. Even apart from this potential equivocation, Kant has created enormous difficulties for any reflection on God's relationship to the world by denying that space and time are characteristic of things in themselves, or reality as such. As Kant himself bluntly puts it, God "cannot be the cause of time (or space) itself...." in any case.[102] This point implies in turn that "the relation between God and things in themselves cannot be a causal relation": because Kant has "denied the temporality of things in themselves, the relation of God to them and, a fortiori, to their temporal appearances is not one of cause."[103] A sudden reversion to the idea that God is the ground of the highest original good hardly mitigates the speculative difficulties he has introduced with these considerations. Certainly Kant cannot simply assume the relation between the world and God that animates the cosmological proof, even apart from his criticism of the proof itself. For he has himself eliminated the role of causality in this relation through his transcendental turn.

More importantly, Kant's defense of divine transcendence from a presumed subordination to rationality depends upon rationally understanding and depicting God's intentions and efforts: the force of the very idea of rationality precedes the conception of God. Not only does there remain a profound gap between divinity and rationality here, but the former is rendered and understood in terms of the latter. The connected notions of God's not failing to satisfy the demands of the highest good and God's not willing to break the moral law are intelligible only in light of Kant's conception of rationality. Accordingly, the appeal to an underlying metaphysical ground of unity between nature and moral action is simultaneously an "explanation" of the divine intention. By Kant's procedure, it would be impossible to give such an explanation if God's actions and intentions were "unreasonable." Rationality – including, in this case, its straightforward yet important sense of "giving good reasons" – remains the governing feature of his account. Since the defense of divine transcendence once again turns out to be derivative from this deeper commitment to rationality, any suspicions about God's fate in the course of the moral argument are surely reinforced rather than eliminated. The stark contrast here with Luther's readiness to appeal to the mysterious and inscrutable nature of God's intentions simply underscores the sense in which the bondage of the will has been transferred from humanity to God.

Moreover, the conception of God as the highest original ground is the paradigmatic instance of Kant's tendency to posit underlying "unities" that serve as the idealized contrast case to humanity's finite and fragmented situation. In multiple contexts, God functions for Kant as the ideal flip side of a human limitation: God possesses an "intellectual" intuition in contrast to our sensuous intuition, a "holy" will as opposed to our fallible will, and pure "creativity" as opposed to the combination of receptivity and spontaneity characterizing human cognitive capacities. God's uniquely divine traits thus insure that, beyond the limitations, imperfections, and fragmentariness of human life, there is a single, archetypal principle that insures the possibility of an ultimate harmonizing of nature and freedom, a "metaphysical ground for their reunion."[104] Yet in such a conception of the divine role, the purely instrumental character of the God of the moral argument is surely radicalized rather than mitigated. God's role as an underlying metaphysical ground of unity is an abstraction intended to encourage finite rational agents to work to overcome their limitations, especially their moral ones. Any larger role that God viewed in this light might play would require something like the cosmological argument – the "first cause" argument – to expand the conception of God beyond these merely abstract and instrumental terms. But Kant himself has of course disclosed the weaknesses of the cosmological argument and can hardly revert to it when invoking the idea of God as the underlying ground of unity.

In addition, apart from the design of Kant's own moral theology, there is no particular reason to posit "God" as the source of an underlying unity of opposites. Kant himself suggests as much in his often revealing account of the "Limitation of the Validity of the Moral Proof" in the *Critique of Judgement*.[105] it is hardly surprising to find Kant emphasizing here that "the final end of creation is such a constitution of the world as harmonizes" with the final ends of practical reason – in short, a unity of nature and freedom indicative of the "moral justification" we enjoy for assuming "a final end of creation."[106] Yet in his elaboration of the idea of God as the moral author of this very possibility, Kant states at one point that "we have to assume *something* that contains the ground of the possibility and practical reality, or practicability, of a necessary final end," arguing that "we may conceive this 'something' as a wise Being ruling the world according to moral laws."[107] As Yovel has pointed out, the force of Kant's reference to "something" is that, as "a matter of principle, one could have pictured that factor in some other way, for instance, as a principle of *internal finality* that rules the universe."

> The fact that we represent it as the product of a God and project upon the latter some semi-anthropological attributes is inessential, and depends on our subjective limitations. For the same reason, the concept of God cannot *explain* the origin of ability. The ability in question is a real ontological power, whereas "God" and his attributes are merely modes of representation by which we picture the source of this ability to ourselves.[108]

In other words, Kant's reference to God as the necessary metaphysical ground of final purpose in nature is not only highly abstract and apparently parasitic on an argument Kant has himself repudiated, but it is perhaps arbitrary as well. At such points, it seems nearly impossible to separate out a definable theism from Kant's prior commitment to autonomous rationality.

One result of this overall picture is the way it suggests that, in the following century, Kierkegaard is not simply engaging in empty caricature when he has his pseudonymous author of *Fear and Trembling* link the idea that the "ethical is the universal" with the insight that "then ... I actually have no duty to God."[109] The obvious element of artifice at work in the composition of *Fear and Trembling*, as in all of Kierkegaard's pseudonymous works, requires careful handling when drawing such morals. Still, the connection Kierkegaard posits between the subordination of individual instances of moral choice to a universal (and universally communicable) principle, and a God who is an "invisible vanishing point, an impotent thought," appears quite apt in light of what we have just surveyed.[110] In effect, Kierkegaard has perceived that God's commandment to Abraham to sacrifice Isaac is the rough equivalent of God's refusing to proportion happiness and virtue. Kierkegaard has thus traced out the implications of Kant's own postulation process, concluding – not unconvincingly – that if something is a moral duty by virtue of being tracked back to the universal, then there is no truly robust sense in which I can be said to have a duty to God.

> If in this connection I then say that it is my duty to love God, I am actually pronouncing only a tautology, inasmuch as 'God' in a totally abstract sense is here understood as the divine – that is, the universal, that is, the duty. The whole existence of the human race rounds itself off as a perfect, self-contained sphere, and then the ethical is that which limits and fills at one and the same time.[111]

The underlying scaffolding supporting this position involves a snug interface between limits on what God can command (as set by the principle of universality) and the increasing abstraction of the very idea of God. The absorption of the divine will by the principle of universality effectively deracinates God in ways that foreshadow more recent criticisms of universalizing thinking as covertly hostile to valuable human differences. As Kierkegaard sees and Kant himself argues, the shift in metaphysical weight produced by this situation is entirely to the benefit of the moral agent, who grows in importance even as God gradually recedes from the scene as a dominating presence. When, in a different though related context, Kierkegaard says that in ethical existence "the individual is simply and solely interested infinitely in his own actuality" and cannot "ask about an actuality that is not one's own,"[112] his point seems puzzling if not viewed in this wider context.

While such matters are more typically surveyed in order to clarify the relation of religion and morality, or the relation between Kant and Kierkegaard,[113] they serve also to reinforce the general lesson of this study, which concerns the movement from divine transcendence to the domain of an immanent rationality in Kant's account of God. What I have suggested is that the "back door" God of the *Critique of Practical Reason* – already diminished by virtue of the lean terms of the moral argument and implicated in a new bondage of the will – is indeed a kind of vanishing point within Kant's scheme. This is why it is perennially difficult to say much about Kant's God, as opposed to the God of the metaphysics handbooks, and perhaps why his actual view of God is not among those key themes that come to mind when we speak of the Kantian legacy within modern theology. Such results follow quite naturally once God, too, comes under the requirements of the moral law.

The chief reason so much metaphysical interest has shifted from God to the moral agent is the radically enhanced concept of autonomy that leaves the agent in unmediated contact with his or her moral fate. The diminishing of the divine is not the occasion for this enhancement but its consequence; God is secondary to our moral fate and not primary to it. We thus find replicated at the purely conceptual level the transfer of worldly authority from the religious to the secular realm that is generally characteristic of European culture after 1600.[114] In both contexts, the issue at stake is autonomy from illegitimate religious intrusion and control.

Here, with the issue of autonomy itself, we come upon what is for some "the most central and profound concept in moral philosophy, but to others . . . an inapplicable relic of an unduly optimistic age, a desperate metaphysical flight from the implications of science and critical philosophy."[115] Either way, the issue is at the very center of Kant's vision, and it persists as one of the most vexed and troubled themes associated with the idea of modernity. The human capacity for "self-invention" implicit in Kant's theory of autonomy is,[116] of course, potentially the forfeiture of the divine ground so fundamental to the definition of the pre-modern West. Quite obviously, the current study can hardly do justice to historical and theological issues of such magnitude. The following chapter will content itself with the more modest task of clarifying several ways in which Kant's theory of autonomy is perhaps the key element in his principle of immanence, resulting in yet a deeper sense of the diminishing of God.

CHAPTER THREE

Autonomy's Autonomy

ROUSSEAU'S PROBLEM

The eddying effects generated by the moral argument evoke the underlying dynamic associated with Kant's principle of immanence. Clearly, Kant's intention in the *Critique of Practical Reason* is to offer a theologically positive account, one that rescues theism from superstition and religious enthusiasm on the one side, and from uncritical efforts to prop up theism with dubious metaphysical arguments on the other. Kant pursues this ambitious project in the conviction that a certain kind of insight into the moral life is the key to religious faith, in contrast to the more familiar tradition of viewing the moral life as the natural entailment of a given set of religious beliefs. The most obvious sense in which Kant effects this alteration in the relation between religion and morality is conveyed by the commitment to "the priority of the practical" over the theoretical, for it is this commitment that finally authorizes the prioritizing of moral faith over scientific knowledge in the consideration of religious claims. With respect to the intellectual integrity of the religious life, this conception of the relation between the theoretical and the practical informs the transition between the first two *Critiques* in ways that presumably give philosophical underwriting to theism without falling into the errors of metaphysical dogmatism.

At the same time, however, those features of the principle of immanence disclosed by the preceding examination of the moral argument suggest that a more fundamental prioritizing process is at work, one less congenial to the theological recovery required by the results of the first *Critique*. The manner in which a self-interested, self-guided rationality sets terms that define even the parameters of divine action displays this more fundamental process in dramatic form. Consequently, even though Kant nowhere makes the kind of direct assault on theistic belief that – taken out of context – one could read into the pages of the *Critique of Pure Reason*, his effort to restore theism to intellectual respectability exacts an enormous price from philosophical theology. The preeminence of God in the thought patterns of the pre-modern West is displaced by a new thought pattern tellingly revealed by the order in which Kant renders the postulates of practical reason: freedom, immortality, and – finally – God. The rational demonstration of the metaphysical validity of the second and third postulates depends entirely on the unique standing in philosophical reflection that Kant accords human freedom. It has been said that "freedom occupies a privileged place among the ideas of pure reason," for we truly "know" freedom as a condition of the moral law that is, in turn, itself a sheer "fact of reason." "By contrast, we neither know nor perceive the possibility and reality of God and immortality, since they are not conditions of the moral law but merely conditions of the highest good. ..."[1] The manner in which this subordination of the cognitive significance of theism to the prior apprehension of freedom subtly informs post-Kantian developments helps to account for the entirely new cultural atmosphere that succeeds the Enlightenment.

Kant shifts the locus of philosophical interest from divine action to human autonomy not arbitrarily, but because the latter constructs the moral community that is evidently the very telos of reason itself. The creation of such a community, with its members acting out of respect for the moral law and, thus, out of respect for one another, could be said to be autonomy's true vocation. Whether rendered as the "kingdom of ends," the "ethical commonwealth," or the "kingdom of heaven on earth," some such vision steadily takes shape in Kant's mature philosophy as humanity's own creation and ultimate goal. In a manner suggestive of the challenges facing the wider culture, the problem for Kant gradually becomes that of somehow fitting God into a process that, by definition, is governed by human freedom. By Kantian ground rules, a genuinely "moral" community is much easier to describe and account for through appeal to human freedom than through appeal to divine action. Freedom could never be for Kant a lingering appendage, carried along through cultural habit and calling for awkward incorporation into a moral vision that has its motivating impulse elsewhere. The same cannot be said for God.

There is no deeper or more difficult topic in Kant's philosophy than his theory of freedom, and recent scholarship tracing the emergence of Kant's position has created fresh imponderable issues even as it has settled or illuminated old ones.[2] Foremost in importance for the current study is the fact that, by refining his theory of freedom in terms of the idea of autonomy, and by then conceiving of autonomy as our capacity to give to the will ends not given to us by nature, Kant insures a deepening of the sense in which God is a problem for his total standpoint. Forged in a context in which he attempts to maintain a commitment to human freedom alongside his equally strong commitment to Newtonian determinism, Kant's account of autonomy creates a momentum that is at times difficult to reconcile with traditional theism. The fact that the creation of a moral community emerges as the very point of autonomy's exercise compounds this already difficult problem of – in effect – making God a part of this moral community in a coherent way.[3] In effect, God's role in the realization of the moral community replicates the role God plays in the full rendering of the highest good: it is a role that is secondary, subordinate, and very nearly an afterthought, in relation to the sustained attention devoted to the free will. The murky question of the extent to which Kant ever believed such a community to be a truly historical goal, as opposed to an unreachable ideal, does not affect the marginalization of God intrinsic to this vision – either way, God is a problem. In a somewhat odd but historically significant sense, the problem of incorporating God into Kant's vision of the moral community could be viewed as the cumulative inheritance bestowed by the theological tradition's protracted effort to reconcile human freedom with divine power and goodness. The issue of theodicy is never far from the surface of Kant's religious thought.

However unintentionally, then, the Kantian conception of autonomy introduces a variation on the idea that, with respect to humanity's highest aims and purposes, appeals to divine action are potentially redundant, if not actually harmful. They are potentially redundant in so far as, once decoded in terms of their authentic, inner meaning, appeals to divine action turn out to be references to humanity's own moral obligations and ethical possibilities, perhaps aided by God in mysterious ways that the truly good will does not count on; and they are potentially harmful, because dependence on divine rather than human effort may undercut actual moral progress by inducing passivity and servility. Versions of such insights run in powerful streams through seventeenth- and eighteenth-century deism long before they assume deepened philosophical complexity in Feuerbach, and a radicalized, subversive form in Nietzsche.[4] In very general terms, we can see here the rise to prominence of a special sort of attention to the self-governing, if not self-positing, character of the human will that becomes a fundamental trait of the "modern" West through social and cultural forms as otherwise diverse as democratic liberalism, existentialism, and expressionistic views of artistic creation.[5] We might even say that the modern idea of autonomy is the vehicle by which the Cartesian insight into reflexivity or self-relatedness assumed its most socially urgent and historically influential forms.

Whether one claims that Kant "discovered"[6] or "invented"[7] the modern idea of autonomy, his preoccupation with the issue implicates him deeply in these broader historical developments, including the marginalization of God in relation to the culture's main projects. Crucial in the depiction of both these broader issues and the more specific question of Kant's emerging viewpoint is the figure of Rousseau. Rousseau's general influence on Kant's approach to issues of freedom, morality, and human nature is well known, having been notoriously conveyed by Kant's own comment that Rousseau did for our understanding of the moral world something analogous to what Newton did for our understanding of the natural world.[8] While we often capture this influence in the familiar idea that Rousseau gave Kant a deeper appreciation for the common person's moral awareness, this aspect of Kant's debt is in fact parasitic on a more broadly based concern. Specifically, Rousseau helped Kant to grasp a serious difficulty intrinsic to the dominant theory of rationality sustaining the European Enlightenment. In effect, Kant's theory of autonomy becomes his solution to this difficulty.

In particular, Rousseau helped Kant to grasp the negative, indeed destructive, implications of the basically instrumentalist conception of rationality that had come to dominate progressive thought in the eighteenth century. The reasoning powers that had produced such impressive results in mathematics and the natural sciences since the early seventeenth century were demonstrated chiefly through calculation and experiment. As we see clearly in retrospect, the exhilaration produced by accelerating intellectual progress was closely associated with a sense of freedom from unwarranted authority, which is symbolized by Descartes' systematic skepticism toward all received wisdom and, more generally, by the secular settings in which serious intellectual work was increasingly pursued. The sort of "progress" we associate with modernity is unthinkable in the absence of what Amos Funkenstein has called the "de-theologization of science."[9] This is why the modern effort to "harness inquiry to the increase of human utility, welfare, and power" is typically correlated with the liberation of humanity from the arbitrariness of revealed truth.[10]

At the same time, however, the self-confidence associated with elite European intellectual life following the scientific revolution largely obscured the important fact that an instrumentalist, experimental conception of reason is powerless to define the proper or ultimate "ends" of reasoning itself. Some such point as this is the abstract version of the frequently observed truism that, whatever else its explanatory powers may reveal, natural science cannot give an account of the "good life." Despite all that one might say about the drag effect on intellectual progress of religious tradition, an appeal to tradition at least discloses the ends and goals of human endeavor, intellectual or otherwise. But without re-introducing an appeal to tradition, the descendants of Bacon, Galileo, and Newton could hardly address this broader issue, however remarkable the results of their investigations might be in other respects. Almost by default, then, Enlightenment Europe increasingly appealed to a conception of reason that receives its ends or goals from the passions, or sentiments. Someone such as Hume readily grasped this point and managed to incorporate it into his philosophical vision with character-istic candor and good cheer, as conveyed by his famous remark that "reason is, and ought to be, the slave of the passions."[11] Here as on numerous other issues, however, Hume turned out to be the exception, not the rule.

It would be Rousseau's special achievement to understand that sub-jecting us to our own passions may as easily lead to the deepest unhappi-ness and leave reason at odds with itself, an insight that tacitly redefines the Enlightenment as a failed promise.[12] Without the capacity to define or otherwise generate humane ends for its own endeavors, reason may end up enslaving us to its own product, thereby leading as easily to our alienation or even destruction as to our fulfillment. At the heart of Rousseau's account is a kind of Weberian nightmare, in which reason leaves us locked in the "iron cage" described by Weber as the result of historical developments in which we have blindly participated. The prophetic element in Rousseau's thinking is still working its way through modern history.

Crucial for my purposes is the fact that Rousseau's complex impact on Kant is certainly felt in connection with this general crisis of the proper "ends" of reason in ways that will have profound implications for the interplay between human autonomy and divine transcendence.[13] The issue raised by Rousseau sheds valuable light on the sense in which Kant's overall theory of rationality develops within a moral context, while also explaining why his specific theory of autonomy is devised with a view to the "good" will's capacity to prescribe ends opposed to those given by nature, including natural human passions and sentiments. These inten-tions lie behind Dieter Henrich's claim that "Kant considers his entire philosophy an attempt to refute the sophistry of reason that is in the service of pleasure."[14] At stake here is the moral telos of the will, the most serious lacuna left by mathematical and experimental reasoning. Rousseau's influence insures that Kant will solve this problem by unhooking the good will from external influences in ways that lead to the prioritizing process I have previously described in connection with the moral argument. The will's capacity to prescribe to itself laws derived from the very "form" of the rational will is the specific development guaranteeing that God's will assumes a secondary status. Once this move is made, it becomes virtually impossible to reconceptualize the relation between God and human freedom in a way that restores preeminence to the former. This "autonomy of autonomy" is important to pinpoint, for the issue of reconciling human freedom and divine transcendence is hardly new with Kant. What changes with him is the radical nature of autonomy that subsequently gives spontaneous human practice and creativity a bold new authority in European culture. The promise of Pico's "Oration on the Dignity of Man" comes to a powerful if belated fulfillment in Kant's theory of autonomy.[15]

It is in this regard that one might say that Kant's conception of autonomy closes the circle of Cartesian reflexivity, resulting in a purely human horizon for the culture's ongoing reflections about its highest projects. Just as there is little or no room for God within this closed circle, there is little room for God in the midst of modernity's most significant cultural projects, save the ideologically driven lip service God receives in order to generate social legitimacy for those projects. In the mid-twentieth century, the doomed theologian Dietrich Bonhoeffer perceptively identified how a "God of the gaps" was increasingly excluded from accounts and explanations of the natural world, as the various sciences filled in the remaining gaps still calling for explanation, such as sudden healings of the sick. As the Cartesian circle also closes, a parallel process occurs at the level of human subjectivity, enormously aided by Kant's conception of autonomy. By accounting for the depiction of a human destiny that had once been framed in providential terms, autonomy closes the circle of explanations in a way constituted solely by human subjectivity and activity, leaving God on the outside, at one with the supernatural God excluded by the filling in of Bonhoeffer's explanatory gaps and fundamentally irrelevant to modern life.

The more negative and radical implications of this set of developments could not have occurred to Kant himself, in part because his account of autonomy remains tied optimistically to the vision of a moral community. As autonomy's vocation, the moral community embodies the form in which humanity "completes" itself as its own project, signaling the final displacement of divine transcendence through the ongoing ripple effects of the principle of immanence. The full sense in which this displacement process occurs cannot be appreciated without further examination of the idea of autonomy itself, together with a consideration of the "needs" and "interests" of reason that create the very notion of a "vocation" for autonomy and disclose the ethical commonwealth as reason's self-generated goal. The latter issue will be addressed in the following chapter, while the former is the main concern of the remainder of the current chapter.

AUTONOMY'S AUTONOMY

"Autonomy of the will," Kant tells us in the *Foundations*, "is that property of it by which it is a law to itself independently of any property of objects of volition."[16] Kant depicts this self-legislative conception of freedom as the "positive" contrast to freedom understood simply "negatively" – that is, as independence from determination by an external cause.[17] In the well-worn but still helpful expression, freedom in the negative sense is "freedom from" outside interference or constraint. Implicit in the conception of the *positive* sense of freedom is Kant's deep commitment to "the property of the will to be a law to itself."[18] In contrast to mere "freedom from," the sense in which positive freedom is "freedom for" is the manner in which it is freedom for a special kind of agreement of the will with itself. This self-referential feature is already an important clue to autonomy's collusion in Kant's principle of immanence. Moreover, the self-referential feature signals Kant's part in a broader eighteenth century effort to break away from dominant conceptions of morality as a form of *obedience* and reconceptualize morality as a form of *self-governance*.[19]

One way to clarify Kant's understanding of autonomy is to focus on the idea of the "good will." This is because the goodness of such a will is the clearest manifestation of autonomy at work – the good will makes itself good through an act of self-reliance that follows a rule, rather than through the intercession of an additional agency.[20] This is not to perpetuate the mistaken notion that the will is acting autonomously *only* when it is acting morally, a mistake finding its source in the idea that, if I am not acting autonomously, I must be acting out of sensuous inclination and am thereby no more free (or culpable) than the bear that kills a camper. Such a view not only makes impossible the imputing of moral evil to the agent, but it disregards Kant's insistence that *both* sensuous *and* moral incentives are always present as I engage in maxim-making.

> Hence the distinction between a good man and one who is evil cannot lie in the difference between the incentives which they adopt into their maxim (not in the content of the maxim), but rather must depend upon *subordination* (the form of the maxim), *i.e., which of the two incentives he makes the condition of the other*.[21]

This refinement of Kant's account of the relation between incentives and moral agency underscores the agent's independence from determining influences, apart from the agent's own act of will. This "subordination" process may ultimately be deeply mysterious and embedded in the recesses of the agent's moral character, but at least the process is the agent's own.

The notion of the good will thus brings into sharp focus the important sense in which Kant's concept of autonomy implies motifs of self-invention and self-sufficiency that, in turn, signal the independence of the good will from God's will. To be sure, as a holy will, God's will is itself always good, but its being good is not the source of the moral agent's good will: as Kant remarks rather tartly at one point in the *Religion*, "godliness is not a surrogate for virtue."[22] Rather, the agent's own autonomy is virtue's source – the agent's own bootstraps are the only ones to pull. What we need to understand is the way in which a prominent Western thinker, produced in large part by north European Protestantism, devises a viewpoint that ultimately leads to a characterization of divine commands as heteronomous at best and, perhaps, finally irrelevant.

For Kant, the good will is defined by its form rather than by its content or object. His entire position flows from this basic principle. The reasons for this claim are embedded in the complex developments in Kant's thinking that finally culminate with the publication of the *Foundations of the Metaphysics of Morals* in 1785.[23] Here we find Kant's famous comment that the "good will" is the only thing that can be considered to be unconditionally good in and of itself.[24] The peculiar genius of Kantian ethics resides in the way Kant analyzes this claim in isolation from a consideration of the products of this good will; his famous anti-consequentialism finds its defining moment in the manner in which he renders the idea of the good will. This is not to imply that Kant's ethical theory involves no consideration of the "ends" of ethical action, a misleading stereotype of Kant that exemplifies Barbara Herman's complaint that "Kant's ethics has been the captive of its critics."[25] After all, larger "ends" are at stake both in Kant's Rousseau-like concern to overcome the limits of instrumentalism and in his depiction of the highest good as the final end of moral action. Indeed, as though conscious of this mistaken view of his position late in his career, Kant states flatly in *Religion within the Limits of Reason Alone* that

> in the absence of all reference to an end no determination of the will can take place in man, since such determination cannot be followed by no effect whatever; and the representation of the effect must be capable of being accepted, not, indeed, as the basis for the determination of the will and as an end antecedently aimed at, but yet as an end conceived of as the result ensuing from the will's determination through the law.[26]

In other words, the force of Kant's anti-consequentialism resides, not in the elimination of all concern for the ends of willing, but in the specific depiction of motivation itself, with particular emphasis on the conception of the will as susceptible to the influence of a rational principle. This rational principle is not mediated as a certain content resulting in an "end," but as a certain form embodied as a rule.

It is, of course, the principle of universalizability that is the form definitive of the good will: the will is good in so far as it prescribes to itself a form for its willing that could be replicated across all possible wills, regardless of any differences of autobiography or circumstance. We might say that the good will does for our conception of moral endeavor what the laws of physics do for our apprehension of the natural world, providing underpinnings of objectivity as well as regularity for both. The Kantian thesis that the moral law embodied in the universalizability principle "is objectively necessary relies on the same type and degree of objectivity he earlier claimed for scientific knowledge."[27] In both cases, Kant is proposing a vision of regularity that discredits whatever is irregular or exceptional – in both cases, in other words, we "spontaneously impose lawfulness on the world in which we live and thereby create its basic order."[28] The obvious fact that irregularity in the moral world is prevalent, while irregularity in the natural world is ruled out virtually by definition, does not affect the underlying parallel here that speaks eloquently of Kant's overall philosophical vision. The parallel itself sheds valuable light on Kant's arresting remark that, in the matter of determining the will, "[m]an conceives himself... in analogy to the deity...."[29]

In the increasingly complicated theory of the will accompanying this viewpoint, Kant even devises a means of replicating on the human side a conception of the will that mirrors the constancy of nature, but without jeopardizing either his commitment to freedom or his realistic grasp of our moral failures. Kant achieves this through his distinction between *Wille* and *Willkür*. Will understood as *der Wille* denotes the power to act out of a sense of moral obligation, which is to say, out of a sense of respect for the moral law. *Wille* is my fundamental rational potential that helps to explain how I could ever experience "obligation" in the first place, suggesting that *Wille* illuminates the very idea of a "rational being." In Schneewind's felicitous expression, *Wille* is the will construed "as the rational demand for consistency in action," a characterization that illuminates the connection between the good will and universalizability.[30] Will understood as *Wille* cannot itself act, but, if it could, it would always act rationally, as a virtual "moral natural law" for itself. Will understood as *die Willkür*, on the other hand, denotes my actual "power of choice" by which I in fact choose maxims exhibiting whether or not I have a good will.[31] If *Willkür* acts out of respect for the moral law, it makes real the potential of *Wille*. If not, then I transgress the moral law, but I do not thereby forfeit my ongoing capacity to be moral, since *Wille* remains intact.[32]

In an important sense, then, *Wille* is to the moral life what natural law is to the physical world: it suggests the idea of "constancy" over against which the notion of an exception or irregularity takes shape in pejorative ways. Unlike the mechanistic regularity of Kant's Newtonian world, however, the human will does not always abide by its own regularizing mandate. Truly rational agency is not *necessitated*, which is why moral lapses are so fundamental to our experience. Kant is effectively explaining these moral lapses in terms of an account of the will being at odds with itself. The relationship between the two aspects of the will is further conveyed by a remark in Kant's *Metaphysics of Morals:* "The Will [*Wille*] itself has no determining ground; but in so far as it can determine will [*Willkür*], it is practical reason itself."[33] The implication here of the metaphysical independence of the will is as important as the clarification of the relationship between the two aspects of the will. For whatever the exact relationship may be between the will in its wholly rational aspect and the will as the actual power of choice, it is clear that Kant is arguing that the will is providing itself with its own determining ground. In doing so, it acts autonomously.[34]

A further clue to the connection between the good will and autonomy is offered by what Kant calls our "predisposition to personality" in his inventory of human nature in *Religion within the Limits of Reason Alone.* "Personality" here connotes "personhood" – what makes us "persons" instead of beasts. As one of three basic "predispositions to good" in human nature, the predisposition to personality denotes "the capacity for respect for the moral law as *in itself a sufficient incentive of the will* [*Willkür*]."[35] The predisposition to personality, Kant tells us, is what underwrites the very concept of our being "accountable" beings.[36] The capacity to experience obligation and the state of being accountable go hand in hand. This combined effect of the two-aspect theory of the will and the predisposition to personality clarifies the important point that we are accountable to our own wills, rather than to some external agency or third party. Kant underscores this "internal" source of our sense of obligation in his effort to clarify our predisposition to personality:

> Were [the moral law] not given us from within, we should never by any ratiocination subtilize it into existence or win over our will [*Willkür*] to it; yet this law is the only law which informs us of the independence of our will [*Willkür*] from determination by all other incentives (of our freedom) and at the same time of the accountability of all our actions.[37]

In other words, the only incentive for the will that is a truly moral incentive is self-given.

Kant's complex theorizing about the nature of the will and the source of our experience of moral obligation is basically an extended gloss on his cardinal insight that the good will is determined by its form rather than by its content or object. The imposing terminological edifice constituting Kant's moral theory both clarifies this basic claim and underscores the self-given nature of obligation itself. The famous universalizability principle sheds valuable light at just this point, for it illuminates the theme of self-sufficiency while also explaining what Kant means by the "form" the moral agent gives the will. In moments of moral agency, I fashion maxims – or rules for acting – that either can or cannot be universalized.[38] In testing maxims for their universalizable form, I utilize the categorical imperative as the relevant template: always act so that the maxim of my action could be made into a universal law. As a rational agent, I reach "inside" myself to access this form of universalizability, subordinating to its influence that part of me – natural, physical, historical – that is on the "outside." The experience of autonomy is my experience of truly being able to do this, which is what is at stake in the notorious dictum, "ought implies can."[39]

In large part, Kant's point is that universalizability is something the moral agent can recognize simply by virtue of being rational. As in the case of recognizing philosophical necessity in a syllogism, recognizing universalizability in a maxim is not an acquired "skill," like the ability to name plants and animals, but is for Kant definitive of what it means to be a rational being. In this respect, the a priori character of moral knowledge in Kant's philosophy becomes plain. The autonomous agent is thus transparent to itself in the sense that, in the course of maxim-making, the agent prescribes universalizable rules *reflecting the agent's own rational structure*.[40] The form of universalizability definitive of the good will does not come from a source external to the agent but is a feature of the agent itself. This motif of "transparency" is an important counterbalance to the more common conception of Kant's ethics as leaving the agent divided against itself, with duty in a constant struggle with inclination. Hegel's famous complaint that Kant's ethics leaves behind a bifurcated conception of human nature likewise shields from view the unifying element in Kant's effort to make ethics autonomous.[41] This is not to say that being virtuous is an easy matter – Schneewind is clearly right when he confirms that Kant views morality as "always a struggle."[42] Rather, the key point concerns the agent's expression, through moral practice, of a quality that is the agent's own, a kind of rationalist/universalist precursor to romantic/individualist conceptions of expressivism that would follow Kant.

This remains true whether or not the agent succeeds in actually becoming virtuous.

This transparency is what is at issue in the suggestion that Kant's theory of autonomy completes in more aggressive form Cartesianism's reflexive turn. The moral agent's transparency to itself in the course of moral agency is at the same time a kind of recognition of self – rather than a subordination of self to an other – thus rendering in moral terms the element of reflexivity that Descartes makes definitive for epistemology. Despite the mature Hegel's eventual criticisms of Kant's moral theory, just such a moment of recognition is what is involved in the young Hegel's struggles with positivity in his grappling with Christianity's claims to truth.[43] Implicit in Kant, as explicit in the young Hegel, is the idea that a moral claim that is truly binding on me must have some natural fit with my innermost self, as opposed to a claim that forces itself on me in heteronomous fashion, in a manner analogous to the imposition of an unbelievable religious claim. Indeed, the metaphor of transparency here suggests the ideal relationship between moral obligation and my own rational structure. Something such as this transparency is presumably the point of Dieter Henrich's characterization of moral awareness in Kant as based upon a "self-agreement of the will."[44] The good will exploits its own rational structure when it imposes on itself the form of universality in discrete acts of maxim-making. It is, in a word, "autonomous."

Working together, these themes of universality, self-agreement, and self-recognition reinforce in powerful ways the emerging note of self-sufficiency in Kant's moral vision.[45] Together with the idea of philosophical necessity, the idea of universality is for Kant one of the hallmarks of rationality itself. No doubt the rise to prominence of the principle of universality also reflects the inevitable strategy of those early modern philosophers committed to the view that self-governance in political matters requires a moral epistemology based on equal access to needed moral concepts.[46] Obviously, the principle of universality is the natural vehicle for advancing this effort to overcome conflict-ridden sectarianism in ethics, even as it trades off of the prestige of the universalizing tendencies of mathematics and natural science. Rather ironically, we can thus begin to trace out the contingent historical circumstances that will elevate to prominence a principle often criticized for its ahistorical tendencies.

We gradually see here a deeper sense in which the theme of self-sufficiency runs through Kant's basic conception of autonomy as the will's capacity to prescribe to itself ends not prescribed by nature. The animating force moving Kant in this direction may have been Rousseau's problem regarding reason's proper end or goal, but the free-standing nature of Kant's eventual concept of autonomy surely reflects deeper historical forces at work as well. For Kant has not only radicalized the very notion of moral "obligation," making it a fundamental feature of rationality itself, but he has also insured that, as a moral agent, I am fundamentally obligated to *myself*. My capacity for respect for the moral law, provided by the predisposition to personality, is at the same time my capacity for respect for rational agents as ends in themselves, *beginning with myself*. Although, inevitably, actual moral agents grasp the moral law with the aid of socializing instruction provided by the surrounding culture (including religion[47]), Kant is adamant that the agent's relation to the moral law is unmediated: it is a "fact of reason" that almost has a sense of mystery about it.

> [T]he moral law is given, as an apodictically certain fact, as it were, of pure reason, a fact of which we are a priori conscious, even if it be granted that no example could be found in which it had been followed exactly. Thus the objective reality of the moral law can be proved through no deduction, through no exertion of the theoretical, speculative, or empirically supported reason; and even, if one were willing to renounce its apodictic certainty, it could not be confirmed by any experience and thus proved a posteriori. Nevertheless, it is firmly established of itself.[48]

As a "fact of reason," the moral law functions as a kind of Kantian analogue to Luther's second use of the law. In both cases, self-knowledge is the result. But whereas for Luther the law reveals me to be a desperate sinner incapable of saving myself, for Kant the fact of reason discloses a law requiring my autonomy as the condition of its very intelligibility. In so doing, this fact of reason licenses the crucial transition needed in Kant's practical philosophy, and in the *Critique of Practical Reason* in particular: namely, the transition from the question *whether* practical reason can have the moral law as an incentive to the claim that it can.[49] Implicitly, the most dramatic theological result arising out of this transition is not really the moral argument for the existence of God. Rather, the key result resides in Kant's remark that it is "not to be understood that the assumption of the existence of God is necessary as a ground of all obligation in general (for this rests, as has been fully shown, solely on the autonomy of reason itself)."[50] Once again, divine existence is subordinated to the larger interests of an autonomous rationality.

Consequently, my most profound insight into myself, mediated through a fact of reason, underscores the moral law's independence from wider metaphysical entanglements, including a divine will that could be conceived apart from rationality's own mandate.[51] In Pierre

Hassner's characterization, since the law that the moral actor respects "is an expression of the subject's autonomy, it stands not for an external authority but for his own will." As "good in itself independently of any effect it might have," the good will "in some measure replaces God and nature."[52] Metaphorically speaking, we might say that, in performing its particular act, the moral law needs no net just as freedom itself needs no cause. Subsequently, given the immediacy of access to the moral law enjoyed by rational agents, final confirmation is bestowed on the connection between the autonomy indubitably conveyed through my awareness of the moral law and my self-sufficiency as a moral agent. Self-sufficiency is precisely what is at issue when Kant explains the idea that "pure reason can be practical" by saying "that *of itself* and independently of anything empirical it can determine the will."[53]

In a revealing though obviously problematic attempt to account for the unmediated manner in which the moral law impinges on my awareness, Kant invokes the expression, moral "feeling." The moral law, he tells us in the second *Critique*, "is an object of the greatest respect, and thus the ground of a positive feeling which is not of empirical origin. This feeling, then, is one which can be known a priori."[54] The a priori character of my apprehension of the moral law connects up with the notion of "respect" that becomes more explicit in the account of the predisposition to personality in the *Religion*. This a priori feeling of respect for the moral law is all that I need to be autonomous – it is the source of my self-sufficiency as a moral agent. My sense of autonomy somehow resides in this self-understanding *as an agent*, rather than in my supposed "possession" of a valued trait or metaphysical quality. In Thomas Hill's helpful characterization, we should view Kant's idea of autonomy "less as a metaphysical account of what we are like than as a normative idea about the task, attitudes, and commitments of *rational* agents when deliberating about what to do." That is, Kant's view "has more to do with what we should count as reasons for acting, and with what we should hold ourselves responsible for, than with how human action fits into a metaphysical picture of what there is in the world."[55] In a certain sense, the entire burden of the present study is to suggest that much the same point emerges in connection with Kant's view of God.

The free-standing character of the Kantian account of moral agency is further underscored by the fact that the thread connecting moral feeling and the capacity for respect for the moral law also runs through Kant's idea of an "intellectual causality." This expression is Kant's odd way of accounting for the fact that freedom is the source of moral agency, without there being any prior "cause" residing behind the free act that would undermine its spontaneous character. "Respect for the moral law," Kant tells us, "is a feeling produced by an intellectual cause, and this feeling is the only one which we can know completely a priori and the necessity of which we can discern."[56] The concept of an intellectual or noumenal causality, which goes back to the first *Critique*, has caused no end of difficulties for Kant's commentators. The issue initially arises out of Kant's effort in the Third Antinomy of the first *Critique* to wrestle with the question of whether there is a way to conceive of causality apart from the mechanistic conception at stake in the Second Analogy of Experience. In the context of the Second Analogy, Kant offers his famous refutation of Hume's skepticism regarding the very notion of causality, thereby saving nature's strict causal connections. The Third Antinomy, in turn, basically poses the problem of whether the response to Hume that saves mechanism in nature also dooms the idea of freedom. Here, Kant proposes the idea of "transcendental freedom" that "stands opposed to the law of causality" and which is "not itself determined, in accordance with necessary laws, by another cause antecedent to it...."[57] His eventual resolution of the Antinomy in a manner that allows us at least to conceive of freedom alongside natural necessity is at the same time an endorsement of the notion of an intellectual causality.[58]

Yet understanding the rationale behind Kant's strategy hardly positions us to grasp what he could mean by an intellectual causality. After all, by Kant's own standards, the expression is profoundly self-contradictory: the very notion of "causality" is for Kant relevant only to the phenomenal world of appearances, yet he clearly wishes to import its main connotations into the noumenal or intelligible world that is freedom's domain.[59] Put differently, the very idea of a "cause" is for Kant a pure concept or category which, by definition, can have no role or application apart from the world of appearances. The awkwardness of Kant's position is signaled by, among other things, his admission that "there can be no *before* and *after*" in connection with actions understood as the result of an intellectual causality, since "time" is a pure intuition having purchase only on the phenomenal world.[60] In the second *Critique*, Kant struggles to salvage his account of an intellectual causality through an argument by analogy:

> The moral law is, in fact, a law of causality through freedom and thus a law of the possibility of a supersensuous nature, just as the metaphysical law of events in the world of sense was a law of the causality of sensuous nature; the moral law thus defines that which speculative [i.e., theoretical] philosophy had to leave undefined. That is, it defines the law for a causality the concept of which was only negative in speculative philosophy, and for the first time it gives objective reality to this concept.[61]

Despite Kant's efforts to suggest that the idea of an intellectual causality is in fact a way of cashing in on a promissory note left behind by the first *Critique*, the suspicion lingers that he is trying to say too much when discussing freedom as a cause. Yet the thorny specifics of Kant-interpretation are less important here than the additional light shed on the element of self-sufficiency associated with the authentic exercise of autonomy. For Kant's whole point in linking together moral feeling, the capacity of respect for the moral law, and an intellectual causality is to emphasize that the moral agent is in an immediate relation to all that informs or otherwise produces the good will. The good will's power to act autonomously is generated by the moral agent's capacity for moral feeling which, in turn, imparts an awareness of respect for the moral law. This awareness is the very source of my sense of moral obligation and can never be eradicated.[62] Finally, my sense of moral obligation is a kind of window on my autonomy, since autonomy is for Kant necessarily entailed by the very moral law producing my sense of obligation.[63] As the notion of moral feeling implies, the elements of a moral psychology are clearly present in Kant's account of moral agency, but the psychological feature never supersedes or dilutes the emphasis on rational necessity sustaining Kant's ethics. As the two sides of the same rational capacity, necessity and universality thus insure my free-standing capacity as a moral agent. I am already profoundly intimate with my own moral touchstone, which is to say, I am "autonomous."

AUTONOMY AND DIVINE COMMANDS

Kant's conception of autonomy takes us onto mysterious ground, in part because his Newtonian sense of a good explanation prohibits him from ever "explaining" autonomy, since to do so would involve placing autonomy in a causal sequence that would rob it of its point. Closely associated and similarly mysterious is the question of the metaphysical status of the moral law itself. The force of the familiar idea that Kant's ethics is concerned with "the" moral law – and not with specific moral *laws* – is to draw attention to the universalizability principle informing the categorical imperative. The moral law itself becomes real *as* a form and not as a content. Yet as challenging as these difficulties are, they do not finally obscure the fact that, in his moral theory, Kant is fashioning a powerful vision of humanity's self-reliance. Indeed, what we might call the "autonomy of autonomy" – its free-standing character as a feature of a will motivated by respect for the moral law – needs no additional metaphysical supports. Kant's principle of immanence finds its most complete expression just here, and the tension with received notions of humanity's dependence on God is considerable.

In fact, it is not only freedom in its positive aspect – as autonomy – that creates theological tension. If we recall that freedom in the less refined but still significant negative sense is defined by Kant as that property of the will "by which it can be effective independently of foreign causes determining it,"[64] we confront the interesting possibility that divine commands not subsumable under the moral law are simply incompatible in principle with human freedom, even apart from the special considerations introduced by the theory of autonomy. The tension between human freedom and God may have its most arresting aspect in connection with the self-legislative mandate introduced by Kant's positive conception of freedom, since the suggestion of a usurping of the divine prerogative is most evident here. But a baseline difficulty is injected at the outset if we consider that divine commands perhaps qualify as versions of the "foreign causes" determining the will that are inimical to the interests of freedom in the negative sense. At the very least, the two senses of freedom taken together underscore the anthropocentric frame of reference out of which Kant is operating.

As in the case of the moral argument, God remains incorporated into Kant's overall vision, yet it is a God oddly muted by the potent strivings of an autonomous rationality. By hinting at the bondage of the divine will, the details of the moral argument convey this point in subtle but unmistakable ways. Similarly, Kant's account of autonomy and the good will leaves no room for a divine command that derives its obligatory status apart from the moral law, or that overrides my own exercise of autonomy. The fact that, for Kant, God would never *want* to corrupt either the moral law or autonomy does not reinstate a robust conception of divine transcendence so much as it confirms the image of a transfer of final authority from God to an immanent rationality. God is here subject to the same universalizability principle as we are.

Kant thus stands at a culminating juncture in connection with the long debate over the linkage between God's will and natural law, and between voluntarism and antivoluntarism in the account of the relation between religion and morality.[65] His theory of autonomy does not contribute to this debate so much as it sets fresh terms for it in ways that will permanently alter the European cultural landscape. The force of his position is readily evident when we acknowledge that traditional conceptions of divine commands as sources of moral motivation are, in principle, as heteronomous in nature as are sensuous inclinations. Any external material influence that cannot be assimilated to the principle of universalizability is incompatible with Kant's conception of properly exercised autonomy; and any such external influence that *is* assimilated by the principle of universalizability disappears from view once the assimilation is complete, exemplified by Kierkegaard's God-of-universalizing-ethics who becomes a "vanishing point." In a curious sort of way, traditional divine command theory for Kant possesses too much concreteness and not enough abstraction. The only *moral* sense in which I can be said to be obeying God's will is the sense in which God's will may be identical with the universalizability principle expressed by the categorical imperative. But of course this leaves us in much the same situation we previously observed in connection with the *Critique of Practical Reason*.

In fact, there can be little doubt that, for Kant, God's will for me is indeed in strict conformity with the principle of universalizability, for such a position is firmly embedded in the numerous variations on Kant's comment that "religion is the recognition of all duties *as* divine commands."[66] The force of this remark is not to argue that God's commanding a duty is what makes it moral, but that its being universalizable makes a duty a divine one: in Kant's own words, "we shall not look upon actions as obligatory because they are the commands of God, but shall regard them as divine commands because we have an inward obligation to them."[67] The "inwardness" of our relationship to the rational character of a moral requirement precedes and informs the more narrowly theological feature. Indeed, regarding the very idea of God's will, Kant goes so far as to observe that "we have no conception of such a will, except as formed in accordance with" the moral law.[68] In short, we shall

> believe ourselves to be acting in conformity with the divine will in so far only as we hold sacred the moral law which reason teaches us from the nature of the actions themselves; and we shall believe that we can serve that will only by furthering what is best in the world, alike in ourselves and in others. Moral theology is thus of immanent use only. It enables us to fulfill our vocation in the present world by showing us how to adapt ourselves to the system of ends, and by warning us against the fanaticism, and indeed the impiety, of abandoning the guidance of a morally legislative reason in the right conduct of our lives, in order to derive guidance directly from the idea of the Supreme Being. For we should then be making a transcendent employment of moral theology; and that, like a transcendent use of pure speculation, must pervert and frustrate the ultimate ends of reason.[69]

Originally staked out in the first *Critique*, this association of an uncritical view of divine commands with what Kant calls "fanaticism" eventually receives its definitive expression in *Religion within the Limits of Reason Alone*, where Kant depicts the notion of unmediated "communications" from God as "the moral death of reason."[70]

To be sure, Kant's account is not immune to some confusion on this point. In an interesting moment foreshadowing the second *Critique*'s postulation process, Kant remarks in the *Critique of Pure Reason* that God is in fact the "condition of the possibility" of the "obligatory power" of morality. Yet he immediately subsumes this observation under the same reasoning process by which proper claims to God's existence flow from morality, as in the second *Critique*:

> At some future time we shall show that the moral laws do not merely presuppose the existence of a supreme being, but also, as themselves in a different connection absolutely necessary, justify us in postulating it, though, indeed, only from a practical point of view.[71]

Presumably, this inchoate attempt to relate God to the binding authority of the moral law is a preview of Kant's eventual effort to display the unity of God's will with the aims of the highest good through the notion of the "highest original good."[72] And it is surely fair to say that Kant's actual intention is to devise a moral vision depicting the rationality of the moral life in a manner that respects the prerogatives and autonomy of both God and humanity. However, as in the case of our previous examination of Kant's appeal to the "highest original good," the momentum of his conception of an autonomous rationality is clearly outpacing Kant's apparent effort to strike a balance between traditional theism and the aggressive mandates of his own emerging position. "Even the Holy One of the Gospel must be compared with our ideal of moral perfection before He is recognized as such," Kant remarks at one point in the *Foundations*, adding: "But whence do we have the concept of God as the highest good? Solely from the idea of moral perfection which reason formulates a priori and which it inseparably connects with the concept of a free will."[73] Reason is, as it were, on its own, with God by contrast dependent on an idea that "reason formulates a priori." We might say that Kant's conception of an autonomous rationality introduces an almost unmanageable propellant that gradually builds up pressure elsewhere in his philosophy, forcing to the margins other claims Kant apparently wants to make and threatening to expel them altogether. As in the case of the moral argument, the diminishing of the divine occurring in conjunction with Kant's account of autonomy is no doubt a spin-off effect rather than a directly intended result of his line of argumentation. But it is a very real effect nonetheless.

In the course of the previous chapter's examination of the details of the moral argument, we had occasion to ask, "What would happen if God refused in a given instance to proportion happiness and virtue?" In the current context, concerning the relation between divine commands and an autonomous rationality, the parallel question is, "What if God proposed an immoral command?" As in the previous case, to respond simply by arguing that a truly good God would not *want* to propose an immoral command begs the question at stake by presupposing a principle of goodness. Once again, the Kierkegaard of *Fear and Trembling* had just the right point in view when he suggested that God's commandment to Abraham to sacrifice Isaac involved a "suspension" or complete bracketing of ethics as a recognizable cultural form. There is simply no way that an ethical theory that subsumes particular duties under a universalizability principle could assimilate or intelligibly relate to God's command to Abraham: the command literally makes no sense. "Ethically speaking" – which is to say, speaking from the standpoint of universalizability – Abraham truly *is* either a murderer or a madman.[74] Apart from these options, the only way to address such a command is to "set aside" the ethical, forgoing the attempt to make any sense of it in terms that could be shared or communicated publicly. Abraham's dramatically rendered silence is the flip side of the universal communicability of the Kantian rational principle.

The implications of this biblical example are confirmed by Kant's actual remarks about biblical interpretation. With the self-grounding character of our sense of moral obligation in the background, Kant effectively enjoys the benefits of a theory of biblical interpretation already embedded in the very definition of religion as the "recognition of all duties *as* divine commands." Scripture yields to the hermeneutical principle evident in Kant's rhetorical question: "I raise the question as to whether morality should be expounded according to the Bible or whether the Bible should not rather be expounded according to morality." The resulting acts of biblical interpretation, Kant candidly admits, may not only "appear forced" but "may often really be forced." And yet "if the text can possibly support" the moral interpretation, "it must be preferred to a literal interpretation which either contains nothing at all [helpful] to morality or else actually works counter to moral incentives."[75] Far from offering a world in which we "live, and move, and have our being," the biblical world is subject to being subsumed under autonomy's own mandate. Kant's moral world thus absorbs the Bible itself, a development suggestive of the limitless possibilities associated with the autonomy of autonomy in the decades ahead.

CONCLUSION

We might summarize the issues raised in this chapter in the following way. Sensitive to the problems inherent in the Enlightenment's dominant conception of rationality, Kant frames the critical philosophy in terms of a theory of autonomy that insures a moral telos for human endeavor. In effect, Kant's theory of autonomy displays reason's true "end." Kant achieves this result by unhooking the exercise of the free will from any external determinant, or even from any particular feature of human nature; instead, the truly moral will freely determines itself by giving itself its own end. What establishes the morality of an autonomous act is a formal, not a material consideration, as displayed in the rule the will legislates for itself.

Significantly, this way of insuring the independence of the free will from a material determining ground is simultaneously a declaration of human independence from a divinely ordained conception of good willing or even of our moral telos taken as a whole. If we in fact *do* reconcile the notion of the good will with the classic idea of God's will, we find that the latter can only be construed in terms of a universalizing rational principle that repeats the domesticating of divine transcendence that has previously been disclosed in connection with the moral argument. In short, the fact that Kant can claim that his moral outlook is compatible with religious belief is simply parasitic on his subordination of traditional religious claims – even including claims bearing on divine existence itself – to reason's demand for universalizability. His own view of biblical interpretation confirms this result.

Autonomy's usurping of moral authority is perhaps the most potent expression of Kant's principle of immanence. The compromise of divine transcendence is occasioned in this instance by the idea of a rational will giving itself its own end, making the note of independence from external determinants both stark and complete. The link between the idea of self-governance and "God-likeness" is virtually explicit, as Kant "transposes onto human practical reason the relation he tried to work out ... between God and the goodness of the outcomes of his choices."[76] What gradually comes into view here is the fact that an appeal to the divine will in the definition of humanity's proper goals is not simply heteronomous but something even worse: it is redundant. For what need could there be for divine prescriptions on the part of a moral agent that can give itself its own ends? Yovel has helpfully captured the heart of the matter by pointing out that, in connection with the duty to promote the highest good, "God has been explicitly transformed into the assistant of man." But Kant's way of effecting this transformation results in Yovel's rather haunting question: "does God really assist in anything?"[77]

The manner in which Kant's conception of autonomy thus absorbs traditional divine prerogatives is ultimately confirmed by the fact that autonomy not only has a vocation, it actually has a "career" – not simply a calling, but a calling that becomes a task undertaken over time. By this I mean to highlight how Kant finally concentrates the proper ends of autonomous rationality in his conception of an emergent moral community, which he finally calls the ethical commonwealth. Mediating between this ultimate goal and individual spontaneous acts of free willing is a battery of shaping devices insuring that, over time, moral acts will not simply be random, episodic, and disconnected, but will in fact be funneled intelligibly toward a specifiable moral goal. These mediating devices are rendered metaphorically by Kant in terms of such notions as the "interests" and "needs" of reason, reflective of the structured quality of reason's quest for completion and totality. It is precisely this drive toward totality that enables an immanent and autonomous rationality to displace the historical dynamic traditionally associated with divine providence. In light of this displacement process, we might say that the Kantian metaphors mediating between discrete instances of moral agency and their total product in the ethical commonwealth illuminate the avenues or pathways along which transcendent activity is transformed into human agency. Kantian "needs" and "interests" of reason, far from being marginal or philosophically "soft" notions, are in fact the very devices by which Kant contributes to the creation of a "modern" world. They are not "mere" metaphors, but nothing less than expressions of the independence of reason itself from any external conditioning agent.

Consequently, Kant's account of the direction reason takes in its search for ultimate satisfaction is not only important for an understanding of the ethical commonwealth, but is significant in itself. The aim of the next chapter is to provide a transition between this account of autonomy and the discussion of the ethical commonwealth by clarifying the metaphorical devices that mediate this very transition in Kant's own thinking. Autonomy does not simply arrive spontaneously at its goal but devises that goal through the same self-structuring capacity that gives it its point. The interplay between metaphors of "activity" and metaphors of "construction" discloses reason's ability to do this and is the appropriate prelude to an in-depth account of the consummation of Kant's principle of immanence in his ideal moral community.

CHAPTER FOUR

Reason's Interest

RATIONAL METAPHORS

In her characteristically provocative way, Onora O'Neill has argued that "a series of connected political and juridical metaphors constitute the deep structure of the *Critique of Pure Reason*," making the *Critique* a "profoundly political" work.[1] Whatever the merits of her bold claim of a political dimension, O'Neill's reading of Kant helpfully draws attention to the powerful role metaphors do in fact play in Kant's account of reason and its "employment." The very idea of a "critique" of reason turns out upon inspection to convey not simply the familiar notion of reason's powers and limits in the effort to avoid the pitfalls of philosophical dogmatism. For alongside this obvious feature of Kant's undertaking is the striking fact that the investigation into the powers of reason depends heavily upon metaphors of "construction" and "activity." The very familiarity of the resulting rhetorical devices has doubtless contributed to an underappreciation of them as a source of insight into Kant's understanding of reason.

Certainly this is O'Neill's view, particularly with respect to the theme of "construction." In a summary that she takes to be in fundamental contrast to the Cartesian starting point for philosophy, Kant speaks of the "sum of all knowledge of pure speculative reason as a building for which we have at least the idea within ourselves." In Kant's view, the problem turns out to be that, in its speculative ambitions, previous philosophy has been unconstrained by an accurate inventory of our building materials in its construction projects. In a highly suggestive development of this thought in the "Transcendental Doctrine of Method" at the very end of the first *Critique*, Kant observes that we have made an estimate of the materials, and have determined for what sort, height and strength of building they will suffice. Indeed, it turned out that although we had in mind a tower that would reach the heavens, yet the stock of materials was only enough for a dwelling house – just roomy enough for our tasks on the plain of experience and just high enough for us to look across the plain. The bold undertaking had come to nothing for lack of materials, quite apart from the babel of tongues that unavoidably set workers against one another about the plan and scattered them across the earth, each to build separately following his own design. Our problem is not just to do with materials, but even more to do with the plan. Since we have been warned not to risk everything on a favorite but senseless project, which could perhaps exceed our whole means, yet cannot well refrain from building a secure home, we have to plan our building with the supplies we have been given and also to suit our needs.[2]

The "supplies" in question, Kant says specifically, are "the pure a priori concepts," and he subsequently warns that, in the "critical estimate of what may be expected from our faculties," there in fact arises the question "whether we are in a position to build at all; and to what height, with the material at our disposal...we may hope to carry the edifice."[3]

However much this imagery may differ from Descartes' preoccupation with secure "foundations," it shares in common with Cartesianism the modern European tendency to devise philosophical method through appeal to some combination of images of "building up" and "tearing down." In a loose but perhaps telling sense, Kant's account is a precursor to Wittgenstein's proposal that we can dismantle our conceptual framework and construct a completely new one, so long as we do not attempt to dismantle everything at once. For his part, Kant employs metaphors of construction to emphasize not only his central point about the speculative modesty of his results, but also his own, post-Cartesian version of the reflexive quality of reason itself. Just as a planned building must be realistically suited to our inventory of materials and personal resources, reason's ambitions must be adjudicated with full awareness of its powers and limits, which can only occur through a "critique" of reason. The perennial puzzlement over the very possibility of Kant's project – the question of how a "critique can be undertaken without presupposing some conception of reason"[4] – is implicitly addressed by the terms of Kant's imagery, as he distinguishes between the "materials" and the "plan" associated with his building project.

Thus, the Critique's preceding "Transcendental Doctrine of Elements" turns out to have been a kind of inventory of materials, resulting in those restrictions on the size and scope of philosophical building projects that rationalist philosophers, in particular, failed to appreciate. In O'Neill's words, "rationalism failed because it took no account either of the paucity of materials or of the disagreements about the plan among the fellow workers."[5] Yet we must embark on *some* sort of construction, despite our limited inventory, which underscores the importance of a "plan." Our problem, Kant insists, has "not just to do with materials, but even more to do with the plan," meaning that "we have to plan our building with the supplies we have been given and also to suit our needs." The very idea of having "needs" requiring accommodation is the crucial element here, for this metaphor, in particular, signals reason's special role. Since we need to "live" somewhere, the question is not *whether* we shall build an edifice, but what sort of edifice we shall construct. Our undertaking will necessarily be limited by our inventory of supplies, yet the construction project itself is not an option, but the result of our needs. Reason in turn generates these needs since, after all, reason is for Kant fundamentally characterized by its needs rather than by any cognitive results. Similarly, reason will provide the plan that reveals how the materials in reason's own inventory will be utilized, aided by its unique capacity for self-discipline, as opposed to the external discipline or control that might be exercised by an outside authority. Appropriately aware of its own needs, reason is and must be its own authority.[6] In short, reason gets its own house in order.

Kant's metaphors are thus suggestive of a personification of reason in ways that implicitly aid autonomy in pursuit of its vocation.[7] Truly rational activity is not haphazard and episodic, like the erratic behavior of a child; rather, it is related to a "plan," like the vocational efforts of a mature adult who is capable of establishing and pursuing goals. Kant's own philosophical plan is rational precisely because it is generated by reason itself and not imposed by an external agency or heteronomous force. Reason itself "acts freely," Kant tells us.[8] In principle, at least, humanity thus holds its destiny in its own hands and needs no plan, blueprint, or marching orders coming from the "outside." Heretofore, the problem has not been insufficient materials for executing the plan, but an inaccurate and unrealistic inventory of what those materials are, resulting in a plan much too ambitious for an autonomous yet finite being. By this argumentative route, metaphors subtly become the vehicle by which reason's own structure becomes apparent: reason's structure reveals the activity of "self-structuring." This activity of self-structuring, in turn, discloses the ultimate goal of autonomy's vocation, which will assuredly be a genuinely autonomous result because the original plan was self-given.

There is in fact remarkable consistency in Kant's deployment of the motif of construction and its associated metaphors.[9] The first *Critique* demonstrates that, in its purely cognitive efforts, reason constructs a world of experience by rendering it in terms of space, time, substance, and causality. Kant's moral philosophy, in turn, distills out for our attention a categorical imperative that is effectively an invitation to construct universal laws. I am not required to imitate the behavior of my peers or accept the orders of a presumed superior. Instead, I particip- ate in the construction of the moral universe itself by devising maxims that could become universal laws. Finally, viewed from the totalizing perspective of reason, moral endeavor turns out to have a collective or social dimension involving the construction of an ideal moral commun- ity. Reason's natural drive toward construction not only reveals its self- sufficiency but turns out to be the clue to the meaning of history itself.

As a further manifestation of Kant's principle of immanence, rhetorical devices thus reinforce in powerful ways the insight that, in Kant's overall philosophy, reason takes on the characteristics traditionally associated with divine agency. Indeed, one might justifiably suggest a providential character implicit in reason's role in both depicting and generating humanity's authentic, final end in the ideal of the ethical commonwealth. In this as in other instances, reason's restlessness reveals itself in the totalizing tendencies that seek out the absolute or unconditioned object of any given set of conditions, such as the unconditioned product of moral endeavor. As we have already seen, it is precisely this totalizing activity that is at work in Kant's depiction of the highest good. In such instances, the "need" of reason to seek out the unconditioned defines reason's "task" and holds out the prospect of certain "satisfactions" for reason to enjoy. What is finally noteworthy is the fact that, in taking on these "tasks" and seeking its own "satisfaction," reason leaves less and less for a transcendent agency to do, beginning with the very "planning" of autonomy's vocation. Kant's own metaphors disclose the transfer of this task to the immanent domain of rationality itself.

In short, Kant's invocation of metaphor in the account of reason turns out upon inspection to be a valuable clue to reason's self-sufficiency.[10] The aim of the remainder of this chapter is to clarify certain aspects of Kant's account of reason that lead in this direction, thus shedding further light on the resulting connection between metaphorical usage and reason's self-sufficiency. The theme of self-sufficiency, in turn, leads naturally to an examination of the ethical commonwealth itself, which turns out to be a truly "ethical" commonwealth precisely because of its self-invented character as autonomy's true vocation: Kant's metaphors serve as a natural bridge between autonomy and the ethical common- wealth as the final realization of his principle of immanence. The culmi- nation of the principle's effects resides in the fact that, for Kant, we give ourselves the command to build the ethical commonwealth in ways disclosed by the metaphors of construction, interest, and need. As a result, "providence" comes from within, not from without. Kant has himself framed the decisive question this way: "What may I hope?"[11] In yet another variation on the patterns of Cartesian reflexivity, Kant's answer to his own question resides in reason's ability to draw on its capacity for self-structuring in the construction of a moral universe. The irresistible movement toward separating humanity's best hope from transcendent agency is nearly complete.

The "Interest" of Reason

The string of Kantian metaphors and their specialized employment in relation to reason's activities serves initially to remind us of one of the most puzzling features of the *Critique of Pure Reason*. The puzzlement resides in the fact that the apparent subject matter in the book's title comes last in the order of Kant's exposition, appearing long after lengthy analyses of our cognitive powers through the accounts of sensibility in the "Transcendental Aesthetic" and the understanding in the "Transcendental Analytic." Indeed, the latter is, for many commentators, the true heart of the *Critique*, with the account of reason in the subsequent "Transcendental Dialectic" often portrayed as of greater historical than philosophical interest. Frequently, the "Transcendental Dialectic" is treated as though it is Kant's catalogue of errors committed by his predecessors, following the completion of his account of the truly important matters in the *Critique*. At the same time, it cannot be denied that it is only here that Kant explicitly discusses the apparent topic of the book, which makes for a puzzling combination.

The conundrum surrounding the presumably central issue of reason goes even deeper. As John Sallis once observed, the fact that the *Critique* appears from the very start to be dealing in some broad sense with reason and its powers, and yet embarks on an examination of "reason" as such only in the "Transcendental Dialectic," actually means that the very subject matter of the book is ambiguous. Sallis goes on to identify two different senses in which Kant speaks of reason.

> According to the broader of the two senses, the Aesthetic and Analytic belong to the critique of pure reason no less than does the Dialectic, for this broader sense corresponds to the mere "contrasting [of] the rational with the empirical" – that contrast to which Kant comes by beginning "from the point at which the common root of our power of knowledge divides and throws out two stems" (A835/B863). This sense is to be distinguished from the narrower sense according to which reason is only

one of the higher faculties of knowledge, to be contrasted especially with the understanding.[12]

Sallis himself suspects that the "ambiguity is anything but a mere equivocation" on Kant's part but is "grounded in the issue of reason itself."[13] By this reading, not only is the very subject matter of the *Critique of Pure Reason* ambiguous by its very nature, but its proper expression will likely assume metaphorical or some other indirect form. That is, Kant's apparent inability to be either direct or univocal in connection with the central question of "reason" is telltale in an important way: it means that reason's "activity" is itself elusive. Kant is attempting to "critique" reason, but clearly this turns out not to be the same thing as domesticating it. In thus slipping out of his explanatory grasp, reason confirms its own nature as both active and restless in a way that Kant attempts to capture metaphorically.

Interestingly, then, Kant has an easier time offering direct remarks about reason taken beyond its proper boundaries than about reason viewed in its legitimate role. His effort to balance the cautionary remarks that explain the philosophical dead ends of the past, with positive remarks concerning reason's rightful employment, runs through the "Transcendental Dialectic" as a kind of emblem of the entire critical philosophy. Reason's characteristic activity involves the quest for unity and totality, but Kant argues simultaneously that such activity is non-cognitive, which gives his theory of reason its unique quality. As we have already seen, prior to this section of the *Critique*, all matters pertaining to the cognitive process – that is, to "knowledge" itself – are not, for Kant, matters of "reason" but of the interaction of sensibility and understanding – not *Vernunft*, but *Sinnlichkeit* and *Verstand*. Familiar as necessary background to Hegel's criticisms of Kant, this point underscores the special quality of those features of reason Kant is at pains to clarify in the "Transcendental Dialectic." While Kant characterizes the "understanding" as the "faculty which secures the unity of appearances by means of rules," he depicts "reason" as the "faculty which secures the unity of the rules of understanding under principles."[14] In effect, then, reason in Kant's specialized sense is once-removed from the authentically cognitive activities of the understanding: reason does not connect up with experience so much as it organizes and systematizes the principles by which the understanding participates in cognitive encounters. This activity is epitomized in the generation of the "ideal" of pure reason we surveyed in chapter 2.

The key element in Kant's account is reason's active quest for wholeness and totality, or what Roger Sullivan has helpfully labeled reason's "quest for finalities."[15] As Kant explains in a characteristic remark, reason "concerns itself exclusively with absolute totality in the employment of the concepts of the understanding," endeavoring to "carry the synthetic unity...up to the completely unconditioned."[16] We might think of this as Kant's way of saying that reason is that aspect of our intellectual capacity that cannot tolerate the absence of closure. Reason makes its demand for totality

> in accordance with the principle that *if the conditioned is given, the entire sum of conditions, and consequently the absolutely unconditioned* (through which alone the condition has been possible) *is also given.*[17]

A major interest of the "Transcendental Dialectic" is to demonstrate the many ways in which philosophers have traditionally confused this fundamentally organizing or regulative activity with a cognitive one, producing the illusion of knowledge rather than knowledge itself – as though they really had constructed a "tower that would reach the heavens" rather than a more modest "dwelling house."

Simultaneously, Kant is eager to demarcate the genuinely legitimate domain of reason's unifying regulative activity, acknowledging that reason's drive to systematize or totalize the concepts that come into view is natural, unavoidable, and – properly considered – philosophically useful. What is deplorable is not reason's natural tendency to drive beyond the bounds of sense, but the readiness of school metaphysicians to make knowledge-claims for what Kant calls their "random groping, and, what is worst of all, a groping among mere concepts."[18] Such an uncritical attitude is, for Kant, the very source of the antinomies signaling the impasse into which thought is then inevitably driven. Kant's own examples show the dead ends down which traditional reflection stumbles when considering, say, freedom and determinism or the question of whether or not the world has a beginning in time. Because directly opposing claims can be successfully argued, Kant remarks, "reason therefore perceives that it is divided against itself."[19] Indeed, the very notion of "antinomy" – the argumentative form in which we can demonstrate reason making equally justifiable but contradictory claims – is not only at the heart of the "Transcendental Dialectic" but a major source of Kant's decision to undertake a "critique" of reason's powers in the first place.[20] In this sense, the antinomies turn out to be what has been called "the saving grace of philosophy,"[21] for they serve as the occasion for demonstrating reason's non-cognitive activity which, in turn, helps to bring into view the proper ends of reason. The antinomies are to Kant's philosophy what Descartes' "evil demon" is to his, yet "the discovery that reason brings about its *own* greatest self-deceptions" surpasses even the

Cartesian evil demon, "because it no longer uncovers only a hypothetical consequence but rather the reality of the immanent movement of reason" itself.[22] Kant thus finds himself attempting "to limit reason's ambitions by enhancing its self-knowledge."[23] The two go hand in hand.

Kant's overall assessment of the antinomies brings vividly into view his near personification of reason. The section of the "Transcendental Dialectic" designed as a summarizing overview of the account of the antinomies bears the revealing title, "The Interest of Reason in these Conflicts." Kant depicts this interest in a nearly dramatic form.

> Unfortunately for speculation, though fortunately perhaps for the practical interests of humanity, reason, in the midst of its highest expectations, finds itself so compromised by the conflict of opposing arguments, that neither its honour nor its security allows it to withdraw and treat the quarrel with indifference as a mere mock fight; and still less is it in a position to command peace, being itself directly interested in the matters of dispute. Accordingly, nothing remains for reason save to consider whether the origin of this conflict, whereby it is divided against itself, may not have arisen from a mere misunderstanding.[24]

Evidently, Kant cannot make any of his key points without the help of metaphors. He is telling a cautionary tale, and implicit in this tale is a vivid depiction of reason as an "activity." The activity itself turns out to be a kind of "movement," with reason remaining restless and unsatisfied as long as this movement falls short of the unconditioned, which is its goal. Though operating for Kant at a lower level, deductive logic is at least suggestive of reason's restlessness at the level of transcendental logic, as rational activity moves inexorably through the syllogism, where the relation among premises sustains an irrepressible progression toward a necessitated conclusion, producing the pressure of an irresistible hydraulic system. To thwart reason's natural drive toward totality would be as frustrating in its own way as to stop just short of the proper conclusion of the syllogism. At either level, reason's "needs" require movement toward a resolution. The alternative would be an intrusive, unhealthy stoppage inimical to reason's active, progressive nature.[25]

Kant's account of reason's activity in metaphorical terms is, in turn, reliant on reason's "interested" character. Here, we have a deepened sense in which metaphors both frame Kant's account and suggest the independent, self-sufficient quality of reason. Kants tells us in the *Critique of Practical Reason* that an "interest" can "never be attributed to a being which lacks reason."[26] Closely connected with Kant's preoccupation with teleology, reason's interested character is what puts life into its activity. Unlike a child, reason *stays* interested in its own projects, sustaining ongoing momentum. The result is what has been called "a new kind of teleology" based upon a teleological ideal confronting the fact that "the rational powers develop in a chaotic and conflicting way without the legislation of an organizing end."[27] But whereas such a teleological ideal might have once had its source in the divine commands of scripture or revelation, "this ideal originates solely in reason," meaning that the "revival of teleological thought in Kant is based on freedom and the spontaneity of reason."[28] Once again, the ultimate ends of life are self-given. Significantly, the full explication of the connection between reason's interest and its goal depends on the complementary nature of theoretical and practical reason, a complementarity that Kant perhaps masks from view as successfully as he articulates. But this ultimate unity of reason itself is both fundamental to his outlook and often the main issue at stake when reason's aims and activities are rendered metaphorically through appeal to its interests.

Just how fundamental this point is to Kant's outlook is readily evident in his argument in the second *Critique* for what he calls the "primacy of the pure practical reason in its association with speculative" or theoretical reason.[29] In some respects, this argument, even more than the postulation of immortality and God, is the key moment in practical reason's recovery from the negative consequences of the first *Critique*'s dismantling of natural theology. For the issue Kant faces here concerns the potential entitlement of practical reason to claim cognitive respectability for a result that theoretical reason had put into serious question. As one commentator has aptly framed the point, the primacy of practical reason "brings relief from the unknowability of the world as it is in itself."[30] Obviously, Kant wishes to claim that belief in God and immortality are not simply subjectively satisfying but objectively valid, yet without transgressing his own epistemological restrictions and suggesting we thereby have theoretical knowledge of them. Instead, we have practical certainty, and the only way to give this insight cognitive significance and save it from the realm of wishful thinking is to establish the primacy of practical over theoretical reason.

Kant's way of achieving this result both underscores the important argumentative role played by the idea of "interest" and sheds valuable light on the relation between the theoretical and practical aspects of what is, for Kant, finally a unified reason. "Primacy" in what Kant calls its "narrower sense" refers to "the prerogative of the *interest* of one so far as the *interest* of the others is subordinated to it. ...."

Reason, as the faculty of principles, determines the interest of all the powers of the mind *and its own*. The interest of the speculative use consists in the knowledge of objects up to the highest a priori principles; that of its practical employment lies in the determination of the will with respect to the final and perfect end. That which is needed in general for the possibility of any employment of reason, i.e., that its principles and assertions not contradict one another, is not a part of its interest but is rather the condition of having any reason at all; only its extension, and not the mere agreement with itself, is reckoned as its interest.[31]

As long as there is no outright contradiction, such as the proposal of a square circle, reason is open to adjudicating potentially competing interests emerging from its own theoretical and practical employment. Kant thus poses the key question: what if practical reason generates a priori principles "with which certain theoretical positions are inseparably bound but which are beyond any possible insight of the speculative reason (though not contradictory to it)"? As Kant puts it, "Which *interest* is superior?"[32] Rhetorically, Kant asks if theoretical reason would be "justified in stubbornly following its own isolated interest...however much it is interwoven with the interest of the practical (pure) use of reason. ..."[33]

Kant resolves the question in telling fashion by appealing to the unified nature of reason. He reminds us that the second *Critique* has already demonstrated that reason can in fact be practical, since the "fact of reason" conveyed through consciousness of the moral law places before us an obligation which we must be able to satisfy through free will. Somehow, the sheer demonstration that reason can be practical as well as theoretical suffices by itself for Kant to show that "it is only one and the same reason which judges a priori by principles, whether for theoretical or for practical purposes."

> Then it is clear that, if its capacity in the former is not sufficient to establish certain propositions positively (which however do not contradict it), it must assume these propositions just as soon as they are sufficiently certified as belonging imprescriptibly to the practical interest of pure reason. ...It must remember that they are not its own insights but extensions of its use in some other respect, viz., the practical; and that this is not in the least opposed to its interest, which lies in the restriction of speculative folly.[34]

Kant thus concludes that, in matters where practical reason has a clear "interest" that involves no contradiction for theoretical reason, the former has primacy. He adds that we could not "reverse" this order "and expect practical reason to submit to speculative reason, because *every interest is ultimately practical*. ..."[35]

Obviously, reason's "interested" character is what makes it active, gives it life, and provides it with a direction. It is theoretical reason's interested character that might incline it to go "stubbornly" in its own way, yet reason's larger interest guarantees a settlement involving the primacy of the practical with no transgression of the prerogatives of the theoretical. Since Kant finally deploys this resolution in order to claim objective validity for the postulates of practical reason, we can even say that the interested character of reason becomes the vehicle by which theism regains intellectual respectability. The priority of rational mandate to divine agency that we previously encountered in connection with the moral argument for God's existence here receives subtle but powerful reinforcement. For Kant, God does not reappear on the philosophical map through revelatory power or transcendent agency, but by virtue of an interest of reason.

But of course this is to say that the interested and unified character of reason is closely associated with reason's self- sufficiency, involving its capacity both to generate and to act upon its own ends. What Yovel has helpfully called reason's "motivational power" arises out of its own prescriptions and not from commands imposed from the outside. "Since it is fundamentally an *interest*, reason can spontaneously generate the motivating principle needed for its actualization."[36] We might even say that it is because of a unified reason's interested character that there is such a thing as autonomy. Such an insight seems plausible because reason's interests include a concern for the satisfaction of its self-sufficient character through the realization of autonomy's vocation. It is through just this set of connections that Kant's highly metaphorical account of reason's activity leads ultimately to the idea of the ethical commonwealth.

The tie between reason's self-sufficiency and its interested character assumes an even more provocative form in light of one commentator's suggestion that the needs arising from reason's interested character might change.[37] Such a possibility resides in Kant's remark in the second *Critique* that "the manner in which we are to think of [the highest good] as possible is *subject to our own choice,* in which *a free interest of pure practical reason* is decisive for the assumption of a wise Author of the world. ...."[38] The free and interested character of reason, which governs the postulation process yielding the claims of immortality and God, might redirect itself toward another content; there is nothing external to reason to prohibit such a shift in the manner in which it will pursue its interests. In this possibility, we have a powerful reminder that "rational faith does not concern the *objects themselves* but *our moral needs and capacities.*"[39] The "objects" or "content" of rational faith, including God, are in the service of this larger moral end. In principle, then, Kant

might well allow that the content of the postulates could change while the form of the argument for their necessity remained the same. Thus, it might be the case that reason's needs have changed to the point that we do not, two hundred years after Kant, need to represent to ourselves a personal God to sustain our moral convictions but can make do with some more general assumption. The extreme indeterminacy of Kant's postulate of God's existence lends weight to this idea.[40]

The contrast case to the indeterminacy of the postulate of God's existence is the enduring role played by reason's interested character. Reason's formal properties remain constant but do not necessarily find satisfaction in a single, unchanging content. On this basis, it becomes conceivable that the "very minimal postulation of God's existence" might "be replaced by the postulate that the world as a whole is progressing toward the best."[41] Obviously, such a conceptual possibility would only reinforce the transfer of reason's interest from the otherworldly domain of the second postulate to the less pristine but more accessible world of history itself.

As we have seen more than once, Kant often teams references to reason's interested character with an appeal to the "needs" of reason. Needs of reason are perhaps best thought of as the most pressing expressions of reason's interest. Already in chapter 2, for example, we confronted the needs of reason in connection with the argumentative machinery surrounding Kant's moral argument, including the idea of the highest good. The very notion of the highest good, so instrumental in Kant's generation of the postulates of immortality and God, is an expression of a need of reason to think its way to the unconditioned total product of moral endeavor. The argumentative force of the metaphor of needs is readily evident in its obvious connection with what Kant speaks of as reason's "tasks," "strivings," "requirements," "claims," "satisfactions," and "destiny." Although it is reason's interested character that makes it active in the first place, the notion of the "needs" of reason perhaps functions more explicitly as a kind of "root" metaphor in Kant's actual argumentation, as in his account of "assent" to the postulates of practical reason "arising from a need of pure reason."[42] For not only does the theme of "needs" introduce motifs of "desire" or "longing" that, in turn, perpetuate reason's activity, but the activity thus generated provides Kant with good ways to keep philosophical arguments in motion. To a great extent, this generation and maintenance of argumentative momentum is precisely what the metaphor of the needs of reason does. The legitimacy of the needs of reason is underscored by Kant's ascription to these needs of certain "rights" that license the passage from objective uncertainty to subjective certainty – precisely the move involved in Kant's own moral argument for God's existence. The *"right of the need* of reason supervenes as a subjective ground for presupposing and accepting something which reason cannot presume to know on

objective grounds, and hence for *orientating* ourselves in thought...
purely by means of the need of reason itself."[43]

Viewed, then, in terms of its metaphorical expressions, Kant's account
of reason in its specialized sense is both instructive with respect to Kant's
larger aims and illuminating as an expression of his principle of immanence. We might say that the element of personification involved in Kant's
treatment of reason is an indirect way of moving divine intentions off the
philosophical map, particularly with respect to humanity's highest aims
and goals – such, at least, is what I shall be arguing in connection with
Kant's account of the ethical commonwealth.

At a minimum, this canvassing of Kant's view of reason and its metaphorical expressions places in a fresh light the philosophical suggestive-
ness of the "Transcendental Dialectic" and its overall importance for the
current study. Often, there is a tendency to approach Kant's distinction
between reason and understanding by reading backwards, as it were,
through subsequent developments within German idealism, beginning
with Hegel's criticism of Kant's distinction and his complaint that Kant
forfeits the philosopher's true vocation by so limiting reason's cognitive
powers. The result is an impression of reason as a kind of instrument of
philosophical "policing" and restrictiveness that accounts for Kant's
metaphysical modesty in comparison with Hegel's philosophy. As a consequence, we often gain a better understanding of the philosophical aims
of Kant's successors than an accurate assessment of the role of reason in
Kant's own philosophy.

But if we read forward, against the background of Kant's own received
tradition, we see that his distinction between reason and understanding
signals an important reconception of the nature of reason. As suggested
recently by Susan Neiman, the "basis of Kant's reconception is his
insistence upon the unity of theoretical and practical reason," and the
"route to that reconception is the denial that the rational is, or is centrally
concerned with, the cognitive."[44] Kant means this denial of cognitive
application to be a strong and not a weak point, since the overriding issue
is not really one of epistemological limitation but, rather, of the "unity"
of reason.[45] The unity of theoretical and practical reason is precisely
what is at stake, not only in Kant's account of the primacy of the
practical, but also in connection with his response to Rousseau's problem, involving the question of the proper "ends" of reason as the
alternative to viewing reason as simply the slave of the passions. In
other words, something about the unity of the theoretical and practical
insures that the limitations of a merely instrumentalist conception of
reason are overcome and not simply repeated in fresh form. To be sure,
the non-cognitive character of reason remains a sign of epistemological

caution, but, even more, it also insures Kant a means of lubricating the links between the theoretical and the practical as they proceed in a unified effort toward a single end. Correctly grasping autonomy's vocation does not depend upon "reason" making "knowledge-claims" but upon reason mediating the distinct yet complementary tendencies of its own theoretical and practical aspects.

For my present purposes, the most significant aspect of Kant's theory of reason is its independent and self-reliant status. In generating a clear "plan" and building affordable "constructions," reason may evince epistemological modesty but it does so on its own terms. Reason's activity requires no wider or underlying metaphysical substrate to account for itself, even as it comments in a cautionary manner about traditional claims concerning such metaphysical visions. This is not to say that Kant's account is without deep philosophical puzzles, for it is by no means clear how his philosophy manages to say so much about matters that it is simultaneously claiming are beyond all philosophical comment. Kant's "negations" often seem to transgress the very limits they are intended to announce, a tendency most notoriously evident in his theory of the noumenal. But the effect of Kant's strategy is clear enough: a theory of reason apparently intended to rein in our philosophical ambitions and cure our dogmatic ills is at the same time a demonstration of reason's independence from external determinants.

Not incidentally, this clarification of reason's role in Kant's philosophy also helps to explain much Continental philosophical activity following Kant. It remains both convenient and, for the most part, accurate to say that Fichte's quest for the absolute ego and Hegel's own dialectical idealism take shape largely as responses to Kant's distinction between reason and the understanding. Both thinkers took this distinction to be illicit and troubling in itself, just as they also argued that Kant held an excessively limited view of reason's true powers. Their attitude toward the critical philosophy is nicely captured in Quentin Lauer's depiction of Hegel's presumed response to the very title of Kant's *Religion within the Limits of Reason Alone.*

> "Within the limits" will signify to Hegel that, for Kant, philosophical thinking is essentially "finite" and, therefore, incapable of coming to grips with an "infinite" object; and "mere (*blossen*) reason" will tell him that Kant's "reason" is not reason at all but only "understanding" trying to stretch itself beyond its limited capacities.[46]

Taken by itself, however, such an account of post-Kantian developments perpetuates the one-sided view of Kant's theory of reason itself as a kind of philosophical policeman. The same can be said for the connection that is often made between the productive quality of Kant's theory of mind as the source even of our notions of space and time, and the constructive powers of mind we see in later idealism. Once again accurate in itself, this connection is usually described as though the later thinkers make "constitutive" what for Kant had been a merely "regulative" capacity, which is to perpetuate the one-dimensional view of Kant's theory of reason as primarily a philosophical brake or constraint.

Underestimated or missed altogether in these readings is the independent, self-directed quality of Kant's theory of reason, which makes his theory something more than an epistemologically cautious precursor to later, more ambitious developments. In retrospect, as we survey German thought from about 1780 to 1830, there is an important and complex connection between construing reason as a self-sustaining activity and giving reason a "life" that becomes the very purpose of history itself.[47] The personification of reason through the metaphorical expressions Kant adopts to describe its aims and activities is itself suggestive of this link to later developments. The bearing Kant's theory of reason has on these developments is inextricably entwined with the difficulties he has introduced concerning the relationship between autonomous rationality and God. The combined effects of (1) the diminishing of the divine in the moral argument, (2) the full exercise of autonomy's autonomy, and (3) the personification of reason through metaphor, finally leave unclear the status of Kant's God as an independent metaphysical entity. But this is precisely the problem we more typically associate with Hegel's conception of *Geist* as the fusion of immanence and transcendence in the philosophy of "spirit" itself, with the problem in Hegel's case portrayed as though Kant's moral argument holds up an obvious contrast case.[48] Yet the confusion of immanence and transcendence is already well advanced in Kant's philosophy, in light of the prerogatives he has given autonomous rationality. Kant's theory of reason may not be able to generate building projects on the scale of Hegel's. However, the real point here is not the size of the structures, but the capacity of reason to design and construct without dependence on an external authority. In this regard, Kant's own break from his received metaphysical tradition forms a more important bridge with later developments than we often acknowledge.

REASON AND PROVIDENCE: TOWARD THE ETHICAL COMMONWEALTH

Inexorably and systematically, then, Kant makes his way toward the ideal ethical community by means of reason's totalizing activity, his account shaped and driven rhetorically by metaphors of need and interest. The fully fashioned idea of an actual ethical commonwealth, of the sort that eventually raises interpretive issues surrounding the question of its potential historical realization, arises in the much thinner and more abstract atmosphere of Kant's initial discussion of the categorical imperative in the *Foundations of the Metaphysics of Morals*. This discussion, in turn, is foreshadowed in the first *Critique* by Kant's brief account of "a *moral world*, in so far as it may be in accordance with all moral laws; and this is what by means of the freedom of rational beings it *can be*, and what according to the necessary laws of morality it *ought to be*."[49] While acknowledging that this moral world is a "mere idea," Kant argues in that context that such an idea "really can have, as it also ought to have, an influence upon the sensible world, to bring that world, so far as may be possible, into conformity with the idea." As though to underscore his ambivalence regarding the potential transformation of the sensible world into a moral world, Kant refers to the moral world as "a *corpus mysticum* of the rational beings in it, so far as the free will of each being is, under moral laws, in complete systematic unity with itself and with the freedom of every other."[50] The eventual transformation of the *corpus mysticum* into the realm of ends and, finally, the ethical commonwealth, is simultaneously an account of Kant's increasing effort to conceptualize the moral transformation of history itself.

In the *Foundations*, the realm or kingdom of ends comes into view as the third version of the categorical imperative: "[E]very rational being must act as if he, by his maxims, were at all times a legislative member in the universal realm of ends."[51] The first version of the imperative requires that I act so that the maxim of my action could become a universal law, while the second version requires me to act so that I treat humanity "always as an end and never as a means only."[52] Less familiar than these first two versions of the categorical imperative, the third is nonetheless simply a variation on the same underlying rational insight. That is, in Kant's view, all three versions are "fundamentally only so many formulas of the very same law, and each of them unites the others in itself."[53]

Commentary on the categorical imperative is of course its own full-time industry, and the problems associated with connecting these three seemingly distinct versions of a presumably single imperative clearly add to the labors.[54] Yet it is perhaps especially revealing that Kant's own effort to justify his claim that the three are "only so many formulas of the very same law" by tracing out their connecting linkage is itself an example of reason's totalizing tendencies. In keeping with his core insight that the good will is constituted by its form and not by its content, Kant renders the first version of the imperative by distilling out the abstract, formal property of the moral principle, which is universalizability. This property is what makes self-legislation based on the categorical imperative "capable of being a law" for all agents in a manner analogous to the operations of natural law.[55] The second version, in turn, seeks out the material element contained in the imperative, thus introducing consideration for "humanity" and disclosing the important connection between universalizability and respect for other rational beings as ends in themselves. Finally, the third version combines the formal and material considerations in a totalizing formula leading toward "the systematic union of different rational beings through common laws"[56] which, in this case, would be laws fashioned according to the categorical imperative itself. In other words, reason's natural drive toward the absolute and unconditioned term resulting from a set of conditions yields in this case the concept of a community of rational agents who always treat one another as ends in themselves and never as a means only. More significantly, Kant's procedure introduces the social dimension of the moral life as an aspect of morality's foundational principle. Indeed, the social dimension is sufficiently significant that it qualifies as a version of the categorical imperative itself.

The *Foundations* thus offers what amounts to a deduction of the realm of ends (*Reich der Zwecke*), with reason's totalizing activity mediated in part by the metaphor of the "whole."

> Because laws determine ends with regard to their universal validity, if we abstract from the personal difference of rational beings and thus from all content of their private ends, we can think of a whole of all ends in systematic connection, a whole of rational beings as ends in themselves as well as of the particular ends which each may set for himself. This is a realm of ends. ... For all rational beings stand under the law that each of them should treat himself and all others never merely as a means but in every case also as an end in himself. Thus there arises a systematic union of rational beings through common objective laws. This is a realm which may be called a realm of ends (certainly only an ideal), because what these laws have in view is just the relation of these beings to each other as ends and means.[57]

On purely a priori grounds, then, in an effort to think through the ramifications of an imperative that is categorical and binding rather than hypothetical and contingent, Kant is able to sketch the outlines of a community of moral agents. In effect, he has integrated the universalizability principle (the first formula of the categorical imperative) with a conception of rational beings as ends in themselves (the second formula) to produce a systematic conception of the interrelations among all moral agents. By drawing on the politically charged notion of a "realm" to label the outcome, Kant evokes the law-like quality of the resulting form of human organization. Things fall into place in a law-like manner when every moral agent prescribes universally. In Sharon Anderson-Gold's helpful expression, Kant is arguing that if "the moral law were the supreme incentive for the human will, the human condition would be spontaneously socially integrated as if 'by nature.'"[58]

Kant's procedure here has several striking features. Not the least of these is the fact that the element of totalization characterizing his theory of reason impels us toward a goal of nearly God-like moral perfection, which is in marked contrast to the more modest aims of those influential moral theories of Kant's day that simply aim toward the satisfaction of natural desires.[59] Mimicking providence, reason displays its fully teleological nature by providing a more dignified successor to the biblical eschaton than the appeasement of our appetites. Moreover, it is also reason's totalizing activity that leads Kant beyond the purely formal and even arid atmosphere surrounding the first version of the categorical imperative to an acknowledgment of the social nature of moral endeavor.[60] Reason's own totalizing tendencies insure that the idea of the individual autonomous moral agent is supplemented immediately in Kant's consideration by reflection on the very idea of a community of moral agents. This of course means that concern for the social dimensions of moral agency is implicit in Kant's ethical theory at the outset. By the terms of Kant's own explanation of the links among the three versions of the categorical imperative, reflection on the idea of a moral community is necessarily entailed by the very idea of morality's formal principle, which we see most clearly with the help of reason's totalizing tendencies. And finally, the apparently analytical relationship between an imperative that is categorical and participation in a community means that the individual's pursuit of virtue is inseparable from participation in a community. At the same time, the delicacy of this relationship between the individual and the community is conveyed by Schneewind's reminder that the "moral need for autonomy" is simply "incompatible with certain kinds of social regulation." Everything hangs on the fact that the "structure of society must reflect and express the common and equal moral capacity of its members."[61]

Consequently, Kant's interest in the social aspects of morality is neither an afterthought nor an artificial or otherwise extrinsic factor in his ethics. As we shall see in more detail in the following chapter, this point is important because of the way other moral agents gradually take on a role that Kant once ascribed to God, particularly with regard to the idea of moral perfection. If the basis of this shift is the categorical imperative itself, then the transfer of interest from a transcendent to an immanent arena is for Kant a systematic development from first principles rather than a random or piecemeal response to a sudden conceptual difficulty. The problem involved in moral agents relating to and interacting with one another is already embedded in the notion of morality's single most formal principle. Kant's subsequent discussion in the *Religion* of the ethical commonwealth will thus be an elaboration of this abstract starting point, developed in the context of a more self-conscious concern for the historical fate of rational agents confronting serious worldly challenges to their moral fulfillment. The account in the *Religion* surely opens up lines of thought not developed in the thinner discussion in the *Foundations*, yet the accounts share in common a systematic Kantian interest in the social dimensions of morality which has the force of drawing attention away from God and toward humanity's own historical endeavors. Moreover, the imperative's depiction of a community in which each member is always "legislating universally" immediately injects Kant into the tradition of social contract theory, which hints broadly at the secular context in which his account has its most natural fit.[62]

The fact that Kant insists that the several versions of the categorical imperative are interconnected is also important for the way it insures the self-legislating character of the ethical community thus depicted. As we saw in chapter 3, autonomy's special character is evident in the moral agent's ability to recognize the principle of universalizability in the formation of maxims, and to fashion maxims accordingly. In so doing, the agent legislates for the moral world in a manner analogous to the rule-giving activities of the categories in the construction of experience itself: the parallel within Kant's philosophy between creating a moral world and creating the world of experience is both powerful and significant. After all, the force of the first version of the categorical imperative is that I act so that the maxim of my action could be made into a law for an entire moral universe. Furthermore, I am capable of totalizing the implications of this rational insight in a way that presents me with the idea of a realm of rational beings, all of whom are following the same categorical imperative and defining a moral world for me as well. Consequently, I am simultaneously "giving" and "receiving" universal laws in the course of my membership in this community. "A rational being belongs to the realm of ends as a member," Kant explains, "when he gives universal laws in it while also himself subject to those laws."[63]

But since universalizability, like philosophical necessity, is infinitely transferrable among rational beings regardless of individual circumstance or accidents of autobiography, my own autonomy is intact even if I "receive" legislation from other agents. "Paradoxically if you like, my ends and actions are most truly my own when they are chosen under the restrictions of a possible reciprocal relation – a kind of friendship – with everyone."[64] Similarly, my "giving universal laws" does not interfere in my neighbor's exercise of autonomy but helps to fulfill it. As fellow members of the kingdom of ends, we "exchange" the universalizability principle in much the same manner that members of a mathematics seminar share or "exchange" deductive procedures in the course of constructing proofs. Far from being oppressive, legislating rationally for my fellow members of the kingdom of ends is salutary in just the same sense involved in correcting the mistaken steps my colleague may have taken in the course of a mathematical proof. In both settings, there is complete commensurability with respect to the appropriate rational procedures. Furthermore, in neither context do I need to draw on an external authority to produce the right result. Instead, I am my own authority to the extent that I can recognize and respond to the demands of universality and necessity.[65]

Here, we have journeyed about as far as possible from Hobbes' state of nature, arriving in an idealized world that, not entirely by chance, Kant will eventually refer to as the "kingdom of heaven on earth."[66] In the *Foundations*, he is not yet so biblical in his rhetorical flourishes, remaining content to exploit a more nearly aesthetic motif of harmony. "A complete determination of all maxims" in accordance with the categorical imperative, he tells us, "ought to harmonize with a possible realm of ends as with a realm of nature."[67] The suggestion of harmony dovetails with the implicit theme of self-agreement that is operating here at two levels: the individual moral agent's agreement of the will with itself in the adoption of the categorical imperative; and the agreement of the wills of all individual agents with one another, as each is treated as an end in itself and never as a means only. Embodied in this idealized image is one commentator's observation that Kant "invests certain moral themes with a direct political bearing, and political themes with a sacred moral dignity."[68]

The result is the idealized concept of a community that not only insures the autonomy of its members, but is self-invented as well. As, in effect, the cumulative product of mutually reinforcing individual acts of autonomy, the kingdom of ends does not pattern itself after a preordained model but "creates" its own social blueprint. No doubt there is a serious dilemma regarding the relation between "rights" and "duties" embedded in this Kantian vision, a dilemma that haunts the liberal political tradition to this day.[69] And in the next chapter, we will have occasion to examine more closely certain remaining tensions between the individual moral agent and the wider community, with a view to their theological importance. My point for now is simply to underscore the lesson implicit in Kant's demonstration of an analytic connection between a theory of individual acts of maxim-making and a concept of a moral community by rooting them both in the categorical imperative. The lesson is that Kant thereby manages on his terms to maintain the element of autonomy on the social as well as the individual side, insuring that his eventual "kingdom of heaven on earth" will be a kingdom designed and produced by our own hands, rather than one delivered by the divine hand.

Reason's self-sufficiency is thus indistinguishable from the autonomy of autonomy. Perhaps oddly but certainly significantly, the metaphors of construction, interest, need, and satisfaction that frame Kant's theory of reason find a culminating partnership with the metaphor of a realm. Reason's own totalizing tendencies, which occasioned such epistemological caution and restraint in the first *Critique*, bring about this partnership, just as Kant's metaphors illuminate the pathways by which he promotes a vision of human destiny that avoids the pitfalls of speculative metaphysics. The fact that ours is a collective rather than a purely individual destiny has considerable significance, for the social perspective will force God further and further from the scene of moral action. As we shall see, this last point is perhaps exemplified by the eclipsing of the postulate of immortality by the corporate hope embodied in the ethical commonwealth, as other moral agents assume the role originally ascribed to God in the unending but obligatory quest for moral perfection. As heaven comes to earth, and an earthly version of the kingdom of heaven becomes the locus of a moral perfection once projected into each individual's noumenal afterlife, the systematic role played by God becomes increasingly questionable. As we have seen in the present chapter, the basis of this telling possibility is clearly established in the third formula of the categorical imperative itself. It thus remains for us to chart out in more detail the important linkage between Kant's further development of the social context of moral agency and the diminishing of the divine.

CHAPTER FIVE

Heaven Comes to Earth: The Ethical Commonwealth

INTRODUCTION: *RELIGION WITHIN THE LIMITS OF REASON ALONE*

At one level, Kant's concept of the ethical commonwealth is simply the systematic development of issues already present in the third formula of the categorical imperative, the realm of ends. Sustained reflection on the idea of moral agents legislating universally for themselves and one another yields a community of virtue that is different in kind from a traditional political community, because its laws are generated autonomously from "within" rather than imposed heteronomously from the outside. As though he had in mind certain twentieth-century efforts to legislate morality, Kant says at one point, "woe to the legislator who wishes to establish through force a polity directed to ethical ends!"[1] This is not to say that a community of virtue is inconceivable, but simply that "the very concept . . . involves freedom from coercion."[2] "In such a commonwealth," Kant explains, "all the laws are expressly designed to promote the *morality* of actions (which is something *inner*, and hence cannot be subject to public human laws). . . ."[3] The originating idea for such a concept is present in Kant's earliest efforts to distill out and isolate morality's most formal principle.

At another level, however, the ethical commonwealth is what we might characterize as the most public manifestation of Kant's principle of immanence. The movement from the abstract considerations accompanying Kant's account of the realm of ends to the more robust conception of the ethical commonwealth is shadowed by an especially obvious transition in Kant's thinking from an otherworldly to a this-worldly frame of reference. If, as I plan to argue in this chapter, the concept of the ethical commonwealth in fact displaces Kant's postulate of the immortality of the soul in the depiction of moral perfection, then even the thin theological commitment of the *Critique of Practical Reason* would appear to be considerably compromised. The clear implication of such a transition would be that, as Kant's sense of the social aspect of moral agency assumes greater refinement, his account of divine transcendence becomes even more attenuated. The already limited divine intervention that is associated with the realization of the highest good is now further diluted by corporate moral agency within the immanent sphere of history. In this new context, the theological question becomes the rather odd one concerning whether, or in what sense, Kant's God is a "member" of the ethical commonwealth. While there may be a certain ambiguity about whether moral perfection will actually be achieved – or only increasingly approximated – through immanent human action, the "duration" at issue is no longer depicted noumenally, as in the second *Critique*. Consequently, even if there remains a role for God to play in the achievement of moral perfection, it is a role that has been brought down to earth from the noumenal realm and is inextricably bound up with human history itself. One way or another, heaven is absorbed by earth.

Kant's most sustained treatment of the ethical commonwealth occurs in *Religion within the Limits of Reason Alone* (1793), published eight years following the appearance of the *Foundations of the Metaphysics of Morals*. All three *Critiques* had by then already been published as well, leaving only *The Metaphysics of Morals* among Kant's major works yet to appear. The *Religion* is a rich, odd, and highly suggestive work, characterized by points of both continuity *and* discontinuity with Kant's other works. Theologian Hans Frei once wrote that "Immanuel Kant's *Religion within the Limits of Reason Alone* is a Book I would pack for a long stay on a desert island,"[4] suggesting the work's many layers of meaning and provocative lines of connection with subsequent theological developments. The *Religion* is, for example, the work in which Kant develops the theme of "radical evil" in human nature in a manner strangely reminiscent of the Christian doctrine of original sin – strange, because ideas such as original sin were precisely the sorts of received dogmas that Enlightenment thinkers usually repudiated. Frederick Beiser's enumeration of the core commitments uniting oftentimes diverse Enlightenment thinkers in fact *begins* with the claim that "people are not innately vicious but naturally virtuous, capable of doing good and knowing the truth through their own efforts without the assistance of divine grace."[5] Kant's doctrine of radical evil raises serious questions about every aspect of that core commitment. Thus, despite the rule-bound and systematic nature of Kant's general outlook, the *Religion* reflects his competing tendency to take up fresh leads, to punctuate his main train of thought with provocative asides, and to demonstrate a breadth of intellectual vision that spills over the borders of his own philosophical territory. It is a work that fits neatly neither into Kant's overall authorship nor into the Enlightenment as a whole.

Certainly the *Religion* offers Kant's fullest statement of the possible connections between his rational account of religion as the "recognition of moral duties *as* divine commands" and historical religions as actually practiced. As such, the work is Kant's most explicit contribution to the more general eighteenth-century debate over the relationship between natural and revealed religion. Although Kant attempts to represent the *Religion* as a rational inquiry into the latent moral element potentially present in any historical religion whatsoever,[6] it is clear that he is basically proposing a moral interpretation of Christianity. Not only is the work filled with examples of how the seemingly contingent truths of Christian faith can be reconciled with the necessary truths of Kant's own moral theory, but Christianity itself is promoted as the "vehicle" of pure moral faith. Indeed, the very composition of the *Religion* through a structure of four "Books" is transparently based on the traditional Christian doctrines of creation and fall, justification and christology, ecclesiology, and sanctification.[7] Drawing especially on the theological manuals of his own Pietist teacher, F. A. Schultz, as well as on the multi-volume *Foundation for the True Religion* by the Swiss Calvinist J. F. Stapfer, Kant rather ingeniously devises points of contact between their concern for sincerity of belief, spiritual struggle, and the experience of rebirth, and his own emphasis on the inner, moral dimensions of authentic religious faith.[8] His procedure is a model of a liberally minded mediating theology and sets a powerful precedent for Protestant theologians in the nineteenth century.

In addition, although Kant never mentions Jesus by name, he proposes what is clearly a moral interpretation of the life of Jesus by means of a complex and nuanced account of what he calls the "personified idea of the good principle."[9] Not surprisingly, Kant's is a christology emphasizing moral action and not dogmatic claims, for Jesus is the embodiment of an "archetype of the moral disposition in all its purity," an idea available to all rational beings apart from any particular historical occurrences, presumably including those reported in the Gospels.[10] While there is evidence of an effort to attend to the historical and philological issues that were increasingly important in biblical and theological studies in his day, Kant conveys his general attitude toward such techniques when he tartly remarks that we "must not quarrel unnecessarily over a question or over its historical aspect, when, however it is understood, it in no way helps us to be better men. ..."[11] The source of our becoming "better men" is our capacity for respect for the moral law rather than any particular collection of historical information. To view Jesus as the archetype of the moral disposition is to remind us of this rational potential in us all.

Despite the suggestion of a disinterested theoretical inquiry into historical religions as such, then, the *Religion* qualifies as Kant's most sustained treatment of Christianity and of the main issues surrounding Enlightenment criticisms of traditional theological authority. The slippage between a putatively neutral, philosophical examination of what Kant rather disingenuously calls "some alleged revelation or other"[12] and a more normative appraisal of Christianity is especially evident in a rhetorical question he both raises and answers:

> What period in the entire known history of the church up to now is the best? I have no scruple in answering, *the present*. And this, because, if the seed of the true religious faith, as it is now being publicly sown in Christendom, though only by a few, is allowed more and more to grow unhindered, we may look for a continuous approximation to that church, eternally uniting all men, which constitutes the visible representation (the schema) of an invisible kingdom of God on earth.[13]

Comments such as this indicate not only the Christian idiom with which Kant is largely operating, but subterranean connections between a moral vision of Christianity and the ethical commonwealth itself. Indeed, one important measure of Kant's success in making a rational account of Christianity the most obvious issue at stake is the fact that this work produced grave, if momentary, difficulties for him with the office of the Prussian censor.[14]

As I have already suggested, the ethical commonwealth is best viewed as the concretized result of Kant's continuing reflection on ideas lodged in his concept of the realm of ends and his theory of the highest good, framed now in terms of his explicit concern for our recovery from radical evil. Kant's sustained account of radical evil takes the pursuit of moral perfection out of the philosophically ideal atmosphere of his earlier discussion of the highest good and interjects a major challenge to the very possibility of moral progress. At the same time, the discussion of radical evil is notorious for its obscurity, for the cumbersome terminological scaffolding that accompanies it, and for the sheer shock effect produced by its appearance at this late point in Kant's authorship. At a time when leading Enlightenment thinkers were united in attacking ignorance as the source of evil, embodied especially in outmoded traditions and superstitions, the aging Kant clearly argues that evil arises out of the will.[15] Such a view effectively pits humanity against *itself* instead of against the royalty, priests, and their associated henchmen whose social dominance derives from the perpetuation of unexamined traditions. As a result, the theory of radical evil implicitly calls into question the entire Enlightenment project of intellectual emancipation and unchecked human progress.

Obviously, the issues and problems raised by Kant's account of radical evil spill well over the boundaries of the present study. For my immediate purposes, I need only clarify the meaning of radical evil as a premise for the sort of moral progress that is at issue in Kant's depiction of the ethical commonwealth.

Kant claims that rational beings possess an "original predisposition (*die Anlage*) to good" and yet inevitably succumb to a "natural propensity (*der Hang*) to evil."[16] To borrow from the formula made popular almost two centuries later by Reinhold Niebuhr's description of original sin, Kant is arguing that radical evil is inevitable but not necessary. That is, our "fall" has for Kant the force of something virtually "innate,"[17] although we always remain accountable for it. Kant effectively remains agnostic on the question of *why* we inevitably fall while (somewhat paradoxically) claiming that this fall is universal.[18] Moral evil itself for Kant is understood as the subordination, through a free act of the will, of the moral incentive to the incentive of self-love – the subordination, that is, of the incentive arising out of my capacity for respect for the moral law to the incentive of sensuous inclination. The specific locus of moral evil is thereby the free act by which I order my incentives in the formation of my maxims.[19]

"Radical" evil, in turn, is the result of adopting a *general* policy of such subordination – the result, that is, of adopting a "supreme maxim" that poisons my individual acts of maxim-making.[20] Kant calls this supreme maxim the underlying moral "disposition" (*die Gesinnung*), for which the agent is accountable because it has also been adopted by free choice.[21] The obvious problem of a potential regress here – introduced by the question of what grounds the free choice of the disposition that grounds the choices I make in individual maxim-making – is evidently of less concern to Kant than the opportunity to provide an account of a *unified* moral agent whose agency expresses itself in characteristic ways eliciting either praise or blame. The notion of an underlying moral disposition allows him to do this, whereas a mere cataloguing of individual acts of maxim-making does not. The concept of the disposition also underwrites the idea of an evil that is "radical" and pervasive rather than simply episodic. "This evil is *radical* because it corrupts the ground of all maxims. ..."[22]

Since the ground of radical evil is itself freely chosen, we are always free in principle to make ourselves good again. Such a transformation may be tremendously difficult, but it is not impossible – the difference is the same as that at stake between being radically evil and being a "devil," rebelling against the moral law *because* it is the moral law.[23] The moral capacity always remains intact, because radical evil infects the disposition but does not eliminate *Wille*, which, as we have seen, involves our capacity for respect for the moral law. With this set of considerations in place, Kant is in a position to discuss the process of moral recovery or regeneration from radical evil. Consequently, Book I of the *Religion* lays out the problem of radical evil and introduces the topic of moral regeneration. Book II is largely an account of moral regeneration viewed in personal and individual terms on a transparently pietist model, while Books III and IV are largely, though not exclusively, devoted to an account of moral progress viewed socially. In these latter two Books, Kant's account is intertwined in provocative ways with his discussion of the gradual evolution of historical or revealed religion into a religion of pure reason, with Christianity once again the obvious central concern. His discussion of the ethical commonwealth itself is concentrated in Book III.

The linkage connecting the ethical commonwealth with Kant's earlier ideas embedded in the realm of ends and the highest good indicates a systematic development in his thinking about the corporate aspect of moral agency. As I have proposed, this development reveals a suggestive correlation between deepened reflection on the social dimensions of moral striving and the diminishing of the divine. Explaining this point and making a case for it will be the main burden of the remainder of this chapter.

The Ethical Commonwealth as Corporate Salvation

Kant defines the ethical commonwealth as a society that enjoys the "sovereignty of the good principle," which is to say, the moral law. The "sovereignty of the good principle is attainable, so far as men can work toward it, only through the establishment and spread of a society in accordance with, and for the sake of, the laws of virtue."

> A union of men under merely moral laws, patterned on the above idea, may be called an *ethical*, and so far as these laws are public, an *ethico-civil* (in contrast to a *juridico-civil*) society or an *ethical commonwealth*. It can exist in the midst of the political commonwealth and may even be made up of all its members; (indeed, unless it is based upon such a commonwealth it can

never be brought into existence by man). It has, however, a special and unique principle of union (virtue), and hence a form and constitution, which fundamentally distinguish it from the political commonwealth.[24]

Kant proposes that "there is a certain analogy between" the ethical and political commonwealths, "in view of which the former may also be called an *ethical state, i.e., a kingdom [Reich]* of virtue (of the good principle)." He adds rather cryptically that, although the "idea of such a state possesses a thoroughly well-grounded objective reality in human reason," we can "never hope that man's good will will lead mankind to decide to work with unanimity towards this goal."[25] Whether this means that the goal will never be reached, or only that there will always be those working against its attainment, is not clear.

As Kant's own allusion to a "kingdom" or "realm" indicates, at stake here is an amplification of ideas already latent in his account of the realm of ends in the *Foundations*. At the same time, the concreteness of Kant's discussion of the ethical commonwealth, including comments about its relationship to actual, real-world political arrangements, is an obvious departure from the skeletal account in the earlier work. Kant's concept of the highest good, developed in the course of the moral argument in the second *Critique*, helps to mediate this transition from the realm of ends to the ethical commonwealth. Whether or not it is too much to say that Kant is increasingly concerned to specify the worldly manifestations of the highest good,[26] such a characterization aptly conveys the general effect of the progressive movement in Kant's philosophy culminating in the ethical commonwealth. The mediating role of the highest good is explicit in Kant's Preface to the first edition of the *Religion*. As though stung by the always misleading charge that his moral philosophy takes no account of the ends of moral endeavor, Kant states that

> although for its own sake morality needs no representation of an end which must precede the determining of the will, it is quite possible that it is necessarily related to such an end, taken not as the ground but as the [sum of] inevitable consequences of maxims adopted as conformable to that end.[27]

While we do not need to envision the end of moral endeavor in order to have the motivation to be moral, such "an end does arise out of morality."

> Hence the end is no more than an idea of an object which takes the formal condition of all such ends as we *ought* to have (duty) and combines it with whatever is conditioned, and in harmony with duty, in all the ends which we *do* have (happiness proportioned to obedience to duty) – that is to say,

the idea of a highest good in the world for whose possibility we must
postulate a higher, moral, most holy, and omnipotent Being which alone
can unite the two elements of this highest good.[28]

This obvious variation on the moral argument of the second *Critique* is
noteworthy in itself for its explicit reference to a highest good "in the
world," as opposed to the noumenal frame of reference that structures
the earlier argument. As we shall see, the mimicking here of the moral
argument's exploitation of the highest good to postulate a theistic claim
is deceptive, for the parallel breaks down as the individual's moral fate in
the second *Critique* is displaced in the *Religion* by Kant's concern for the
moral community.[29] Given the decisive role that moral agents will play
for one another in the formation of this community, the role left for God
is not nearly so clear as the instrumental role God plays in the proportioning of virtue and happiness for the individual.

But the important preliminary point is the sheer fact of Kant's invocation of the highest good in the effort to think through the total end of
moral action. For we see in this gesture the controlling role assumed by
reason's totalizing activity which, in this case, will give definite shape to
the ultimate ends of moral striving. Our striving yields the ethical commonwealth, which becomes the content of reason's providential activity:
the ethical commonwealth is the shape in which providence arrives or, at
the least, is approximated.

As I have already indicated, the specific occasion for the more
extended discussion of the social aspect of morality leading to the ethical
commonwealth is Kant's account of radical evil. The connection between
radical evil and the ethical commonwealth resides in Kant's presentation
of the latter as the only social arrangement providing "hope for a victory
of the good over the evil principle."

> In addition to prescribing laws to each individual, morally legislative
> reason also unfurls a banner of virtue as a rallying point for all who love
> the good, that they may gather beneath it and thus at the very start gain the
> upper hand over the evil which is attacking them without rest.[30]

Prior to his effort to depict a corporate victory over radical evil, Kant had
already described moral regeneration or recovery in strictly personal or
individual terms. There is no neat integration of his view of moral
regeneration in individual and corporate terms.[31] At the same time, a
different atmosphere appears to accompany the shift in perspective from
individual to social considerations. The change in atmosphere is signaled
by Kant's own metaphorical usage as he describes moral regeneration.
When speaking of our recovery from radical evil in individual terms,

Kant draws in obvious ways off his pietist background and speaks of a personal "change of heart" involving a complete alteration of the underlying moral disposition. With an eye to what he calls his "rigorist" as opposed to a "latitudinarian" ethical position, Kant maintains that the disposition must be viewed as *either* good *or* evil and not as some sort of mixture or hybrid: it is, he tells us, "of great consequence to ethics in general to avoid admitting, so long as it is possible, of anything morally *intermediate* ... for with such ambiguity all maxims are in danger of forfeiting their precision and stability."[32] As a result, Kant invokes metaphors of "revolution" whenever he addresses moral change in the individual. The agent "becomes a new man only by a kind of *rebirth*, as it were a *new creation* (John III, 5; compare also Genesis I, 2), and a *change of heart*."[33] Significantly, there can be no gradualism with respect to the change in the individual's disposition. The desired change "cannot be brought about through gradual *reformation* so long as the basis of the maxims remains impure, but must be effected through a *revolution* in the man's disposition. ... "[34] In matters of the underlying moral character, so it would seem, there can for Kant be no gray areas. The revolutionary metaphors reflect this ethical rigorism, this Kantian "either/or."

By contrast, moral improvement viewed corporately draws on precisely the motifs of evolution and gradualism that Kant avoids in the case of the individual. The "victory of the good over the evil principle" announcing the section of the *Religion* that elaborates on the ethical commonwealth involves a "gradual establishment of the sovereignty of the good principle on earth."[35] In stark contrast to Kant's earlier revolutionary imagery, the motif of gradualism here is reinforced by Kant's invocation of the image of a "vehicle" evoking the idea of a "visible church" that purifies itself over time through increasing orientation toward the moral law rather than toward arbitrary and history-based "statutory" laws.[36] The visible church construed in such a way thus becomes the precursor to the ethical commonwealth, a role it assumes because of the presumably voluntary nature of membership in the church, in contrast to the coercive mechanisms associated with the enforcement of laws in the political realm. As Kant envisions the moral purification of the church, followed in turn by the transformation of the invisible church into the ethical commonwealth itself, the revolutionary imagery associated with personal rebirth has been replaced by a clear emphasis on an ongoing and gradual historical process.

The gradualism implicit in the corporate recovery from radical evil thus hints at a deeper commitment to history and historical processes, in contrast to the otherworldly conception of moral progress associated with the postulate of immortality in the second *Critique*. By itself, Kant's concern for the social aspect of moral agency serving as the source of this deeper commitment represents no real shift in his thinking, simply because the social consideration is broached in principle in his account of the categorical imperative. What *is* a shift is the more sustained attention Kant now devotes to the idea of the individual moral agent's responsibilities to the wider moral community, together with the suggestion that this community is in fact emerging and taking shape in time. Suggestions along these teleological lines are evident in some of Kant's occasional writings on the philosophy of history,[37] and they receive more sustained treatment in the discussion of the ethical commonwealth in the *Religion*. In contrast to the discussion surrounding the postulate of immortality, Kant now forges powerful connections between the individual's moral perfection and the fate of the entire group. The changed atmosphere signaled by the switch from revolutionary to evolutionary metaphors implies that the individual moral agent's destiny becomes inseparable from that of the entire moral community. Simultaneously, the shift in metaphorical usage marks the transfer of interest from a transcendent, noumenal context for moral perfection to the immanent arena of historical action.

One important source of Kant's altered frame of reference is the second of the three "predispositions" to good that he enumerates in the *Religion*, as he expands on the philosophical anthropology informing his theory of radical evil. These predispositions constitute Kant's way of taking stock of original human nature prior to the exercise of human freedom. They are good in themselves, which is why moral evil can ultimately be imputed to the moral agent, since evil must then be the result of an act of will rather than the predetermined consequence of a given state of human nature.[38] One of these three predispositions, the predisposition to "personality," is the sheer capacity to respect the moral law discussed in connection with Kant's theory of autonomy in chapter 2. In addition, the predisposition to "animality" constitutes the physical "self-love" insuring our preservation as a species. Standing between these two in Kant's account is the predisposition to "humanity" which produces the inclination to *"acquire worth in the opinion of others."*[39] Kant suggests that

> we judge ourselves happy or unhappy only by making comparison with others. ... This is originally a desire merely for *equality*, to allow no one superiority above oneself, bound up with a constant care lest others strive to attain such superiority; but from this arises gradually the unjustifiable craving to win it for oneself over others.[40]

Here we have what is effectively a *social* obstacle to moral progress, since a social context is required for the relevant comparisons to occur.

Accordingly, a solution to the problems thus posed must be social in nature. We might say that the collusion between the predisposition to humanity and the propensity to radical evil serves as the occasion for the need of the ethical commonwealth. In the words of one commentator, "the attainment of virtue must take the form of efforts to create a more perfect social union," which is to say that because of "the corruption of the original end of our social nature, the task of moral perfection for the individual is inseparable from a reorientation toward others."[41] Attaining my own virtue becomes coincident with promoting a certain kind of community.

In a different context some years earlier, Kant proposed what he called the "unsocial sociability of men" as a description of the source of antagonism among persons living together in a social setting.[42] Kant there defines unsocial sociability as people's "tendency to come together in society, coupled, however, with a continual resistance which constantly threatens to break this society up." He further depicts the "unsocial" or selfish side of this tendency as the individual's "unsocial characteristic of wanting to direct everything in accordance with his own ideas."[43] Curiously, this unsocial sociability becomes the basis of social and cultural advancement, since the individual's awareness of "resistance" from others "awakens all man's powers and induces him to overcome his tendency to laziness."

> Through the desire for honour, power, or property, it drives him to seek status among his fellows, whom he cannot *bear* yet cannot *bear to leave*. Then the first true steps are taken from barbarism to culture, which in fact consists in the social worthiness of man. All man's talents are now gradually developed, his taste cultivated, and by a continued process of enlightenment, a beginning is made towards establishing a way of thinking which can with time transform the primitive natural capacity for moral discrimination into definite practical principles; and thus a *pathologically* enforced social union is transformed into a *moral* whole.[44]

We thus have a depiction of moral progress based in part on appeal to a negative characteristic of humankind that gets put to good use. In a sense, Kant is deriving a moral result from a basically cosmopolitan account of moral agents living together in society.[45]

Something similar and more detailed is at stake in Kant's account of the ethical commonwealth. In this new context, the predisposition to humanity plays the role played in the earlier context by the unsocial sociability of man, with the challenges to moral progress now intensified by the account of radical evil. In what is for Kant the primordial "ethical state of nature," we "mutually corrupt one another's moral predispositions," for despite

the good will of each individual, yet, because they lack a principle which
unites them, they recede, through their dissensions, from the common goal
of goodness and, just as though they were *instruments of evil*, expose one
another to the risk of falling once again under the sovereignty of the evil
principle.[46]

The problem disclosed by the predisposition to humanity is the natural
tendency to compare oneself with others and thus to strive to acquire
worth in the opinion of others. Morally innocent in itself, this predisposition nonetheless becomes the occasion for "jealousy" and "rivalry,"
producing the fall into the vices of envy, ingratitude, and spitefulness.[47]
At the same time, however, the categorical imperative enjoins us to
treat other persons as ends in themselves and never as a means only – the
fact that morality's most formal principle has, from the very start,
included social implications now pays full dividends. In effect, morality's
formal principle generates a social antidote to this socially caused problem, and the idea of an ethical commonwealth emerges from rational
reflection on the effects of this antidote. Comparisons between persons
that degenerate into odious comparisons must be transformed into the
treatment of others as ends in themselves. We might say that *reciprocity*
turns out to be the "principle which unites" that Kant claims we need
when we exist only in the ethical state of nature, a reciprocity disclosing
the identification of the good will with justice itself.[48] With the obligation to overcome radical evil joined now by a depiction of the *social*
conditions of our fall,[49] the idea of an ethical commonwealth becomes
for Kant the necessary vehicle of moral improvement. A solution that is
social in nature is required to address a fundamentally social problem.
Only the harmony of wills present in the idea of a universalizing legislation can heal the rupture between myself and my neighbor, for the
criterion of universality will respect the autonomy and intrinsic dignity
of all parties.
As Kant's thinking crystallizes in the concept of a "union of such
individuals," we find a fusion of the legislative features of the realm of
ends with the totalizing tendencies evident in the very idea of the highest
good. The doctrine of radical evil has apparently injected sufficient
urgency into the situation to impel Kant toward a greater degree of
specificity regarding the otherwise abstract ideals rendered by these
previous themes, for Kant now speaks of "a duty which is *sui generis*,
not of men toward men, but of the human race toward itself."

For the species of rational beings is objectively, in the idea of reason,
destined for a social goal, namely the promotion of the highest as a social
good. But because the highest moral good cannot be achieved merely by the

exertions of the single individual toward his own moral perfection, but requires rather *a union of such individuals into a whole* toward the same goal – into a system of well-disposed men, in which and through whose unity alone the highest moral good can come to pass – the *idea of such a whole*, as a universal republic based on laws of virtue, is an idea completely distinguished from all moral laws (which concern what we know to lie in our own power); since it involves working toward a *whole* regarding which we do not know whether, as such, it lies in our power or not.[50]

Reason's totalizing activity culminates here in the projection into the future of a social "whole" (*ein Ganzes*), a moral community that will serve as the antidote to the social setting in which radical evil so easily arises. At stake is what has been characterized as the "regulative idea of history" itself, wherein Kant's concept of the highest good becomes the principle of integration between a morally idealized world and our own world.[51] Reason's totalizing activity, already evident in the concept of the highest good in the second *Critique*, becomes progressively more comprehensive, yielding a vision informed now by the special challenges introduced by radical evil. More to the point, reason's totalizing activity has shifted from the individual, personal, and otherworldly framework of the postulate of the immortality of the soul to the social, communal, and immanent perspective conveyed by the ethical commonwealth. In the face of radical evil, the providential nature of a self- directed rationality has now defined "providence" with much greater precision.

THE ETHICAL COMMONWEALTH AND GOD

While Kant retains generous references to God in connection with the formation of the ethical commonwealth, certain implications of his increased attention to the corporate aspect of moral agency leave unclear both the exact meaning and the argumentative necessity of those references. As I have been suggesting, the shift from an individualist to a social perspective on moral improvement is shadowed by a gradual displacement of the role of divine agency by the moral community's own activity. The envisioned ethical commonwealth is greater than the sum of its parts – greater, that is, than the sheer aggregate of individual moral strivings or perfections[52] – and the sense in which it is "more than" is coincident with the sense in which divine transcendence continues to recede from view. The two shifts in Kant's perspective reinforce one another.

Interestingly, an important indicator of this pair of shifts resides in an apparent solution that the transition from the second *Critique* to the *Religion* implicitly provides for a problem left unresolved in the earlier work. The second *Critique* leaves unclear the sense in which we might be able to act on Kant's apparent claim that we are obligated to promote the highest good. Although he at times manages to cross-thread in confusing ways an appeal to the moral law with an appeal to the highest good as the determining ground of the good will,[53] Kant claims at several points that "we *should* seek to further the highest good (which therefore must be at least possible),"[54] adding in the *Religion* that "the moral law demands that the highest good possible through our agency should be realized."[55] Yet since the definition of the highest good is the proper proportioning of happiness and virtue, it is frankly unclear what such a moral requirement actually entails for an individual moral agent.[56] If the issue is simply that of endeavoring to perfect one's own virtue, it is not at all obvious why an appeal to the highest good is required or what such an appeal adds to the respect for the authority of the moral law the agent already possesses. As Beck puts it, "suppose I do all in my power"

> to promote the highest good, what am I to do? Simply act out of respect for the law, *which I already knew*. I can do absolutely nothing else toward apportioning happiness in accordance with desert – that is the task of a moral governor of the universe, not of a laborer in the vineyard. It is not *my* task; my task is to realize the one condition of the *summum bonum* which is within my power; it is seriously misleading to say that there is a command to seek the highest good which is different from the command to fulfill the requirements of duty.[57]

However, by fusing together the totalizing tendencies of the highest good with the legislative dimension of the realm of ends in his emerging concept of the ethical commonwealth, Kant initiates a reconceptualization of what it would mean to promote the highest good. If the shape that reason's providential activity takes is ultimately the ethical commonwealth, then any duty I may have to promote that goal turns out to be identical to my duty to enter into rational reciprocity with my fellow moral agents. I find my salvation in the strictly social enterprise of transforming the negative degeneration of my predisposition to humanity into the positive activity of treating all others as ends in themselves. The result is a capacity to engage in universalizing legislation that respects the autonomy of all parties even as it applies to them. The shift from the noumenal frame of reference in the second *Critique* to the earthly task of community-building at stake in the *Religion* thus gives both meaning and content to the injunction to promote the highest good.

But of course such a shift raises serious questions concerning the divine role. As the function of the second postulate is apparently supplanted by the task of creating the ethical commonwealth, that feature of Kant's

moral argument allowing God in by the back door is effectively eliminated. Yovel helpfully captures the shift from the noumenal world to
historical activity – and the compromising of divine transcendence that
results – when he points out that, in Kant's later works including the
Religion, the "highest good and the given world no longer signify two
different worlds but two states, present and ideal, of the same world. In
other words, the highest good becomes a historical goal."

> Only in light of this change can the human duty to realize or promote the
> highest good become meaningful. The highest good is our own world
> brought to perfection. It is not the transcendent world of God, but like
> the given world it has temporal existence and empirical constituents. . . .
> The duty to promote the highest good no longer means that a person
> should make himself good, but that he should also make the *world* good.[58]

Kant himself evidently sees the parallel between the proportioning of
virtue and happiness informing his original moral argument and the
human task of fashioning the ethical commonwealth. For just as the
proportioning process described in the second *Critique* results in Kant's
theistic claim, his depiction of the difficult process of creating a moral
community results in an analogue to the third postulate. As Kant argues
that "the highest moral good cannot be achieved merely by the exertions
of the single individual toward his own moral perfection" but requires a
"system of well-disposed men, in which and through whose unity alone
the highest moral good can come to pass," he adds that we "can already
foresee that this duty will require the presupposition of another idea,
namely, that of a higher moral Being through whose universal dispensation the forces of separate individuals, insufficient in themselves, are
united for a common end."[59] The transfer of interest from the otherworldly noumenal zone of God's activity in the second *Critique* to a
setting in which "the forces of individuals, insufficient in themselves,
are united for a common end," is itself indicative of an important shift
in Kant's thinking. He seems to be proposing a complex and dynamic
interaction among the overcoming of radical evil, community-building,
and trust in a hidden source of divine aid: the interaction of the first two
generates the third in a manner that is reminiscent of the postulation
process in the second *Critique*.

Kant also invokes divine aid in his discussion elsewhere in the *Religion*
of moral regeneration depicted in purely individual or personal terms,
and the comparison is instructive. In the case of the individual's moral
conversion, the truly "radical" quality of the problem is altogether obvious because of the way the underlying ground of our maxim-making,
the disposition, has become polluted. As Kant recognizes, it is not at

all clear how the moral agent can freely subordinate the incentive of sensuous inclination to the incentive of moral duty if the agent has adopted the reverse order as a *general* policy, which is precisely what radical evil is. This grim state of affairs is why, at one point, Kant goes so far as to say that radical evil is "*inextirpable* by human powers, since extirpation could occur only through good maxims, and cannot take place when the ultimate subjective ground of all maxims is postulated as corrupt."[60] It is just here that Kant introduces the idea that "some supernatural cooperation may be necessary to [the individual's] becoming good."[61] Kant apparently has in mind some sort of cooperative endeavor involving both an element of autonomous human effort toward moral recovery and an element of divine grace that makes up for the inevitable shortfall in the fallen agent's moral effort. Moral recovery "must be within our power, even though what *we* are able to do is in itself inadequate and though we thereby only render ourselves susceptible of higher and, for us, inscrutable assistance."[62] We have here something like a postulation of human/divine cooperation in the recovery from radical evil, based on what amounts to a Pelagian appeal to divine assistance for those who do their moral best.

Consequently, in the case of the individual's moral recovery, God plays the role of the hidden accomplice whose grace takes the form of canceling the difference between what the individual is obligated to do and what the agent can in fact do in the recovery from radical evil. Divine aid complements the individual's morally imperfect best efforts. Kant's appeals to hidden divine aid never actually transgress his own stringent epistemological principles, for such aid is an object of hope, not of knowledge. Kant's concept of grace is thus not so much a fully fashioned theological position as it is a form of psychological encouragement for moral agents who might otherwise fall into despair in the face of radical evil.[63] Kant is not really attempting to offer information about God or the divine will so much as he is finding yet another avenue for ethical exhortation.

Similarly, in the case of moral recovery viewed in corporate terms, something of this encouraging "gap-filling" role remains in Kant's proposed "presupposition... of a higher moral Being through whose universal dispensation the forces of separate individuals, insufficient in themselves, are united for a common end."[64] Again, it appears that it is God's role to make up a perceived shortfall. But in the former instance the stark depiction of the individual's desperate situation leaves utterly no alternative but an appeal to hidden grace, while Kant's very formulation of corporate moral agency suggests the *community's* capacity to offset the individual's limitations – the very role God plays for the individual. To repeat the key passage, Kant tells us that the "highest moral good cannot be achieved merely by the exertions of the single individual toward his own moral perfection, but requires rather a union of such individuals into a whole toward the same goal."[65] At the very least, the community is now playing a mediating role suggestive of a strengthened connection between other moral agents and the individual's moral progress.

As a result, the wider community not only competes with God as an object of the moral agent's interest but has the advantage of being publicly available in ways that God is not. In the social task of establishing the ethical commonwealth, rational beings working together offset the limitations of any one moral agent, a role that had been God's alone when the individual was viewed in isolation. In light of the fact that it is difficult in any case to make sense of a traditional doctrine of divine grace alongside Kant's emphasis on human autonomy, this emerging role for the community to play in relation to the individual's moral progress assumes even greater force. For the basis of the individual's relations with other members of the ethical commonwealth has already been established in the second and, especially, the third formulas of the categorical imperative. To be sure, there are deep challenges connected with treating other rational beings as ends in themselves and entering into a relation of universalizing legislation with them. But these challenges promise to fulfill the agent's autonomy, whereas a trust in God's grace, however comforting, always results in confusion about the exact status of autonomy. The advantages to the individual of a corporate conception of moral improvement are increasingly evident in ways that diminish further the divine role.

We might say, then, that moral agents "united for a common end"[66] become the social correlate to divine aid in the process of moral regeneration conceived at the individual level. The role traditionally played by God's will is transformed into a Kantian version of Rousseau's "general will."[67] The actual – if gradual – process of "uniting" along lines originally prescribed by the third formula of the categorical imperative promises a corporate reality that is more than the sum of its parts in the sense that this union for a common end helps to offset the limitations of any individual. With this vision, Kant has set in motion a transition of the agent's object of hope away from a noumenal heaven and toward the always problematic task of community-building on earth, a task no less obligatory for its enormous difficulty. Any lingering appeal to divine action no longer takes the form of a mysterious proportioning process occurring after my death in an unimaginably remote noumenal zone. Rather, God, too, has now been drawn into the earthly business of fashioning the ethical commonwealth, with this "immanentizing" of divine activity itself symptomatic of the further marginalization of transcendence in Kant's shifting account of moral perfection.

Indeed, God is no longer really an "actor" at all, performing a variation on the divine role described in the second *Critique*. Instead, God becomes a spectator or even a placeholder, serving yet again as a kind of background metaphysical premise guaranteeing a rational result for genuinely moral endeavors. The relevant comparison in the second *Critique* is not with the active God who proportions virtue and happiness, but with Kant's highly abstract appeal to God as the "highest original good" that seems parasitic on features of the other theistic proofs left unaccounted for by the moral argument. As we saw in connection with our examination of the moral argument in chapter 2, God's role as a metaphysical ground is in any case more of an acknowledgment of a rational requirement than it is a robust expression of divine activity; it is a way of giving reason its due. At issue is a good example of what has been referred to as the "speculative apparatus of the doctrine of the deity" furnishing "no explanation but only a subjective *decor*," where God and divine attributes are "merely modes of representation by which we picture the source of [an] ability to ourselves."[68] The "ability" in question is, of course, our own, and the scene of action for the promotion of the ethical commonwealth is history.

In other words, God's presumed ability to proportion virtue and happiness in an infinitely distant noumenal realm has become the occasion for referring to our own abilities. When, at the end of Book III of the *Religion*, Kant once again points out that the prodigious task of achieving the highest good impels belief in "the cooperation or management of a moral Ruler of the world, by means of which alone this goal can be reached," he rounds off his own point with a combination of agnosticism and moral exhortation.

> And now there opens up before him the abyss of a mystery regarding what God may do, whether indeed *anything* in general, and if so *what* in particular should be ascribed to God. Meanwhile man knows concerning each duty nothing but what he must himself do in order to be worthy of that supplement, unknown, or at least incomprehensible, to him. ... This idea of a moral Governor of the world ... concerns us not so much to know what God is in Himself (His nature) as what He is for us as moral beings ...[69]

Upon inspection, then, the superficial resemblance between God's relation to the ethical commonwealth and the postulation process in the second *Critique* actually serves to underscore the transfer of Kant's interest away from God and toward the immanent zone of human action. The religious motif accompanying Kant's depiction of reason's drive toward a community of virtue thus exemplifies what has been characterized as "the political and emancipatory intentions of the notion of rational faith."[70] Authentic faith is rational precisely to the degree that it leads us away from an otherworldly frame of reference. His way of conceptualizing the social aspect of moral agency thus turns out to be the source of Kant's chief means of doing justice to history, providing reason itself with a route back into the world from which it was presumably abstracted.

The resemblance between God's relation to the ethical commonwealth and the earlier postulation process appears to undergo an additional iteration when Kant proposes that God should be viewed as the "law-giver" of the ethical commonwealth.[71] Kant remarks rather surprisingly that "if the commonwealth is to be *ethical*, the people, as a people, cannot itself be regarded as the law-giver."

> Hence only he can be thought of as highest law-giver of an ethical commonwealth with respect to whom all *true duties*, hence also the ethical, must be represented as *at the same time* his commands; he must therefore also be "one who knows the heart," in order to see into the innermost parts of the disposition of each individual and, as is necessary in every commonwealth, to bring it about that each receives whatever his actions are worth. But this is the concept of God as moral ruler of the world. Hence an ethical commonwealth can be thought of only as a people under divine commands, i.e., as a *people of God*, and indeed *under laws of virtue*.[72]

In this cumbersome train of thought, Kant seems to be conflating remnants of the original postulation process with his definition of religion as the recognition of duties as divine commands. He then seems to infuse the resulting combination with his view of personal conversion, in which Kant emphasizes God's capacity to "see" the revolutionized and now virtuous moral disposition, in light of God's possession of an intellectual rather than a sensuous intuition.[73] The idea animating this train of thought is Kant's suggestion that the law-giver for the ethical commonwealth cannot be the people, an apparent retreat from his own theory of autonomy.

However, this apparent retreat turns out simply to be Kant's method of distinguishing between "public" and "inner" laws, a variation on his already proposed distinction between a political community and a community of virtue. Kant reminds us that in an ethical commonwealth

> all the laws are expressly designed to promote the *morality* of actions (which is something *inner*, and hence cannot be subject to public human laws) whereas, in contrast, these public laws – and this would go to

constitute a juridical commonwealth – are directed only toward the *legality* of actions, which meets the eye, and not toward (inner) morality, which alone is in question here.[74]

Kant makes the connection between this "public/inner" distinction and God when he claims that there "must therefore be someone other than the populace capable of being specified as the public law-giver for an ethical commonwealth," yet we should not think of the ethical laws "as emanating *originally* merely from the will of this superior being."[75] In fact, the ethical laws at stake arise out of our very own rational sense of duty and are not arbitrary statutes imposed on us from without.

In other words, the sense in which God is viewed as the "law-giver" for the ethical commonwealth does not impinge upon the rational *source* of the laws governing such a community. Rather, God's status as law-giver is a function of God's ability – and God's ability alone – to *pass judgment* on the inner, moral state of individual members of the community. The issue at stake is the integrity of the moral agent's private moral disposition and not a potentially heteronomous source of laws governing the ethical commonwealth. Whether or not a member of the ethical commonwealth is obeying the moral law is not a matter for public debate or adjudication, but only a matter for the "divine eye" to see and judge. Kant's invocation at this point of his definition of religion as the recognition of moral duties as divine commands underscores the rational basis of whatever is morally obligatory: a duty is a divine command *because* it is rational. As Kant himself points out elsewhere in the *Religion*, the "bare idea" of a law-giver is "identical with the general moral concept of duty," and the two are in fact analytically equivalent.[76] Reverting to the ethical commonwealth's precursor in the realm or kingdom of ends, we find confirmation of this point in one commentator's observation that "we still have the right to regard ourselves as sharing the headship of the kingdom of ends with God insofar as we are legislators in that world."[77] We might say that the conception of God as a fellow member of the ethical commonwealth constitutes Kant's final overcoming of the voluntarist tradition's emphasis on the creation of morality through divine fiat. Antivoluntarism suggests the desirability of being in a moral community together with God, under the same moral law.[78]

Consequently, the suggestion that God is the law-giver for the ethical commonwealth is not a diminishment of the community's autonomy but another way in which Kant shows how morality leads to religion. Yet in the very act of so doing, Kant once again underscores the priority of rationality to the divine will. For the sake of the inner integrity of the members of the ethical commonwealth, reason has *conferred* upon God the status of law-giver. In fact, Kant elects just this moment in the *Religion* to observe that a claim that something is a "divine command can never, by any empirical token, be accredited adequately enough to allow an otherwise established duty to be neglected on its account."[79] The clear call of reason always trumps the proposal of a contingent and arbitrary divine command; alternatively, anything that is truly a divine command can be rendered in the rational form of a universal duty. The will's consistency with itself rather than its obedience to an outside power animates Kant's position.

One implication of this position is that, in appealing to God as the law-giver for the ethical commonwealth, we are really addressing our own rational nature. Yet this of course suggests that Kant's very notion of "law-giver" introduces an ambiguity of reference: upon examination, the appeal to God turns out to be a special way of talking about ourselves. We find this point amplified in a reference to God as moral law-giver in the *Critique of Judgment*, where Kant says the "actuality of a supreme morally legislative Author is, therefore, sufficiently proved simply *for the practical employment* of our reason, without determining anything theoretically in respect of its existence."[80] In other words, appealing to God as moral law-giver is in fact a way of redirecting attention to ourselves. One might even say that this ambiguity of reference anticipates some of the argumentative subtleties of Feuerbach's conception of theology, including his investment of divine traits in humanity taken as a whole. To be sure, Feuerbach's argument in *The Essence of Christianity* has a much more fully developed conception of the way appeals to corporate humanity offset the limitations of any individual. Still, his position finds a clear precursor in Kant's invocation of a union of moral agents "in which and through whose unity alone the highest moral good can come to pass," thereby offsetting the imperfect "exertions of the single individual toward his own moral perfection."[81] In both cases, the aim is not to highlight a transcendent "other" but to exhort humanity to the realization of its highest and best historical potential, without the distractions of heaven.

Moreover, in Kant's case, the sense in which God remains "other" is further jeopardized by a lingering implication of God's relation to the "laws" that are at issue in the notion of God as law-giver: these laws are laws for God as well as for humanity. Far from being external to the ethical commonwealth, God is in fact a member *of* it. God, too, is obligated to obey the universalizing legislation of the community in the same way that, in the second *Critique*, God is obligated to meet the demands of the highest good by proportioning happiness and virtue.[82] Somewhat cryptically but nonetheless significantly, Kant provides the basis for this incorporation of God into the moral community in the preface to the *Foundations*, where he argues that everyone "must admit that a law, if it is to hold morally, i.e., as a ground of obligation... does not apply to men only, as if other rational beings had no need to observe it."[83] Such a conception of a law that is common to God and humanity both underscores Kant's own position in a crucial eighteenth-century debate[84] and reaches a culminating moment in his view of the ethical commonwealth. In their battle against the doctrine that morality is simply the contingent and arbitrary creation of God, antivoluntarists such as Kant would need to define moral obligation apart from reference to God while still having a way of incorporating God into the subsequent account of moral action. Yet Kant's aggressive and original approach to the first part of this project so thins out the second part that God finally appears to be little more than a kind of moral partner whose role is clearly secondary to that of the community itself.

Since there appears to be no truly vigorous conception of divine action to replicate the limited yet nonetheless instrumental role God plays in the *Critique of Practical Reason*, the implications involved in the shift in Kant's perspective appear increasingly serious. One might plausibly say that the most important strictly theological development in the *Religion* is the apparent superseding of the postulate of immortality by the theory of moral progress associated with the ethical commonwealth.[85] This is a crucial development, since by the very terms of Kant's moral argument, there is no argumentative bridge to a claim of divine existence without prior appeal to the postulate of immortality. Consequently, in so far as the historical duration required for the full realization of the ethical commonwealth does in fact supplant the noumenal realm as the locus of moral perfection, Kant's most explicit strategy for offsetting the agnosticism of the first *Critique* is seriously compromised. The second *Critique*'s carefully forged connection between theism and the conception of a will that can be motivated by rational principles is now framed by question marks. As I have previously suggested, this point remains true regardless of whether the ethical commonwealth is to be fully realized in history or only ever-approximated over time, like an asymptote. This difference is simply irrelevant to the change in venue initiated by the reasoning associated with the ethical commonwealth.

The full force of the multiple aspects of Kant's principle of immanence comes to bear at just this point, for the jeopardizing of his own moral argument for the existence of God is itself eloquent testimony to the clear priority of non-theistic considerations in his thinking. In particular, the account of radical evil, though clearly a threat to humanity's self-sufficiency, does not finally compromise Kant's concern for human autonomy in the name of a reinvigorated theological commitment. Rather, his account results in a reconceptualizing of autonomy in corporate terms as the best source of human hope. Theistic claims may linger, but they co-exist in an awkward and unsystematic relationship with the more fundamental emphasis on autonomy, as epitomized by Kant's appeals to divine grace when discussing individual moral regeneration. As a result, the peculiar possibility emerges that Kant's most explicitly religious writing turns out to include a train of thought that sabotages his chief argument for God's existence.

The cumulative effect of Kant's "interested," self-directed, and utterly autonomous rationality finds a neat resting point in this irony. Virtually personified and busily engaged in projects of construction, reason restlessly pursues its interests and satisfies its needs in ways that define and circumscribe any reference to God, rather than the other way around. God was once the restless presence, operating unhindered in the desert, jealously protecting the divine prerogative and frankly announcing bold interests and purposes, including some that made no "sense." Now the restlessness is all reason's, as it seeks to satisfy its own interests and fulfill its needs in a setting that remains a desert, except for autonomy's inventiveness. It only remains for Kant's God to align the divine will with the formal constraints suggestive of the domestication of divine restlessness in the uncompromising terms set by rationality. Whether or not this remnant is an adequate content for an authentic theology is no doubt an open question.

CHAPTER SIX

Conclusion

FROM KANT TO MARX

Kant's philosophy demands autonomy, but it only accommodates theism. Such would appear to be the clear moral of the preceding investigation, which has traced the way an "interested" reason devises its own ends, generates its own momentum, and presses towards its self-designed goal. In its multiple aspects, Kant's principle of immanence convincingly demonstrates that "self-consciousness, freedom, and human sociality" are "at the core of the modern project."[1] In his case, the definitively modern feature resides especially in the idea that human subjectivity is ultimately inspired and moved to action by a fact of reason requiring no further ground. Paradoxically, a philosophical effort initially intended to demarcate reason's limitations ends up demonstrating reason's self-sufficiency. Kant's philosophy may take the form of "a rigorously argued self-limitation of reason," but the fact that it is a *self*-limitation reminds us that the critique of reason is "from reason's *own* perspective."[2]

A closely related paradox stands at the very center of Kant's demolition of the traditional proofs for God's existence: an apparent constraint on speculation in fact reflects the very dependence of the "world" on the transcendental conditions of experience, rather than on an act of God. Space, time, and lawfulness in nature come from the structure of our own minds rather than from divine fiat. By simply saying "I think," I implicitly acknowledge that I have already grounded the world itself. The element of pure spontaneity informing Kant's concept of reason thus leads to an entirely fresh configuration of the self's relation to its own world. Now, in Dieter Henrich's words, to "be a self means precisely to be the ground of oneself."[3] In the wake of such a discovery, the disproof of the proofs suddenly becomes possible.[4]

To be sure, Kant's own unquestioned personal religious commitment is cobbled together with this philosophical vision, yet the points of connection are not only strained but they invariably display theism in a second-order relationship to a prior and much clearer account of reason's prerogatives. The religious side of Kant's outlook is best understood as the manifestation of a sensibility rather than as the result of philosophical argumentation; no accusation of hypocrisy is necessary to make such an observation. There is nothing far-fetched about the proposal that the religious dimension in Kant's thought has less to do with philosophical argument than with his "awe before infinity, his respect for the moral law, and...a well-developed and well-characterized sense of the holy which sees the holy primarily as righteous."[5] In such a characterization, the lingering effects of a profoundly pietistic upbringing, rather than the explicit results of philosophical positions aggressively staked out, account for whatever remains of a religious outlook. Without question, something deeply important about Kant himself comes to expression in this description. At the same time, however, such comments invite a distinction drawn between Kant's personal sensibility and the force and implications of his philosophical claims. As we have seen, his actual philosophical claims suggest in multiple contexts a transformation of appeals to God and divine transcendence into fresh ways of acknowledging reason's freely given privileges and, indeed, its very sovereignty. By contrast, the religious aspect of Kant's thinking often seems to remain largely in the form of motifs not easily integrated with his main commitments. The result is not so much a matter of divinizing reason as it is a matter of collapsing the traditional domain of the transcendent into a single arena of moral action. The fact that a truly rational faith must be rendered in terms of its own inner "political and emancipatory intentions"[6] inevitably leaves the lingering religious element appearing strained and potentially dispensable.

Kant's effort to provide theism with improved intellectual footing is thus subtly undermined by his own clarification of why the only secure theism is "moral" theism. Time and again, Kant announces the priority of the moral point of view to the religious, with the conviction that his starting point will always circle back to an affirmation of God's existence. Yet the power of his demonstration of how morality might be construed *apart* from religious convictions potentially short-circuits the route back to God. When, on the opening page of *Religion within the Limits of Reason Alone*, Kant characteristically comments that "for its own sake morality does not need religion at all,"[7] he speaks with the assurance of one who knows how his own book will turn out. At the same time, however, the full implications of this starting point, played out in Kant's account of autonomy and reason's projection of a self-designed goal for humankind, betray the possibility of a purely secular conception of morality. Kant's very point, after all, is to explain the way morality is both intelligible and, consequently, obligatory apart from reference to God, and he largely succeeds. Kant thus embodies the odd but plausible possibility that influential early steps toward a secularizing of morality would not be undertaken by atheists.

Particularly noteworthy is the fact that the diminishing role played by divine transcendence correlates in Kant's thinking with the increasing importance of a historical goal for human moral aspirations. Here, his sustained reflection on what links autonomous moral agents assumes a deepening importance. For the telos arising from an interest of reason may define Kant's account of our moral end, but it is his sharpened sense of the corporate aspect of moral agency that truly brings history and human action into full prominence. The notion that it is only Kant's idealist successors who insist on the role reason might play in actually shaping the historical world perhaps underestimates the power of this idea in Kant himself. A common way to characterize Kant's relationship to his successors is to argue that his theory of freedom may be protected by the distinction between the phenomenal and noumenal worlds, but that the distinction itself leaves moral agents somehow alienated from the external world, existing as a kind of moral "solitary."[8] The resulting sense of spiritual isolation is compounded by a growing despair over the possibility of ever transforming the social sphere in ways that would fulfill our aspirations for freedom. Kant's successors thus devise ways to overcome this intolerable situation, which helps to explain why the phenomena–noumena distinction itself is so often at the center of post-Kantian controversy. But the basis of this transformation of the world is in fact already present in Kant himself. The ethical commonwealth, as incomplete and unsystematic as it may be, is nonetheless a better guide to the direction of Kant's thought than the conceptual machinery surrounding the moral argument for the existence of God. In its suggestion of a transfer of interest from a noumenal to a worldly frame of reference, the ethical commonwealth symbolizes Kant's own advance against other-worldliness.

In short, Kant himself is already making respectable the idea that a purely human frame of reference is sufficient for depicting our highest goals and possibilities. Often strained and conceptually awkward, the religious motifs lingering in his philosophy might be viewed as the residue of an outmoded outlook that invariably characterizes a transitional thinker during a transitional period. For even as he is thinking through the implications of a theory of human autonomy that has no wider metaphysical mooring and needs no compass from an external source, Kant could hardly be expected to cast off the habits of thought that give rise to such speculation in the first place. There are simply no traditions of thought and discourse available to him for thinking through his chosen topics apart from the traditions of a Christian European heritage. Relevant here is Hans Blumenberg's suggestion that the "sphere of sacral language outlives that of the consecrated objects" and is subsequently "conserved and used as a cover precisely where philosophically, politically, and scientifically new thinking is being done."[9] At the least, we can safely acknowledge that the continuity of vocabularies inevitably present whenever an original thinker generates new answers to old problems can sometimes mask from view the magnitude of the proposed changes. Continuity and discontinuity exist side by side in Kant's idea that God and humanity are members of the same moral community. For this seemingly innocent, even pious, proposal, evoking the comforting biblical imagery of the kingdom, turns out to be the "astonishing claim" that "God and we can share membership in a single moral community only if we all equally legislate the law we are to obey."[10] In short, Kant's actual way of rendering the moral community underscores the immanent source of holiness itself. Heaven not only comes to earth, it is progressively displaced by it.

It is in light of the theme of heaven coming to earth that we should view the suggestion, made at the outset of this study, that Kant might profitably be viewed as a way station between Luther and Marx. We can now see more clearly that it is Kant's account of autonomy and its relation both to divine transcendence and to the external world that reveals this linkage. Implicitly, Kant's position is both an adaptation and a criticism of Luther's account of the "freedom of the Christian," in which the Lutheran idea of a highly personal, "inner," and inviolate religious self, beyond all priestly intrusion or manipulation, finds secular expression. The associated Lutheran theme of authentic freedom as submission to the divine will becomes in Kant's hands submission to the demands of the moral law: the full realization of the self depends upon obedience.[11] Moreover, there is nothing privileged about the sense of obligation underwriting our accountability. The democratic conception of access to the divine will embodied in Luther's emphasis on vernacular translations of the Bible is replicated in the universal availability of Kant's moral law. Neither the individual Lutheran believer nor the Kantian moral agent needs a soul-saving gate-keeper.

The continuing linkage between submission and an inviolate personal self would become the occasion for Marx's further alteration of this tradition of reflection. With Kant's postulation process clearly in view,

Marx will complain of the impotence of a privatistic ethical outlook involving an otherworldly concept of autonomy that can in no way alter our actual material circumstance.[12] Notwithstanding the half-truths perpetuated by Marx's criticisms of Kant, the line that can be traced through these three thinkers concerns the question of freedom and freedom's relation to the "outside" world. Kant is himself already probing beyond the boundaries of his own position through his transformation of the postulate of immortality into the worldly striving for the ethical commonwealth. Already with him, the appeal to the divine will has been compromised as the free will becomes the source of its own law. Moreover, Kant's reorientation of the individual and private self to the community of fellow moral agents makes the link with Marx all the more provocative, even as it raises questions about the classically "liberal" Kant.[13] It is thus a significant measure of his breadth of vision that Kant provides resources for overcoming the more severe tendencies of his own moral individualism.

Viewed in this light, Kant turns out to stand in the same relationship to Feuerbach that the latter stands to Marx. Although Kant's philosophy falls short of the explicit translation of theology into anthropology that we find in Feuerbach's *Essence of Christianity*, his principle of immanence provides significant momentum toward just such a translation process.[14] Quite simply, Kant, as much as Hegel, should be viewed as making possible the transformations in European culture that we associate with the rise of humanistic atheism. As I have tried to show, this is true for reasons going well beyond Kant's criticism of the traditional theistic proofs: his criticism of the proofs is symptomatic of a much wider argumentative context with negative implications for theology, rather than an isolated and idiosyncratic moment that is ultimately offset by a positive theological turn. Certainly Kant has no systematic interest in maintaining an otherworldly residue in connection with moral reflection, insisting instead that the practical task of promoting the ethical commonwealth should be humanity's highest priority. Reason's goal is to change the world, not leave it. Kant should thus be understood as providing the clue of self-sufficiency to an emerging tradition of discourse that would attempt more aggressively to bring heaven to earth, aided in due course by Hegelian variations on Kant's own efforts to think in modern terms. The differences in philosophical idiom and ambition introduced by Hegel himself should not obscure the essential lines of continuity between Kant and Feuerbach regarding a human-centered frame of reference for thought and practice.

Reading Kant's philosophy in this way confirms the centrality of his presence in any effort to disentangle the vexed issue of the secularization of Western thought. Certainly the transfer of interest from the scrupulous and penitent regard for the divine will that would have characterized Kant's pietist boyhood, to the self-directed and even providential conception of rationality animating his mature philosophy, tracks in biographical form larger developments in the culture as a whole. In this transition, we see a thinning out of the divine will into something less robust and more abstract, even as we see a continuing teleological trust. Purposeful human action takes the same form but simply has a more immanent content: heaven is displaced by worldly goals, just as a noumenal immortality is displaced by Kant's ethical commonwealth. In the meantime, confidence in the vocabulary of "purpose" remains intact. Whether or not this lingering teleological element is the genuinely definitive way of carrying on biblical thinking, as Nietzsche thought, remains unresolved amidst our debates about the potentially "belated" nature of modernity. The tension in Kant's own philosophy between a mechanistic Newtonianism and a moral transformation of the world – between the "starry heavens above and the moral law within" (*Practical*, p. 166) – is an uncanny preview of our own problem.

KANT AND MEDIATING THEOLOGY

If it is true that "Kant's reinterpretation of Christianity became the prototype for the mediating Protestant theologies of the nineteenth century and their twentieth-century heirs, Roman Catholic as well as Protestant,"[15] then there is an unsettling dimension to my reading of his philosophy. The whole point of mediating theology is to balance or otherwise integrate into a single and articulate vision the competing claims of a modern sensibility and the biblical tradition. By definition, mediating theology holds that Christianity speaks to the modern world with no compromise of either the essential Christian message or modernity's canons of intelligibility. Yet it would appear that Kant's principle of immanence effectively undercuts the very element of "mediation" at stake in this task, raising questions about his place in the mediating tradition and, perhaps, about the very idea of reconciling modernity and Christianity.

Now sometimes referred to as "revisionist" theology, mediating theology typically involves a continuing commitment to what one of its practitioners calls the "noble correlative enterprise" that presupposes an underlying commensurability between faith and culture.[16] The assumption is that there is a fundamental, if admittedly latent, tie between Christian truth-claims and certain modes of secular awareness or anthropological "givens," a tie that can be exposed through the proper conceptual or philosophical analysis. At stake is the disclosure of the meaning – and perhaps even the truth – of Christian faith in terms immediately accessible to the believer, in keeping with the Cartesian–Kantian model of intellectual autonomy. Kant's own moral hermeneutics is in many ways the model for the correlative enterprise, which animates the powerful tradition linking Schleiermacher and Tillich and establishes such concepts as the "experience of absolute dependence" and "ultimate concern" at the center of the dialogue between theology and modern culture.[17] Certainly the idea of a hidden commensurability between faith and the self is the ideal apologetic device, since all the theologian needs to do is uncover that dimension of the self that correlates with faith, and the rest falls into place.

> Maybe moral seriousness, maybe a distinctive experience of "depth" in human life – usually some appeal to a basic incompleteness, basic need, a primordial relation to divine transcendence, or some combination of these – is made in order to persuade us that in our hearts we knew all along what we weren't willing to admit, viz., that we cannot get along without divine succor. *There is always an appeal, in this kind of apologetic, to a conjunction between one's own, autonomous life quest and the divine grace.* Our path toward that conjunction, in terms of which the event itself is at least partially understood, is assumed to be the indispensable condition for understanding Christianity.[18]

Especially (though not exclusively) within Protestant theology, mediation of this sort has maintained a powerful presence since the Enlightenment. Even apart from any morals that might be drawn simply from the present study, the mediating project has evidently entered a period of difficult transitions and challenges that perhaps reflect the social location of the theologian as much as they concern any strictly conceptual developments. A powerful example of the relevant shifts is the fact that many of the clearest examples of contemporary mediating theology are the several forms of liberation and feminist theologies that correlate the biblical message with the historical experience of oppression, domination, and exploitation. These harsh realities replace the indubitable anthropological "givens," such as Kantian moral awareness or existential states, that informed earlier styles of mediating theology. Yet what is most striking about this shift in perspective is the manner in which mediation is pursued in conjunction with an explicit repudiation of the modernist, Cartesian–Kantian conception of the self that helped to launch mediating theology in the first place. Rather oddly, mediation continues unabated, but without the conceptual apparatus that not only made it possible, but that gave mediation its original point by posing the modern problem of intellectual autonomy. In effect, the crisis of plausibility initially induced by religious claims repugnant to the intellect is displaced by a plausibility crisis created by the experience of repugnance toward certain social and political realities. In fact, part of the repugnance is now directed toward the narrow and limited terms in which the Cartesian–Kantian tradition has framed the issue.[19]

Not surprisingly, then, liberation and feminist theologians typically focus their repudiation of the modern model of personal identity on its individualistic, privatizing tendencies. Such tendencies are depicted as the conceptual expression of a controlling, manipulative, and exploitative attitude, and of the denigration of the body as well.[20] Indeed, the powerful and influential image of an incorrigible "ground" or foundation for knowledge characterizing the modern epistemological project may itself be decoded as the tacit justification of the dominant power relations within the social setting: "foundationalism" is not merely bad epistemology, it reflects the injustices perpetuated by unquestioned seats of authority and privilege.[21] Similarly, as the condition of the possibility of depicting "otherness," dualistic thinking turns out to be the hidden and (for that very reason) powerful cultural vehicle for the rationalization of existing forms of oppression. Expressive of an intellectual ethos that "represents," "objectifies," and thereby "controls," the Cartesian–Kantian model is castigated as perpetuating in the polite and abstract terms of academic discourse the historical realities of racism, sexism, and economic exploitation.[22] Yet alongside this rejection of the very conceptual arrangements that originally gave mediating theology its life, liberation and feminist theologians develop fresh avenues of dialogue between contemporary experience and Christian faith. They achieve this mainly by fashioning correlations between tradition and modernity through adaptations of the exodus account, calls to action based upon Jesus' attitude toward the poor, or sustained attention devoted to gender issues in scripture in the effort to overcome the tradition's deep-seated patriarchal tendencies.[23] Indeed, rarely has the Bible itself been so "relevant" as in instances such as these. This time, however, the relevance is to historical realities that are publicly accessible rather than to concealed and deeply private moments of self-awareness.

From the standpoint of the Kantian legacy, it is especially telling that these suspicions of the subject-centered approach to faith and culture sustain a particularly sharp critical focus on the modern concept of autonomy. As an expression of a supposedly illicit privatistic conception of the self, autonomy is often deciphered in a manner that reiterates the moral, though hardly the full message, of earlier unmaskings of human freedom that we associate with Freud and Marx: that is, autonomy itself may be rendered in terms of underlying systems of constraints. Our inability more readily to apprehend the latent coercive element simply suggests the blindness that liberation and feminist theologians now associate with the false consciousness generated by oppressive and patriarchal social arrangements. From this new standpoint, the liberal conception of autonomy falsifies our real situation while perpetuating the harsh conditions of a world of injustice. As an antidote to autonomy's mystifying influence, the authentic Christian message is at once a call to a new form of community and a summons to political and social change. Notwithstanding the diversity and, perhaps, incompatibility of theological programs informed by such a political understanding of Christian faith, there is often a common point of reference in the suspicions directed toward a basically Kantian ideal of personal, individual autonomy.[24] Once again, then, Kant shares with Descartes an uncanny knack for remaining present in the midst of philosophical and theological debate by virtue of being an object of suspicion and criticism.[25]

In more subtle but still important ways, the issue of autonomy is also at stake in the emergence of a self-consciously "postliberal" program for theology.[26] Here, the mediating tradition faces quite a different sort of challenge. The specific way in which autonomy is at issue in this instance can be quite difficult to discern, partly because of the several strands of thinking that are finally drawn together to constitute the postliberal outlook. Particularly relevant to the Cartesian–Kantian model of private selfhood is the influence on postliberalism of Ludwig Wittgenstein's philosophy, with its criticism of the inadequacy of the modern emphasis on individual subjectivity. In his later work especially, Wittgenstein generates an ironic stance toward the very possibility of the systematic doubt with which the Cartesian project begins.[27] He then deploys this irony in a manner that discloses the philosophical emptiness of the mentalistic vocabulary we find in Descartes and Kant, while ultimately undermining the subject–object dichotomy itself in ways evocative of very powerful cultural shifts. The resulting lessons have not been lost on theologians already suspicious of the privatizing tendencies of post-Kantian conceptions of faith.[28] By emphasizing how language and culture precede and determine our very capacity to attribute "inner" episodes to ourselves, Wittgenstein's philosophy reorients us in fresh ways toward the "outside," away from personal subjectivity and toward shared linguistic and social practices. One effect for theology, of course, is to direct attention away from individualistic and privatistic conceptions of faith and to underscore the sense in which being a Christian involves sharing in those linguistic and social practices distinctive of the Christian community.[29] On this view, there is no pre-linguistic route – by way of a reflexive

Cartesian–Kantian consciousness or anthropological "given" – to Christian faith. Consequently, there is no point to the traditional liberal strategy of seeking correlations between Christian faith and natural modes of human insight or understanding.

The repudiation of the privatistic conception of the self thus shapes in important ways the postliberal effort to construct an alternative theological strategy. This alternative will be non-apologetic in nature, reflecting the flip side of the conceptual linkage between apologetics and the modern concept of selfhood. For a postliberal thinker such as George Lindbeck, the "Word" that makes a difference is truly a *verbum externum* and not a Word that strikes a chord of recognition by virtue of something already present "in" the believer, as typified by a Tillichian "shock of recognition."[30] In this dual repudiation of the privatistic concept of the self and the modern apologetic project, we see the debate over the nature of selfhood subtly superimposed on the preoccupation with intellectual autonomy. This time, however, autonomy is subordinated to a norm external to the believer – a point difficult to make, because the Wittgensteinian stance toward selfhood has turned the metaphors of "inner" and "outer" into objects of irony rather than reliable terms of reference.[31]

Still, the link between the reconception of selfhood and the subordination of personal autonomy is clearly evident in the postliberal suggestion that faith emerges out of an idiosyncratic language and set of practices that must be adopted *before* they can be understood: entrance into the Christian form of life is the precondition for understanding it, not the other way around. By this view, faith is anything but a moment of self-discovery, self-recognition, or self-realization – in part because there is less to "discover," "recognize," or "realize" than the broadly Cartesian–Kantian tradition, reinforced by an acquisitive consumerist society, has led us to believe. Faith is instead a form of learning that is dependent, not on what is naturally present in the self, such as Kantian moral consciousness, but on something resembling "ancient catechesis" which "seeks to teach the language and practices of the religion to potential adherents."

This has been the primary way of transmitting the faith and winning converts for most religions down through the centuries. ... Pagan converts to the catholic mainstream did not, for the most part, first understand the faith and then decide to become Christians; rather, the process was reversed: they first decided and then they understood. More precisely, they were first attracted by the Christian community and form of life. ...Only after they had acquired proficiency in the alien Christian language and form of life were they deemed able intelligently and responsibly to profess the faith, to be baptized.[32]

Here we see the liberal trust in an implicit "fit" between the religious message and the natural self replaced by quite a different conception of the Christian life. An external Word that "molds and shapes the self and its world" assumes priority over the intellectual autonomy and psychological comfort of the believer: the self's life is redescribed in terms arising from scripture, in contrast to the view that scripture should be interpreted in terms that meet the demands of the given forms of human consciousness, as in the case of Kant's own moral theory of biblical interpretation.[33] From the postliberal standpoint, to "become a Christian involves learning the story of Israel and of Jesus well enough to interpret and experience oneself and one's world in its terms."[34] Proponents of such a view rely heavily on the analogy between becoming a Christian and learning a foreign language, thereby reinforcing the insight that faith does not meet up with or receive life from something that is already "in" the believer: in neither instance are we dealing with a "Socratic" project.[35] It is precisely this insight that separates postliberal from liberal theology, suggesting the decisive role played by competing views of the need to accommodate intellectual autonomy in the accounting of faith.

At the outset of this study, I invoked what I characterized as John Locke's "spectrum of believability" as a way of symbolizing how the sheer credibility of Christian claims had become a marker of the problem of intellectual autonomy. Since successfully interpreting to the believer religious claims that might be a scandal to the intellect is the very heart of the mediating project, the issue of credibility has itself played a central role within the broadly liberal tradition. Postliberal theology dramatically revises this traditional preoccupation with credibility. In keeping with the emphasis on what is "outside" the self, someone such as Lindbeck redirects attention away from credibility and toward *practice*, with practice now understood in terms of the religious form of life that the believer must learn because it is not naturally apprehended. Here, we see a subtle reintroduction of Kant's own turn to practice, even as we see a radical devaluation of the Kantian emphasis on the hidden and personal dimensions of faith. In effect, the issue of credibility is not so much dismissed as it is redefined: rather than viewing credibility as "adherence to independently formulated criteria," including criteria of believability that are independent of faith, credibility is now understood as "good performance."[36] In other words, postliberalism implicitly makes something like consistency with the publicly available rules of a given form of life the mark of reasonableness in religion, as opposed to believing only what can fit comfortably alongside my natural sense of myself. Postliberalism thus shares with liberation theology a preoccupation with the public sphere, as opposed to the private and hidden existential dramas of the religious self. From the standpoint of the mediating tradition, what is noteworthy about the postliberal outlook is the fact that the Christian form of life can in no way be justified or grounded through appeal to more general truths or experiences, for the same reason that faith does not correlate with given modes of human consciousness. Such is the natural fallout of the claim that a *verbum externum*, and not some foundational universal experience, assumes both logical and theological priority in the formation of faith. Faith is "learned" as one becomes habituated to a form of life, not "discovered" as something that had been present in the self all along.

This sense of the sheer givenness of the Christian form of life stands in stark contrast to the liberal mediating theologian's assumption that faith is grounded in a mode of experience that is generally available. Something like a Kantian trust in the inferential route from confidence in the moral life to practical faith in God is clearly evident in these characteristic remarks of Schubert Ogden's:

> The only way any conception of God can be made more than a mere idea having nothing to do with reality is to exhibit it as the most adequate reflective account we can give of certain experiences we all inescapably share. ... I hold that the primary use or function of "God" is to refer to the objective ground in reality itself of our ineradicable confidence in the final worth of our existence. ... [T]he idea of God alone explicates and makes fully intelligible the presupposed ground of our confidence that life is ultimately meaningful.[37]

The natural corridors justifying the mediating enterprise could hardly be more obvious. Ogden's position exemplifies the confidence that the Christian form of life can indeed be grounded in a wider, publicly accessible context of meaning that insures fruitful continuity between faith and the surrounding culture. This continuity, in turn, protects the modern believer's intellectual integrity, thereby avoiding the sacrifice of the intellect that Ogden views as the death of serious theology. One finds a very similar appeal to faith's commensurability with its secular surroundings in the work of Ogden's Roman Catholic ally in revisionism, David Tracy. Tracy avows that theology should be pursued "in accordance with publicly available criteria for meaning, meaningfulness, and truth." Christian theology, Tracy argues, "is best understood as philosophical reflection upon the meanings present in common human experience and the meanings present in the Christian tradition."[38] An obvious variation on Tillich's "method of correlation," Tracy's position reflects the way his outlook "is intrinsically indebted to and derived from the formulations of the liberal task in theology classically formulated in the nineteenth century."[39]

From such a standpoint as this, the postliberal subordination of natural human understanding to a *verbum externum* not continuous with given forms of human consciousness is a retreat into sectarianism. Indeed, Tracy has characterized Lindbeck's position as "a methodologically sophisticated version of Barthian confessionalism" which would isolate theology from the modern world by leaving it "done purely from 'within' the confessing community."[40] The implication is that postliberal theology of the sort associated with Frei, Lindbeck, and others is a form of backsliding that effectively forfeits the intellectual gains of the liberal heritage.

Contemporary mediating theologians thus continue in revised ways Kant's own effort to correlate the Christian tradition with universally accessible insights, insuring lines of continuity between faith and culture. By contrast, postliberalism goes against the grain of much post-Enlightenment theology by its devaluation of such lines of continuity in the accounting of Christian faith. This is most evident in connection with postliberalism's reframing of the question of faith's intelligibility: intelligibility is not construed in terms of faith's relations with a non-believing surrounding culture but is now understood in relation to the purely internal norms and practices of the worshiping community. Not surprisingly, this alteration in perspective is not driven by philosophical insight, since philosophy and philosophical method are quietly demoted through their association with traditional mediating techniques. Rather, the alteration is driven largely by a freshened sense of a truly "realistic" reading of scripture. A realistic reading turns neither on a prior philosophical anthropology, nor on the question of whether the Bible accurately refers to a history lying behind it, but on the recovery of the biblical narrative itself as the world in which we "live and move and have our being."[41] Once again, the autonomy of human understanding is subordinated to a norm outside itself. While such a reversal may be associated with a fresh conception of selfhood, it can hardly be its consequence. After all, Lindbeck does not reject apologetics simply because he has a different view of selfhood.[42] Rather, a view of selfhood different from the views dominating the mediating tradition becomes an imperative for Lindbeck because of a prior understanding of the individual's relationship to the Christian message. Surely there must be something about the message itself that accounts for Lindbeck's series of reversals of the liberal tradition's priorities. One suspects that an effort to recover *divine* freedom from a universal preoccupation with human autonomy is perhaps a more accurate way to describe the motivation behind postliberal theology.[43] At the same time, the fair characterization of a significant strand of postliberalism as "rigorously opaque" – so that "one senses that the most important point is being shown but not stated" – suggests why many of the central issues remain highly elusive.[44]

One thing that is clear is the set of awkward circumstances surrounding the liberal mediating tradition upon the arrival of a new millennium. On one side, theologies of liberation evidently subvert the very framework for pursuing mediating theology as traditionally conceived. At the same time, such theologies reintroduce mediation in a manner that implicitly raises the question of what all the fuss over intellectual autonomy could possibly have been about. On another front, an openly postliberal initiative severs the proudly fashioned connection between faith and secular culture that had been at the heart of the mediating project. The resulting hint of a renewed intellectual isolation of Christian theology conveys the deepest sort of repudiation of the liberal marriage between faith and culture. The classic liberal heritage is thus bracketed by question marks concerning its very rationale and viability. Simultaneously, these challenges remind us – as, indeed, does the inventiveness of the mediating tradition itself[45] – that the Cartesian–Kantian model of the self is historically contingent, rather than the indispensable conceptual device for properly framing the issue of faith and transcendence. Most important of all, these cases intimate that the sorts of theological judgments that are prior to, rather than conditioned by, a given view of selfhood can be difficult to perceive and assess, in the midst of debates about other matters. This difficulty may be symptomatic of insufficiently shared theological ground for exchanges that move very far beyond discussion of narrow technical details. Relevant here, perhaps, is George Hunsinger's reminder of Karl Barth's insight into the "logical dilemma of modern liberal theology," arising in part from Barth's reading of Feuerbach. "Either liberalism's method could be retained at the expense of its theological content, or its content could be retained (and expanded) at the expense of its theological method."[46] This way of framing the issue implies that the decisive judgment is not itself a *methodological* one, which suggests in turn that much of the extraordinary amount of attention devoted to methodological issues in modern theology may be beside the point. In that case, academic theology may simply mirror in its own way the difficulties afflicting the wider society's efforts to debate serious matters of morality and public policy without falling into immediate misunderstanding and impasse.

If it eventually turns out that mediation is a theological dead end, Kant's own example will have been a powerful harbinger of its fate. Certainly the cumulative impact of the principle of immanence suggests that Kant does not provide a template for liberally minded mediation so much as he exposes the imperializing tendencies of whatever feature of the modern experience the mediating theologian wishes to accommodate. In Kant's own case, of course, this feature is autonomy itself. In the wake of autonomy's assertive activity, little or nothing survives that transcends humanity's experience of its own powers, obligations, and goals. To be sure, Kant may implicitly be fashioning a new conceptuality for divine transcendence generated by this newly apparent human capacity for self-transcendence. Such an attempt, signaling the modern break from spatial conceptions of God's "otherness," might be viewed as the prototype for numerous post-Kantian efforts to conceive of God non-objectively, which is to say, as pure "subject." Kant's own method of exploiting our capacity for something like self-transcendence obviously resides in the intimate link he forges between moral consciousness and consciousness of God. However, Kant inevitably and consistently subordinates the latter to the former in ways that raise genuine questions about any remaining need for language about God – this, I submit, is the whole point of the preceding examination of Kant's actual arguments. In Kant's own hands, the project of self-transcendence turns out to be so successful and all-consuming that there is little or nothing left to ground the idea of the "other," let alone to mediate.

I thus return to my basic claim. The consistent subordination of divine transcendence to the demands of autonomous rationality strongly suggests that Kant's own thought – as opposed to retrospective fabrications of a Kantian "conceptuality" – is moving in a non-theistic direction rather than in a direction with obviously constructive possibilities for theology. His status as precursor to Feuerbach both trumps his place in the tradition of liberal mediating theology and raises subversive questions about mediation itself. Fittingly, appearances here are indeed deceiving. Kant appears to provide legitimacy to the idea that language about anything external to the religious believer, including language about God, gains its very intelligibility by virtue of a preceding appeal to some general and presumably universal feature of human consciousness. In his case, however, once the deeper universal feature of human consciousness is isolated and identified, the possibility of maintaining language about God that is more than a series of motifs is seriously compromised. As Kant's own writings exemplify, the religious feature may remain present, but that is not where the real life is, any more than the twitching body of a beheaded reptile indicates real life. As a result, Kant's own example is hardly a comforting model for those committed to holding divine transcendence and a modern sensibility in proper balance. In his case, the balancing act simply cannot be sustained; his particular way of endorsing modernity is finally too self-aggrandizing. There is in

Kant no enduring alliance or stable partnership between autonomy and divine transcendence, but rather a struggle on the part of the latter to elude the imperializing tendencies of the former. By my reading of Kant, this struggle is finally a losing one, and mediation inevitably grinds to a halt as Kant's own modernity principle gains momentum and fills out the human horizon.

Kant thus exemplifies one of the chronic difficulties facing mediating theology since the Enlightenment: if one is actually successful in displaying the intelligibility of Christian faith in modern terms, the result may be the loss of a distinctively Christian content. Making faith intelligible might also make it redundant, since the mediating maneuver may simply recast what can also be said in purely secular terms.[47] In that event, appeals to divine transcendence are more neatly eliminated than resuscitated, since they merely repeat in unwieldy terms what also comes to expression in neater and more immediately available form. This, after all, seems a fair way to describe the combined impact of Kant's bald claim that "for its own sake morality does not need religion at all," and his admonition that "godliness is not a surrogate for virtue." For if I do not need to refer to God either to recognize or to act on my moral obligations, I may not even need to do so in order to round out my thinking about my life. The last thing the "modern" world needs is redundant explanations. Framing the very idea of divine transcendence in these Ptolemaic terms is perhaps the ultimate expression of Kant's own Copernican revolution. Too cumbersome by half, divine transcendence goes the same way as Ptolemy's model of the heavens, and for roughly the same reasons.

Notes

The standard edition of Kant's works is *Immanuel Kants gesammelte Schriften, herausgegeben von der Deutschen Akademie der Wissenschaften* (formerly *Königlichen Preussischen Akademie der Wissenschaften*), 29 vols (Berlin: Walter de Gruyter, 1902 –). The locations in the Academy edition of works cited in the text are given below, in the order of their original publication. Standard English translations are also indicated, and subsequent citations will be to the translations, with occasional modifications that will be indicated.

As noted below, I have used the following abbreviations for the most frequently cited of Kant's works:

Foundations (*Foundations of the Metaphysics of Morals*)
Judgement (*Critique of Judgement*)
Practical (*Critique of Practical Reason*)
Pure (*Critique of Pure Reason*)
Religion (*Religion within the Limits of Reason Alone*)

References to the *Critique of Pure Reason* follow the standard convention of citing the A and B pagination of the first and second Academy editions, followed by the page number in the Kemp Smith translation.

1755   *Universal Natural History and Theory of the Heavens, or An Essay on the Constitution and Mechanical Origin of the Entire World Edifice Treated according to Newtonian Principles.* Vol. I, pp. 215–368. Trans. Stanley L. Jaki (Edinburgh: Scottish Academic Press, 1981).
1763   *The One Possible Basis for a Demonstration of the Existence of God.* Vol. II, pp. 63–163. Trans. Gordon Treash (Lincoln and London: University of Nebraska Press, 1994).
1764   *Inquiry Concerning the Distinctness of the Principles of Natural Theology and Morality.* Vol. II, pp. 273–301. Trans. David Walford in collaboration with Ralf Meerbote, *Kant's Theoretical Philosophy, 1755–1770* (Cambridge: Cambridge University Press, 1992).
1766   *Dreams of a Spirit-Seer Elucidated by Dreams of Metaphysics.* Vol. II, pp. 315–73. Trans. David Walford in collaboration with Ralf Meerbote, *Kant's Theoretical Philosophy, 1755–1770* (Cambridge: Cambridge University Press, 1992).

140 NOTES

1781   2nd edn 1787 *Critique of Pure Reason*. Vols. III–IV. Trans. Norman
        Kemp Smith (New York: St Martin's Press, 1965). Hereafter cited as
        Pure.
1783   *Prolegomena to Any Future Metaphysics*. Vol. IV, pp. 253–83. Trans. Paul
        Carus (Indianapolis and New York: Bobbs-Merrill, 1950).
1784   "Idea for a Universal History with a Cosmopolitan Purpose." Vol. VIII,
        pp. 15–31. Trans. H. B. Nisbet in Hans Reiss (ed.), *Kant: Political Writ-
        ings* (Cambridge: Cambridge University Press, 1991).
1784   "An Answer to the Question, 'What is Enlightenment?'" Vol. VIII, pp.
        33–42. Trans. L. W. Beck, *Kant on History* (Indianapolis and New York:
        Bobbs-Merrill, 1963).
1785   *Foundations of the Metaphysics of Morals*. Vol. IV, pp. 385–463. Trans.
        L. W. Beck (Indianapolis and New York: Bobbs-Merrill, 1959). Hereafter
        cited as *Foundations*.
1786   "What is Orientation in Thinking?" Vol. VIII, 131–47. Trans. H. B.
        Nisbet in Hans Reiss (ed.), *Kant: Political Writings* (Cambridge: Cam-
        bridge University Press, 1991).
1788   *Critique of Practical Reason*. Vol. V, pp. 1–163. Trans. L. W. Beck
        (Indianapolis and New York: Bobbs-Merrill, 1956). Hereafter cited as
        Practical.
1790   *Critique of Judgement*. Vol. V, pp. 165–485. Trans. James Creed Meredith
        (Oxford: Clarendon Press, 1952). Hereafter cited as *Judgement*.
1791   "On the Failure of All Attempted Philosophical Theodicies." Vol. VIII, pp.
        253–71. Trans. Michel Despland in Despland, *Kant on History and
        Religion* (Montreal and London: McGill-Queen's University Press,
        1973).
1793   *Religion within the Limits of Reason Alone*. Vol. VI, pp. 1–202. Trans.
        Theodore M. Greene and Hoyt H. Hudson (New York: Harper Torch-
        books, 1960). Hereafter cited as *Religion*. A new translation has been
        done by George Di Giovanni and is included in Di Giovanni and Allen
        Wood (eds), *Religion and Rational Theology* (Cambridge: Cambridge
        University Press, 1996).
1793   "On the Old Saw: That Might be Right in Theory but it Won't Work in
        Practice." Vol. VIII, pp. 273–313. Trans. E. B. Ashton (Philadelphia:
        University of Pennsylvania Press, 1974).
1797   *The Metaphysics of Morals*. Vol. VI, pp. 203–493. Trans. Mary Gregor
        (Cambridge: Cambridge University Press, 1991).
1798   *The Conflict of the Faculties*. Vol. VII, pp. 1–116. Trans. Mary Gregor
        (Lincoln and London: University of Nebraska Press, 1992).
1798   *Anthropology from a Pragmatic Point of View*. Vol. VII, pp. 117–333.
        Trans. Victor Lyle Dowdell (Carbondale and Edwardsville, Illinois:
        Southern Illinois University Press, 1978).
1817   *Lectures on Philosophical Theology*. Vol. XXVIII, pp. 525–610. Trans.
        Allen W. Wood and Gertrude M. Clark (Ithaca and London: Cornell
        University Press, 1978).
1924   *Lectures on Ethics*. Vol. XXVII. Trans. Louis Infield (New York: Harper
        Torchbooks, 1963).
1936–8 *Opus Postumum*. Vols. XXI–II. Trans. Eckart Förster and Michael
        Rosen (Cambridge: Cambridge University Press, 1993).

Chapter 1   Kant, Modernity, and Theism

1   E.g., Patrick Masterson, *Atheism and Alienation* (Middlesex: Penguin Books, 1973), ch. 2; Michael J. Buckley, S.J., *At the Origins of Modern Atheism* (New Haven and London: Yale University Press, 1987), pp. 326–33.

2   "The motives for a philosophy of unification can be traced back to crisis experiences of the young Hegel. They stand behind the conviction that reason must be brought forward as the reconciling power against the positive elements of an age torn asunder. What encourage Hegel to presuppose an absolute power of unification, therefore, are not so much arguments as biographical experiences..." Jürgen Habermas, *The Philosophical Discourse of Modernity*, trans. Frederick Lawrence (Cambridge, MA: The MIT Press, 1987), pp. 21–2, 24. See also Georg Lukács, *The Young Hegel: Studies in the Relations between Dialectics and Economics*, trans. Rodney Livingston (Cambridge, MA: The MIT Press, 1976), Part II.

3   These difficulties of exposition are conveyed by Charles Taylor in a summary that captures the problematic interplay of immanence and transcendence in idealist philosophy generally: "Hegel's spirit, or *Geist*, although often called 'God,' and although Hegel claimed to be clarifying Christian theology, is not the God of traditional theism; he is not a God who could exist quite independently of men, even if men did not exist, as the God of Abraham, Isaac and Jacob before the creation. On the contrary, he is a spirit who lives as spirit only through men. They are the vehicles, and the indispensable vehicles, of his spiritual existence, as consciousness, rationality, and will. But at the same time *Geist* is not reducible to man, he is not identical with the human spirit, since he is also the spiritual reality underlying the universe as a whole, and as a spiritual being he has purposes and he realizes ends which cannot be attributed to finite spirits qua finite, but on the contrary which finite spirits serve." Taylor, *Hegel* (Cambridge: Cambridge University Press, 1975), pp. 44–5.

4   For a helpful account of Feuerbach and Marx and their relationship, see Van A. Harvey, "Ludwig Feuerbach and Karl Marx" in Ninian Smart, John Clayton, Patrick Sherry, and Steven T. Katz (eds), *Nineteenth Century Religious Thought in the West*, Vol. 1 (Cambridge: Cambridge University Press, 1985), pp. 291–328.

5   "Editorial Introduction," in *ibid.*, p. 5.

6   Claude Welch, *Protestant Thought in the Nineteenth Century*: Vol. 2, *1870–1914* (New Haven and London: Yale University Press, 1985), p. 2.

7   The dialectical theologians' polemic against the ethical understanding of Christian faith can hide from view the heavily Kantian element that persists, especially in their account of the relation between faith and secular knowledge. Helpful correctives focusing on major theologians include Bruce L. McCormack, *Karl Barth's Critically Realistic Dialectical Theology: Its Genesis and Development, 1909–1936* (New York and Oxford: Oxford University Press, 1995); and Roger A. Johnson, *The Origins of Demythologizing* (Leiden: E. J. Brill, 1974).

8   Alasdair MacIntyre, *A Short History of Ethics* (New York: Macmillan, 1966), p. 110.

9   John Locke, *An Essay Concerning Human Understanding*, Vol. II, ed. A. C. Fraser (New York: Dover Publications, 1959), pp. 412–13. Hans Frei draws a

line connecting John Locke and nineteenth-century German theologian Friedrich Schleiermacher by virtue of their both "suggesting that the meaningfulness of something general or universal is the logical and real precondition for the meaningfulness of the particular," including particular Christian concepts such as "Redeemer." Hans W. Frei, *Types of Christian Theology*, ed. George Hunsinger and William C. Placher (New Haven and London: Yale University Press, 1992), pp. 73–4. Frei's book offers a provocative – if characteristically elusive – account of mediating theology in its several guises. See also Charles Taylor's discussion of what he calls Locke's "rationalized Christianity," which Taylor claims is complicit in "generating what is perhaps the dominant outlook of modern Western technological society." Taylor, *Sources of the Self: The Making of the Modern Identity* (Cambridge, MA: Harvard University Press, 1989), p. 234.

10 Schubert M. Ogden, *Christ without Myth* (New York: Harper and Row, 1961), p. 130.

11 Stephen Toulmin, *Cosmopolis: The Hidden Agenda of Modernity* (Chicago and London: University of Chicago Press, 1990), p. 75.

12 René Descartes, "Meditations on First Philosophy," *Descartes: Selections*, ed. Ralph M. Eaton (New York: Charles Scribner's Sons, 1955), Meditation II, pp. 95–106. See the compressed but very helpful account of Descartes in relation to the reflexivity issue in Mark C. Taylor's "Introduction" to Taylor (ed.), *Deconstruction in Context: Literature and Philosophy* (Chicago and London: University of Chicago Press, 1986), pp. 3ff. For a more extended account, see Anthony Kenny, *Descartes: A Study of his Philosophy* (New York: Random House, 1968), chs 1–4.

13 Helmut Thielicke, *The Evangelical Faith*, Vol. 1, trans. G. Bromiley (Grand Rapids: William B. Eerdmans, 1974), pp. 44–5.

14 The importance of this historical change is readily evident in Ian Hacking's tracing of the shift within European culture from viewing the relative improbability of a claim as counting *for* it to counting *against* it. It is of course difficult for us now even to imagine improbability reinforcing rather than undermining a belief. Yet the shift from the one viewpoint to the other underscores the importance of the emerging sense of intellectual autonomy and the striking difference it begins to make in adjudicating claims of empirical fact – including, of course, biblical claims. See Hacking, *The Emergence of Probability* (Cambridge: Cambridge University Press, 1975).

15 For an excellent overview of this general transition, see Jeffrey Stout, *The Flight from Authority* (Notre Dame, IN: University of Notre Dame Press, 1981).

16 Dieter Henrich, *Aesthetic Judgment and the Moral Image of the World*, ed. Eckart Förster (Stanford: Stanford University Press, 1992), p. 3.

17 Paul Connerton, *The Tragedy of Enlightenment: An Essay on the Frankfurt School* (Cambridge: Cambridge University Press, 1980), pp. 21–2.

18 Andrew Bowie, *Schelling and Modern European Philosophy* (London and New York: Routledge, 1993), p. 15. In order to show that this conundrum of the post-Cartesian tradition remains influential, Bowie makes the interesting connection between the ego philosophy of J. G. Fichte and the basic thesis of Thomas Nagel's book, *The View from Nowhere* (New York and Oxford: Oxford University Press, 1986): "namely that subjectivity cannot be understood in the same manner as the world of objects. ..."

19   Kant, *Pure*, B131–132, pp. 152ff.
20   A good summary is in Bowie, *op. cit.*, pp. 15ff. See also the excellent guide to
     post-Kantian developments offered by Frederick C. Beiser, *The Fate of
     Reason: German Philosophy from Kant to Fichte* (Cambridge, MA and
     London: Harvard University Press, 1987).
21   Kant, *Foundations*, p. 59.
22   Albert Levi, *Philosophy as Social Expression* (Chicago and London: Uni-
     versity of Chicago Press, 1974), p. 244.
23   Kant, "What is Enlightenment?," p. 3.
24   Thomas McCarthy's observation is apt: "The strong conceptions of reason
     and of the autonomous rational subject developed from Descartes to Kant
     have, despite the constant pounding given them in the last one hundred and
     fifty years, continued to exercise a broad and deep – often subterranean –
     influence." McCarthy, "Introduction," in Habermas, *op. cit.*, p. viii.
25   The work of Foucault is an obvious, though hardly unique, example. Some-
     what ironically, Foucault's final, multi-volume history of sexuality seems to
     depend on an appeal to something very much like a human "subject" in its
     ethically charged polemic against the oppressiveness of "normalizing" tend-
     encies in Western sexual attitudes. The problem is that much of Foucault's
     own earlier work evidently dismissed the very subject whose rights are at
     stake in the history of sexuality. See Foucault, *The History of Sexuality*, Vol.
     1, *An Introduction*, trans. R. Hurley (New York: Pantheon, 1978); *The Use
     of Pleasure: History of Sexuality*, Vol. 2, trans. R. Hurley (New York:
     Pantheon, 1985); *The Care of the Self: History of Sexuality*, Vol. 3, trans.
     R. Hurley (New York: Pantheon, 1986).
26   Relevant here is the effort of Kant scholar Dieter Henrich to "restore for the
     present age the power of the classical German themes of self-determining
     reason, subjectivity, and self-consciousness" by rejecting "any claim that
     linguistic interaction and intersubjectivity can supersede the subject [or]
     eliminate or trivialize the self-referential moment in discourse." In his rejoin-
     der to post-Heideggerian fashions on the one hand, and the anti-metaphys-
     ical standpoint of Habermas on the other, Henrich offers a revisionist view
     of Kant as a "second founder of modernity" offering precisely the ethical
     resources required today. See Richard Velkley, "Introduction," Henrich, *The
     Unity of Reason: Essays on Kant's Philosophy*, trans. Jeffrey Edwards, Louis
     Hunt, Manfred Kuehn, and Guenter Zoeller (Cambridge, MA and London:
     Harvard University Press, 1994), pp. 5–6. A similar effort to draw on the
     classical German tradition to address the contemporary debate about the
     "subject" is represented by the collection of essays in Karl Ameriks and
     Dieter Sturma (eds), *The Modern Subject: Conceptions of the Self in Class-
     ical German Philosophy* (Albany: State University of New York Press,
     1995). Consider as well the observation of Onora O'Neill, who remarks
     that "despite long traditions of reading Kant as presenting a 'philosophy of
     the subject,' his starting point is rather that of plurality.... Kant's distinc-
     tiveness lies in the fact that his discursive grounding of reason presupposes
     plurality, and the possibility of community; it does not presuppose 'atomis-
     tic' subjects, actual communities or ideal communities." O'Neill, "Vindicat-
     ing Reason," in Paul Guyer (ed.), *The Cambridge Companion to Kant*
     (Cambridge: Cambridge University Press, 1992), p. 308, n. 17.

27 The motifs of "inside" and "outside" the believer probably also serve as natural corridors with the social, economic, and broadly "material" factors accounting for the modern preoccupation with autonomy. These would of course include the rise of a market economy, the quest by a growing middle class for freedom from royal or priestly intrusion, and the pressure produced by interminable and inconclusive religious wars simply to consider religious belief a matter of private conscience. In other words, I make no claim here that the purely "conceptual" account of the rise of autonomy that I am tracing is exhaustive, but only that it sheds light on a specific aspect of modern theological history.

28 Quoted in Henry Allison, *Lessing and the Enlightenment* (Ann Arbor: University of Michigan Press, 1966), p. 96. The important role played by the metaphors of "inner" and "outer" in the rise of modern moral philosophy is readily evident in Jerome Schneewind's "Introduction" to Schneewind (ed.), *Moral Philosophy from Montaigne to Kant*, Vol. 1 (Cambridge: Cambridge University Press, 1990), pp. 1–30. The distinction is especially crucial in emerging modern accounts of the source of moral obligation, such as the efforts by early modern natural law theorists to account for obligation: "Perhaps the kind of obligation arising from sanctions is not really the kind that is central to morality. It is, after all, merely an *external* sort of obligation, and morality is an *inner* matter" (p. 23, emphasis added). This trend toward linking the authentic source of moral obligation with an "inner" characteristic of the agent of course culminates with Kant's theory of autonomy, which Schneewind has now traced out in impressive detail in *The Invention of Autonomy: A History of Modern Moral Philosophy* (Cambridge: Cambridge University Press, 1998).

29 As I indicated at the outset, recent Hegel scholarship has emphasized the connection between Hegel's quest for unity and the fact that he came of philosophical age during a period of considerable political unrest. See, e.g., the richly detailed study by Laurence Dickey, *Hegel: Religion, Economics, and the Politics of Spirit, 1770–1807* (Cambridge: Cambridge University Press, 1987), Parts I–II.

30 Hans-Georg Gadamer, *Hegel's Dialectic*, trans. P. Christopher Smith (New Haven and London: Yale University Press, 1976), p. 56.

31 McCarthy, *op. cit.*, p. x.

32 G. W. F. Hegel, "The Positivity of the Christian Religion," *Early Theological Writings*, trans. T. M. Knox (Philadelphia: University of Pennsylvania Press, 1971), p. 167.

33 Karl Löwith, *From Hegel to Nietzsche*, trans. David E. Green (Garden City, New York: Doubleday Anchor Books, 1967), p. 324. There is a helpful discussion of positivity and its role in modern theology in Garrett Green, "Kant as Christian Apologist: The Failure of Accommodationist Theology," *Pro Ecclesia* IV (1995), pp. 301–17, esp. pp. 304–5. See also Green's "Editor's Introduction" to J. G. Fichte, *Attempt at a Critique of All Revelation*, trans. Green (Cambridge: Cambridge University Press, 1977), pp. 28–9.

34 The valuable recent study of Feuerbach by Van A. Harvey has deepened our understanding of Feuerbach in ways that make it important to distinguish stages of his authorship, rather than simply subsuming his authorship under his best-known work, *The Essence of Christianity*. Harvey, *Feuerbach and*

the Interpretation of Religion (Cambridge: Cambridge University Press, 1995).

35 Ludwig Feuerbach, *The Essence of Christianity*, trans. George Eliot (New York: Harper and Row, 1957).

36 This is not to say that we cannot say a great deal about the "received" view of God that Kant evidently endorses, as has been very ably done by Allen Wood in *Kant's Rational Theology* (Ithaca and London: Cornell University Press, 1978). Building on his earlier account of moral theism as the necessary consequence of the antinomy of practical reason in his *Kant's Moral Religion* (Ithaca and London: Cornell University Press, 1970), Wood argues persuasively for the "rational inevitability of an *ens realissimum*" in Kant (p. 147). Based in large part on the translation of Kant's "Lectures on Philosophical Theology" that he published at the same time as his study, Wood's account focuses more on Kant's relationship with his received, Leibnizian metaphysical tradition than with Kant's moral argument. I think there can be little doubt that Kant believed in the God of this tradition. But as I shall argue in chapter 2 of this study, it is not at all clear that Kant's own moral argument for the existence of God accounts for all the predicates associated with the God of the metaphysical tradition. Moreover, as Wood openly acknowledges, Kant's "Lectures on Philosophical Theology" are based on the assigned metaphysics manuals of the day, making it difficult at times to distinguish between Kant's actual views and the topics on which he was expected to lecture – a difficulty that compounds the antecedent difficulty of working with a text constructed out of student notes, as are Kant's "Lectures." Wood in fact seems to moderate his position somewhat in the more recently published "Kant's Deism," in Philip J. Rossi and Michael Wreen (eds), *Kant's Philosophy of Religion Reconsidered* (Bloomington and Indianapolis: Indiana University Press, 1991), p. 20: "But by now Kant's God may seem to some very far from omnipotent. For it now appears that God is incapable of revealing himself to human beings except through the operations of reason." Wood's rejoinder is that God thereby shows respect for rational creatures that God has intentionally created "free" and "with the vocation to self-legislation and to thinking for themselves" (*ibid.*). But my own view is that Wood's implicit concession here to divine limitation and to the preeminence of reason in grasping the divine intent simply reinforces the interpretation guiding the present study.

37 Otfried Höffe, *Immanuel Kant*, trans. Marshall Farrier (Albany: State University of New York Press, 1994), p. 123. The standard sort of theological summary of Kant's discussion of the proofs is therefore somewhat misleading, if understandably so. E.g., see Claude Welch, *Protestant Thought in the Nineteenth Century*: Vol. 1, *1799–1870* (New Haven and London: Yale University Press, 1972), p. 45: "Kant reviewed in detail the arguments for the existence of God, showing their fatal defects." Strictly speaking, it is not defects in the arguments but the category mistake involved in attempting to relate "God" and "existence" that constitutes the negative move in Kant's account of natural theology. Kant's approach is thus an interesting precursor to Paul Tillich's effort to eliminate references to God as "existing," since, for Tillich, God is "Being Itself."

38 Karl Barth, *Protestant Thought from Rousseau to Ritschl*, trans. Brian Cozens (New York: Simon and Schuster, 1969), p. 150.

39 Anthony J. Cascardi, *The Subject of Modernity* (Cambridge: Cambridge University Press, 1992), p. 2.

40 Still very useful in this regard is the essay by Hans Frei, "Niebuhr's Theological Background," in Paul Ramsey (ed.), *Faith and Ethics: The Theology of H. Richard Niebuhr* (New York: Harper and Row, 1957), pp. 9–64. The Kantian conceptuality for modern Protestant theology is readily evident in Frei's account of what he calls the "academic tradition in nineteenth-century Protestant theology," pp. 16ff.

41 Rudolf Bultmann, "On the Question of Christology," in *Faith and Understanding*, ed. Robert W. Funk and trans. Louise Pettibone Smith (New York: Harper and Row, 1969), p. 132.

42 H. Richard Niebuhr, *The Meaning of Revelation* (New York: Macmillan, 1941).

43 Paul Tillich, *Perspectives on 19th and 20th Century Protestant Theology*, ed. Carl E. Braaten (New York: Harper and Row, 1967), p. 216.

44 Richard Velkley, *Freedom and the End of Reason* (Chicago and London: University of Chicago Press, 1989), p. 15.

45 Kant, *Practical*, p. 166.

46 Kant, *Foundations*, p. 9.

47 S. Kierkegaard, *Fear and Trembling*, ed. and trans. Howard V. Hong and Edna H. Hong (Princeton: Princeton University Press, 1983), pp. 38ff.

48 These suspicions took their most famous, but by no means only, form in Karl Barth's somewhat ironic essay, "Rudolf Bultmann: An Attempt to Understand Him," in Vol. 2 of *Kerygma and Myth*, ed. Hans Werner Bartsch and trans. Reginald H. Fuller (London: SPCK, 1962), pp. 83–132. Obviously, the role of Heidegger would need to be factored into the supposed loss of a content for theology in Bultmann, but the fact that Heidegger himself was a lifelong reader of Kant simply brings Kant's influence into the picture in another way.

49 J. M. Bernstein, *The Philosophy of the Novel: Lukács, Marxism and the Dialectics of Form* (Minneapolis: University of Minnesota Press, 1984), p. xvii.

50 E.g., Ralph Walker, *Kant* (London: Routledge and Kegan Paul, 1978), p. 137. See also the discussion in Lewis White Beck, *A Commentary on Kant's Critique of Practical Reason* (Chicago and London: University of Chicago Press, 1960), pp. 242ff.

51 Thus, while I do not entirely disagree with Allen Wood's sophisticated efforts over a thirty-year period to demonstrate the cogency, on Kantian grounds, of Kant's "moral faith," I think my reading makes better sense of Kant's theory of autonomy as well as of his legacy. Wood argues that belief in God is finally necessary in Kant in order to make sense of reason itself, let alone to live the moral life. By contrast, I am arguing that, at crucial junctures brought to light by the principle of immanence, rationality operates in a reductionistic, indeed imperialistic, fashion in relation to theism and that Kant's very arguments on behalf of theism (and Wood's recapitulation of them) are often themselves the key instances of this. As Richard Velkley has recently put it, "all supersensible realities and causes are understood [by Kant] as subordinated to freedom's essential projects. *Even the idea of God is so subordinated.*" Velkley, *op. cit.*, p. 144, emphasis added. I am simply trying to draw out the implications of this sort of insight and relate them

to modern mediating theology. In addition to Wood's works cited in note 36, see Wood, "Rational Theology, Moral Faith, and Religion" in Guyer (ed.), *op. cit.*, pp. 394–416; and the very useful "General Introduction" Wood has written for the recent Cambridge University Press edition of Immanuel Kant, *Religion and Rational Theology*, ed. and trans. Wood and George Di Giovanni (Cambridge: Cambridge University Press, 1996), pp. xi–xxiv.

52 Ernst Cassirer, *The Philosophy of the Enlightenment*, trans. Fritz C. A. Koelln and James P. Pettegrove (Princeton: Princeton University Press, 1951), p. 159. Cassirer's fuller explanation of the "exchange of index symbols" captures much of what is at stake in the way Kant's principle of immanence displaces traditional accounts of divine transcendence: "That which formerly had established other concepts now moves into the position of that which is to be established, and that which hitherto had justified other concepts now finds itself in the position of a concept which requires justification."

53 Kant, *Religion*, p. 142, emphasis Kant's. (Oddly, the Greene-Hudson translation does not include the emphasis.)

54 Yirmiahu Yovel, *Kant and the Philosophy of History* (Princeton: Princeton University Press, 1980), p. 16.

55 Sarah L. Gibbons, *Kant's Theory of Imagination* (Oxford: Oxford University Press, 1994), p. 153.

56 Yirmiahu Yovel, *Spinoza and Other Heretics: The Adventures of Immanence* (Princeton: Princeton University Press, 1989), p. 7.

57 I discuss this awkwardness at some length in *Fallen Freedom: Kant on Radical Evil and Moral Regeneration* (Cambridge: Cambridge University Press, 1990), chs 5–6.

58 Kant, *Religion*, p. 40.

59 J. B. Schneewind, *The Invention of Autonomy*, p. 3.

Chapter 2 Kant's Moral Argument

1 Quoted in Allen W. Wood, *Kant's Rational Theology* (Ithaca and London: Cornell University Press, 1978), p. 13.

2 For a helpful overview of this background, see Lewis White Beck, *Early German Philosophy: Kant and His Predecessors* (Cambridge, MA and London: Harvard University Press, 1969).

3 Kant, *Judgement*, p. 128.

4 Kant, *Practical*, p. 51.

5 Cited in Stephen Körner, *Kant* (Middlesex and Baltimore: Penguin Books, 1955), p. 128. Any attempt to generate poignancy out of this (no doubt apocryphal) vignette is considerably undercut by that fact that Kant ultimately dismissed his manservant, Lampe, due to suspicions that he had been stealing from his master.

6 Kant, "Universal Natural History and Theory of the Heavens," trans. Stanley Jaki (Edinburgh: Scottish Academic Press, 1981).

7 Kant, *The One Possible Basis for a Demonstration of the Existence of God*, trans. Gordon Treash (Lincoln and London: University of Nebraska Press, 1994).

8 E. Cassirer, *Kant's Life and Thought*, trans. James Haden (New Haven and London: Yale University Press, 1981), p. 78.

9   J. B. Schneewind, *The Invention of Autonomy* (Cambridge: Cambridge University Press, 1998), pp. 494ff.; Treash, "Translator's Introduction" to *The One Possible Basis for a Demonstration of the Existence of God*, pp. 9–39. Lewis White Beck, *A Commentary on Kant's Critique of Practical Reason* (Chicago and London: University of Chicago Press, 1960), p. 271.

10 Examples include Schneewind, *op. cit.*; and Richard Velkley, *Freedom and the End of Reason: On the Moral Foundation of Kant's Critical Philosophy* (Chicago and London: University of Chicago Press, 1989). Both Schneewind and Velkley cite the important work of Josef Schmucker, *Die Ursprünge der Ethik Kants in seinen vorkritischen Schriften und Reflexionen* (Meisenheim: Anton Hain, 1961). This same softening of the distinction between Kant's pre-critical and critical works is evident in a different and highly original fashion in Susan Meld Shell, *The Embodiment of Reason* (Chicago and London: University of Chicago Press, 1996).

11 Treash, "Translator's Introduction" to *The One Possible Basis for a Demonstration of the Existence of God*, p. 31. Allen Wood helpfully tracks some of the *Beweisgrund*'s influence in Kant's subsequent work in Wood, *Kant's Rational Theology*, pp. 65ff.

12 *Kant: Selected Pre-Critical Writings and Correspondence with Beck*, trans. G. B. Kerford and D. E. Walford (Manchester: University of Manchester Press, 1968), pp. 3–35. It should be noted that Kant was writing in response to a prescribed topic, namely: "Whether metaphysical truths generally, and in particular the fundamental principles of natural theology and morals, are not capable of proofs as distinct as those of geometry; and if they are not, what is the true nature of their certainty, to what degree can the certainty be developed, and is this degree sufficient for conviction [of their truth]?" See the discussion in Beck, *Early German Philosophy*, pp. 441–3.

13 Dieter Henrich, "Hutcheson und Kant," *Kant-Studien* 49 (1957–8), pp. 49–69; Velkley, *op. cit.*, pp. 47–9.

14 Cassirer, *op. cit.*, p. 78. Kant, "Dreams of a Spirit-Seer Elucidated by Dreams of Metaphysics," trans. David Walford and Ralf Meerbote in Walford and Meerbote (eds), *Kant's Theoretical Philosophy, 1755–1770* (Cambridge: Cambridge University Press, 1992).

15 See Cassirer, *op. cit.*, p. 79. A fascinating recent account of *Dreams*, by a scholar eager to break down the firm line between "critical" and "pre-critical" works, is chapter 5 of Shell, *op. cit.*

16 Velkley, *op. cit.*, p. 107. Velkley (pp. 107–8) adds that *Dreams* "is notable for three other features: (1) it is the first work of Kant to offer a description of a will that is 'pure' and of a morality that arises solely from the universal voice of moral reason, rather than from moral sense; (2) it introduces the doctrine of the practical end of all philosophy and rational inquiry, as determined by pure morality; (3) it elaborates the definition of metaphysics ... as the 'science of the limits of reason,' whose aim is to defend common moral reason against distortions by speculative thought."

17 There is a good summary of Kant's likely lecturing schedule in Allen Wood's "Translator's Introduction" to Kant, *Lectures on Philosophical Theology*, trans. Wood and Gertrude M. Clark (Ithaca and London: Cornell University Press, 1978), pp. 13ff.; see also James Collins, *The Emergence of Philosophy*

of Religion (New Haven and London: Yale University Press, 1967), pp. 90ff.; Bernard M. G. Reardon, *Kant as Philosophical Theologian* (London: Macmillan Press, 1988), pp. 76ff.

18 James Collins, "Kant's *Logic* as a Critical Aid," *Review of Metaphysics* XXX (1977), p. 441.

19 Wood, "Translator's Introduction," *Lectures on Philosophical Theology*, p. 13. Wood acknowledges that "there might seem to be a tension between the lectures and the *Critique of Pure Reason*" but adds that he is "inclined to regard the lectures at such points as supplementing rather than contradicting what is said" in that work. By contrast, James Collins warns that the *Lectures on Philosophical Theology* must "be used with some caution," suggesting that we "use only those teachings which can be corroborated and modified by Kant's direct writings." Collins, *The Emergence of Philosophy of Religion*, p. 97 n. 6.

20 Kant, *Opus Postumum*, ed. Eckart Förster, trans. Förster and Michael Rosen (Cambridge: Cambridge University Press, 1993). For a helpful general discussion of the *Opus Postumum*, including problems associated with its composition, see Förster's "Introduction," pp. xv–lv.

21 Kant in a letter to his former pupil J. G. C. C. Kiesewetter, quoted in Förster, "Introduction," *Opus Postumum*, *op. cit.*, p. xvi.

22 Kant, *Opus Postumum*, p. 217. See the analysis of such remarks, together with an assessment of their compatibility with Kant's earlier writings, offered by George Schrader, "Kant's Presumed Repudiation of the 'Moral Argument' in the *Opus Postumum*: An Examination of Adickes' Interpretation," *Philosophy* XXVI (1951), pp. 228–41.

23 Frederick Copleston, S. J., *A History of Philosophy*, Vol. 6, Part II (Garden City: Image Books, 1964), p. 179.

24 Schneewind, *op. cit.*, p. 225; Reardon, *op. cit.*, p. 159. This aspect of the *Opus Postumum* would have to be reconciled with John Zammito's claim that there "is no evidence of any effort on Kant's part to study Spinoza." Zammito, *The Genesis of Kant's Critique of Judgment* (Chicago and London: University of Chicago Press, 1992), p. 231. The connection between Spinoza and atheism became an issue in the notorious "pantheism controversy" that originally developed through a disagreement between F. H. Jacobi and Moses Mendelssohn over the question of Spinoza's influence on G. E. Lessing. Frederick Beiser argues that it "is no exaggeration to say that the pantheism controversy had as great an impact upon nineteenth-century philosophy as Kant's first *Kritik*." Beiser, *The Fate of Reason: German Philosophy from Kant to Fichte* (Cambridge, MA and London: Harvard University Press, 1987), p. 44. Beiser offers a richly detailed account of the pantheism controversy in chs 1–4, including a discussion of Kant's involvement (ch. 4), which took the form of his essay, "What is Orientation in Thinking?"

25 Howard Caygill, *A Kant Dictionary* (Oxford: Blackwell, 1995), p. 216.

26 Allen Wood, "Rational Theology, Moral Faith, and Religion," in Paul Guyer (ed.), *The Cambridge Companion to Kant* (Cambridge: Cambridge University Press, 1992), p. 398.

27 Wood, "Translator's Introduction," Kant, *Lectures on Philosophical Theology*, p. 14.

28 On the unity of reason, see the aptly titled and well argued recent work of Susan Neiman, *The Unity of Reason: Rereading Kant* (New York and Oxford: Oxford University Press, 1994).

29 Kant, *Pure*, BXXX, p. 29.

30 *Ibid.*, A819/B847, p. 644.

31 Plato, *Euthyphro*, in *The Republic and Other Works*, trans. B. Jowett (Garden City: Doubleday, 1960), p. 435.

32 "Many suggestions reached Kant from the Leibnizian school, especially from the discussions of the relations between God's faculties and the world, between God and His 'inner object,' between possibility and necessity in God, etc. It might be added that the Highest Good, too, is described by Kant in Leibnizian terminology – as *the best world*, as a *harmony* of nature and morality (*nature and grace*), as a system which combines the mechanical with the (morally) teleological outlook, and so on." Yirmiahu Yovel, "The God of Kant," *Scripta Hierosolymitana* XX (1968), p. 99 n. 13, emphasis Yovel's.

33 Kant, *Practical*, pp. 112ff.

34 *Ibid.*, p. 112.

35 Kant, *Pure*, A326/B382, p. 318. There will be a fuller account of reason's "totalizing" activity in ch. 4.

36 Y. Yovel, *Kant and the Philosophy of History* (Princeton: Princeton University Press, 1980), p. 40.

37 Kant himself defines happiness as "the condition of a rational being in the world, in whose whole existence everything goes according to wish and will." *Practical*, p. 129.

38 Kant, *On the Old Saw: That Might be Right in Theory but it Won't Work in Practice*, trans. E. B. Ashton (Philadelphia: University of Pennsylvania Press, 1974), pp. 46–7n. "The need to assume a *highest good* in the world made possible with our cooperation, as the ultimate end of all things is due, not to a lack of moral motivations. It is due rather to external conditions in which alone, and in accordance with the motivating forces, an object can be brought forth as an end in itself (as the moral *ultimate end*). For without an end there cannot be any *will*. ...," emphasis Kant's. In her "Translator's Introduction" to Kant's *Metaphysics of Morals* (Cambridge: Cambridge University Press, 1991), Mary Gregor clarifies the sense in which this late work brings into view the relation between "duties" and "ends." See esp. pp. 20ff. A sustained effort to rescue Kantian ethics from systematic misunderstandings (such as the role of an "end" to moral action) is Barbara Herman, *The Practice of Moral Judgment* (Cambridge, MA and London: Harvard University Press, 1993).

39 Kant, *Practical*, p. 113.

40 J. B. Schneewind, "Autonomy, Obligation, and Virtue: An Overview of Kant's Moral Philosophy," in Paul Guyer (ed.), *The Cambridge Companion to Kant*, p. 335 n. 14.

41 Schneewind, "Introduction," *Moral Philosophy from Montaigne to Kant* (Cambridge: Cambridge University Press, 1990), pp. 26ff.

42 H. J. Paton once referred to a "strain which may be described as Aristotelian or teleological" in Kant's ethical theory. Paton, *The Categorical Imperative: A Study in Kant's Moral Philosophy* (London: Hutchinson and Co., 1947), p. 109.

43   One theological commentator who has probed the connection between Kant and Aristotle in relation to the idea of the highest good is Paul Lehmann, *Ethics in Christian Context* (New York: Harper and Row, 1963), pp. 172ff. For an excellent collection of recent studies of Kant in relation to classical sources, see Stephen Engstrom and Jennifer Whiting (eds), *Aristotle, Kant, and the Stoics: Rethinking Happiness and Duty* (Cambridge: Cambridge University Press, 1996), especially Julia Annas, "Aristotle and Kant on Morality and Practical Reasoning" (pp. 237–58) and J. B. Schneewind, "Kant and Stoic Ethics" (pp. 285–301).

44   Kant, *Practical*, pp. 111ff. See Lewis White Beck's clarification and reconstruction of the antinomy of practical reason in Beck, *A Commentary on Kant's Critique of Practical Reason*, pp. 246–8.

45   Kant, *Practical*, p. 113.

46   See Velkley, *op. cit.*, pp. 95ff.

47   *Ibid.*, p. 97.

48   Schneewind, *The Invention of Autonomy*, pp. 492ff.

49   Kant, *Practical*, p. 119.

50   *Ibid.*, p. 126.

51   *Ibid.*, p. 125.

52   *Ibid.*

53   *Ibid.*

54   *Ibid.*, p. 118.

55   *Ibid.*, p.127.

56   *Ibid.*, p. 129.

57   Michel Despland, *Kant on History and Religion* (Montreal and London: McGill-Queen's University Press, 1973), pp. 142–3.

58   Bernard Carnois, *The Coherence of Kant's Doctrine of Freedom*, trans. David Booth (Chicago and London: University of Chicago Press, 1987), p. 69.

59   The personal dimension of Kant's account of faith is conveyed in capsule form in a well-known remark from the *Critique of Pure Reason*: "No one, indeed, will be able to boast that he *knows* that there is a God, and a future life; if he knows this, he is the very man for whom I have long sought. ... No, my conviction is not *logical*, but *moral* certainty; and since it rests on subjective grounds (of the moral sentiment), I must not even say, '*It is* morally certain that there is a God, etc.', but *I am* morally certain, etc." Kant, *Pure*, A828–9/B856–7, p. 650. See the very lucid analysis of the "self-involving" aspect of Kant's epistemology of faith in W. H. Walsh, *Kant's Criticism of Metaphysics* (Chicago and London: University of Chicago Press, 1975), pp. 231ff.

60   Strictly speaking, the postulation of God's existence is the solution to the antinomy of practical reason concerning the tension between our duty to realize the highest good and our awareness of our inability to achieve such a goal. Allen Wood's approach to Kant emphasizes the way the connection between God's existence and the resolution of this antinomy expresses the internal integrity of Kant's philosophical theology and the centrality of divine existence to his entire philosophy. By contrast, Yirmiahu Yovel's view of the resolution of the antinomy points toward an immanentizing emphasis on human action as the key to history, with God increasingly left behind as a secondary and abstract consideration. My own sympathies, obviously, lie with Yovel. Cf. Allen Wood, *Kant's Moral Religion* (Ithaca

and London: Cornell University Press, 1970), esp. chs 3–4; and Yovel, *Kant and the Philosophy of History*, pp. 87ff.

61 Wood, *Kant's Moral Religion*; Richard Kroner, *Kant's Weltanschauung*, trans. John E. Smith (Chicago and London: University of Chicago Press, 1956).

62 F. Nietzsche, *The Gay Science*, trans. Walter Kaufmann (New York: Vintage Books, 1974), parag. 335, emphasis Nietzsche's.

63 In a letter to Herder, Goethe said that Kant "had criminally smeared his philosopher's cloak with the shameful stain of radical evil, after it had taken him a long human life to cleanse it from many a dirty prejudice, so that Christians too might yet be enticed to kiss its hem." Quoted in Karl Barth, *Protestant Thought from Rousseau to Ritschl*, trans. Brian Cozens (New York: Simon and Schuster, 1969), p. 178.

64 Kant, *Pure*, A333/B390–l, pp. 322–3. Jonathan Bennett, *Kant's Dialectic* (Cambridge: Cambridge University Press, 1974), p. 269. A fuller account of reason's "totalizing" tendencies will be given in ch. 4.

65 Kant, *Pure*, A327/B383, p. 318; A567–8/B595–6, p. 485. Kant's self-consciousness in adapting for his purposes Plato's notion of "ideas" is evident from his explicit reference to Plato, A313/B370, p. 310. Following his favorable summary of Plato's viewpoint, Kant remarks that "it is by no means unusual, upon comparing the thoughts which an author has expressed in regard to his subject, whether in ordinary conversation or in writing, to find that we understand him better than he has understood himself." There is a helpful account of Kant's connections with Plato in Patrick Riley, "The Elements of Kant's Practical Philosophy," in Ronald Beiner and William James Booth (eds), *Kant and Political Philosophy* (New Haven and London: Yale University Press, 1993), pp. 14ff.

66 Kant, *Pure*, A576/B604, p. 491. There is a very helpful account of the "transcendental ideal," including its connection to Kant's pre-critical thinking, in W. H. Walsh, *op. cit.*, pp. 214–29. Although dated in many respects, F. E. England's *Kant's Conception of God* (London: George Allen and Unwin, 1929) contains a good account of the ideal of pure reason (pp. 113–25), as well as useful background concerning the Leibniz/Wolff metaphysical tradition out of which Kant was working (chs 1–3).

67 Kant, *Pure*, A577–8/B605–6, p. 491.

68 In his essay of 1786, "What is Orientation in Thinking?," Kant offers a variation on the reasoning yielding the ideal of pure reason: "Since reason needs to assume reality as given before it can conceive the possibility of anything, and since it regards those differences between things which result from the negations inherent in them simply as limits, it finds itself compelled to take a single possibility – namely that of an unlimited being – as basic and original, and conversely, to regard all other possibilities as derivative." He adds that we thereby "find a subjective ground for this necessity, i.e., a need on the part of our reason itself to base all possibility on the existence of an utterly real (supreme) being." Acknowledging the connection between this reasoning and the Cartesian version of the ontological proof, Kant echoes the first *Critique*'s assessment of its cognitive status by stating that this train of thought accomplishes "nothing in the way of demonstration" but is "not for this reason by any means useless." "What is Orientation in Thinking?," trans. H. B. Nisbet in Hans Reiss (ed.), *Kant: Political Writings*, 2nd edn (Cambridge: Cambridge University Press, 1991), p. 241n.

69   Wood, "Rational Theology, Moral Faith, and Religion," p. 398.
70   Beck, *Commentary*, p. 275. Wood offers a rejoinder to Beck in *Kant's Moral Religion*, pp. 133ff.
71   Kant, *Pure*, A80/B106, p. 113.
72   Otfried Höffe, *Immanuel Kant*, trans. Marshall Farrier (Albany: State University of New York Press, 1994), p. 123.
73   The most aggressive effort to sort out these issues in a way that defends Kant's position is no doubt Wood's, in *Kant's Rational Theology*. Among other things, Wood defends Kant against the claim by Kemp Smith and F. E. England that "the concept of an *ens realissimum* is positively ruled out by Kant's critical views" (p. 59). Yet Wood's defense is of Kant's handling of the received scholastic "idea" of God rather than of the God presumably at stake in the moral argument in the second *Critique*. The real issue, in my view, is not the relation between the traditional scholastic deity and the critical views developed in the first *Critique*, but the degree to which predicates associated with the traditional view of God are accounted for by Kant's moral argument. Time and again, Kant appears to fall back on the "concept" of God in ways that go beyond his own moral argument – yet this is the very thing he accuses careless speculative metaphysicians of doing.
74   Ralph Walker, *Kant* (London: Routledge and Kegan Paul, 1978), p. 137. An alternative view is forcefully argued by Wood, who insists that abandonment of pursuit of the highest good (and, thus, of the theistic content that goes with it) is tantamount to "the abandonment of moral volition itself." See Wood, *Kant's Moral Religion*, p. 158. Wood's point seems to be that, without the encouragement offered by the hope that morality makes a difference and virtue will be rewarded, the agent is afflicted with a crippling moral discouragement. But it is difficult to see how Wood's appeal to what we might call the "psychology" of moral motivation affects the objectivity of the moral law and the binding force that accompanies it. That is, it does not necessarily follow that if the moral agent "were to discover that this final end [i.e., the highest good] itself must be abandoned as an impossibility, he could not so abandon it without at the same time ceasing to act purposively in obedience to the moral law." (*Ibid.*) The general question of the extent to which Kant's moral theory requires religious views has been helpfully explored by Terry F. Godlove, Jr, "Moral Actions, Moral Lives: Kant on Intending the Highest Good," *The Southern Journal of Philosophy* 25 (1987), pp. 49–64.
75   Kant, *Judgement*, p. 121. The complex role played by Spinoza in Kant's *Critique of Judgement* is helpfully explored by John Zammito in *The Genesis of Kant's Critique of Judgment*, chs 11–12.
76   Kant, *Judgement*, p. 121.
77   Kant, *Practical*, p. 130, emphasis added.
78   Andrews Reath, "Introduction," Kant, *Critique of Practical Reason*, trans. Mary Gregor (Cambridge: Cambridge University Press, 1997), p. xxx.
79   Kant, *Judgement*, p. 127. Interestingly, Kant develops a more ambitious theory of analogical reasoning about God in the third *Critique* than in the original moral argument itself. At once clarifying and cautionary, his comments about analogy reinforce Kant's insistence that God's existence and attributes may be objects of practical certainty, but they never become objects of theoretical knowledge. Referring to the importance of "preventing

a misunderstanding which might easily arise," Kant states that the "attributes of the Supreme Being can only be *conceived* by us on an analogy. For
how are we to investigate its nature when experience can show us nothing
similar? In the second place, such attributes also only enable us to conceive a
Supreme Being, not to *cognize* it or to predicate them of it in a more or less
theoretical manner." *Ibid.*, p. 126, emphasis Kant's.

80 Kant, *Religion*, p. 130.
81 Wood, *Kant's Moral Religion*, p. 138.
82 Kant, *Pure*, A811/B839, p. 639.
83 Lehmann, *op. cit.*, p. 187.
84 Kant, *Practical*, p. 12n.
85 Regarding this ambiguity, see Beck, *Commentary*, p. 252.
86 Wood, *Kant's Moral Religion*, p. 42.
87 Kant, *Practical*, p. 130.
88 Schneewind, *The Invention of Autonomy*, p. 251. Schneewind argues persuasively and at length that controversies over voluntarism "were central to
the development of modern moral philosophy. Because of its importance in
the theologies of Luther and of Calvin, and in the philosophical thought of
Descartes, Hobbes, Pufendorf, and Locke, the issues voluntarism raised
could be avoided only by unbelievers like Hume, the radical French thinkers,
and Bentham. Everyone else held that God must somehow be essential to
morality. ... The opponents of voluntarism thus had to show that morality
involves principles that are valid for God as well as for us. God and we must
be able to have a common understanding of the rationale or point of the
principles as well as the actions they require," pp. 509–10.
89 *Ibid.*, p. 510.
90 *Ibid.*, p. 511. There is, I think, a significant parallel between Schneewind's
account of the antivoluntarist effort to save the moral life from the contingency and arbitrariness of divine fiat and Hans Blumenberg's thesis that
the modern world is in large part the result of Western humanity's "self-
assertive" reaction to late medieval nominalism's depiction of the utter
mystery and unknowability of the divine will. In both cases, a fresh impulse
toward human initiative and self-sufficiency is sparked by a growing sense of
God's unintelligibility: there is nowhere else to turn but to human effort.
Both developments lay the foundation for powerful tensions between divine
transcendence and human autonomy. See Blumenberg, *The Legitimacy of
the Modern Age*, trans. Robert M. Wallace (Cambridge, MA and London:
The MIT Press, 1983), esp. Part II. Leszek Kolakowski offers remarks that
parallel Blumenberg's in *Modernity on Endless Trial* (Chicago and London:
University of Chicago Press, 1990), pp. 96ff. See also the remark of Richard
Velkley: "The impetus of modern thought to make humanity autonomous or
self-sufficient must be related to some unresolved questions in late medieval
and Renaissance thinking about the 'status of reason in the whole' and the
'dignity of man' (especially after Copernicus) and is not derivable only from
a Machiavellian critique of classical and Christian utopian politics." Velkley,
"The Crisis of the End of Reason in Kant's Philosophy and the *Remarks* of
1764–1765," in Beiner and Booth (eds), *op. cit.*, p. 90, n. 5.
91 Jonathan Berg, "How Could Ethics Depend on Religion?," in Peter Singer
(ed.), *A Companion to Ethics* (Oxford: Blackwell Publishers, 1991), p. 527.
Relevant here is Patrick Riley's claim that the element of Platonism running

through Kant's philosophy finds powerful expression in his antivoluntar- ism. According to Riley, the "most striking instance of an almost orthodox Platonism in Kant – which in this case may well have arrived via Leibniz – is found in those parts of [the *Critique of Pure Reason*] that attack the Cartesian notion that the good and the true are simply products of divine creative will, the effects of God's sheer fiat. It is here that Plato, Leibniz, and Kant stand as one against radical voluntarism." Riley, *op. cit.*, p. 16.

92   Quentin Lauer, S.J., *Hegel's Concept of God* (Albany: State University of New York Press, 1982), p. 26.

93   In the course of arguing that this famous claim is the source of *value* in Kant – in the context of an effort to wean us away from viewing Kant as the founding father of "deontological" ethics – Barbara Herman notes that, for Kant, there is nothing prior to the good will in the definition of goodness – including, presumably, any metaphysical claims or theological truths. Her- man, *op. cit.*, pp. 208–9.

94   Kant, *Foundations*, p. 9.

95   Martin Luther, *On the Bondage of the Will*, trans. J. I. Packer and O. R. Johnston (Westwood, N.J.: Fleming H. Revell, 1957), p. 104.

96   *Ibid.*, pp. 209, 314. Quoted in Schneewind, *The Invention of Autonomy*, p. 31.

97   Schneewind, *The Invention of Autonomy*, p. 25.

98   In his very illuminating account of the "invention of autonomy," Schnee- wind traces the idea that certain moral properties guide even the actions of God at least back to Grotius. *Ibid.*, p. 74.

99   E.g., Kant, *Religion*, p. 3. In her recent study of Hume, Jennifer Herdt makes a persuasive case that Hume's major contribution to the seculariza- tion of moral philosophy resides in a similar displacement of divine provi- dence by an immanent human capacity. In Hume's case, the key concept is "sympathy," not rationality. Herdt, *Religion and Faction in Hume's Moral Philosophy* (Cambridge: Cambridge University Press, 1997).

100 Kant, *Practical*, pp. 129ff. The idea of a "ground" comes from the Leibniz- ian philosophical tradition. Kant used the notion that God grounds poss- ibility as early as 1755. See Schneewind, *Autonomy*, pp. 494ff.; Yovel, "The God of Kant," pp. 99ff.; Yovel, *Kant and the Philosophy of History*, pp. 49–50, 77–8, 133–4, 281–2; England, *op. cit.*, pp. 56ff.

101 Kant, *Practical*, p. 129.

102 *Ibid.*, p. 105.

103 Beck, *Commentary*, p. 206.

104 Yovel, "The God of Kant," pp. 99–103. Yovel goes on to make the interesting point that, in thus serving as a kind of "divine guarantee" that the dualities of human existence can in principle be brought together, God plays a role analogous to that of the schematism in the first *Critique*. In that context, the process of schematizing solves the problem of linking the categories of the understanding to their particular instances in experience: the schema is the "third thing" mediating between pure concepts and empirical reality, insuring the actual application of the categories. Similarly, God's role as unifying metaphysical ground "carries on the tradition of making God the mediating term between the fundamental dualities in reality." *Ibid.*, p. 106. The theme of the human quest for the kind of unity or reconciliation of opposites already enjoyed by God no doubt signals important, if complex, lines of connection between Kant and European romanticism.

156 NOTES

105 John Zammito captures Kant's aim in economical but accurate terms when he states that, in the third *Critique*, "Kant made his most strenuous effort to achieve the unity of reason." Zammito, *op. cit.*, p. 345.
106 Kant, *Judgement*, p. 124.
107 *Ibid.*, p. 127, emphasis Kant's.
108 Yovel, "The God of Kant," p. 121, emphasis Yovel's. Although Yovel does not make the connection, his employment of the "projection" motif in relation to Kant's account of the divine predicates is obviously suggestive of Feuerbach's *Essence of Christianity*. For a very thorough discussion of the theme of "projection" in Feuerbach, see Van A. Harvey, *Feuerbach and the Interpretation of Religion* (Cambridge: Cambridge University Press, 1995), ch. 1. Harvey also relates Kant's transcendentalism to more recent projection theories of religion, pp. 249ff.
109 S. Kierkegaard, *Fear and Trembling*, ed. and trans. Howard V. Hong and Edna H. Hong (Princeton: Princeton University Press, 1983), p. 68. Whether Kierkegaard was engaging in something like plagiarism is a separate issue, recently explored in considerable detail by Ronald M. Green, *Kierkegaard and Kant: The Hidden Debt* (Albany: State University of New York Press, 1992).
110 Kierkegaard, *op. cit.*, p. 68.
111 *Ibid.*
112 Kierkegaard, *Concluding Unscientific Postscript*, trans. Howard V. Hong and Edna H. Hong (Princeton: Princeton University Press, 1992), pp. 323–4.
113 E.g., Gene Outka, "Religious and Moral Duty: Notes on *Fear and Trembling*," in Outka and John P. Reeder, Jr (eds), *Religion and Morality* (Garden City: Doubleday, 1973), pp. 204– 54; Robert L. Perkins (ed.), *Kierkegaard's Fear and Trembling: Critical Appraisals* (Birmingham: University of Alabama Press, 1981).
114 Stephen Toulmin's description of the aftermath of the Thirty Years' War highlights the arresting parallel between historical and philosophical developments. In the wake of the war – a war that "ended as a peace of exhaustion, not of conquest" – Pope Innocent "recognized that the new system of sovereign nations undercut rights and powers that earlier Popes had exercised without challenge. From now on, instead of secular rulers having to conform to the Church's demands, they could interfere freely in ecclesiastical affairs.... authorities had lost the power to enforce their demands." Toulmin, *Cosmopolis: The Hidden Agenda of Modernity* (Chicago and London: University of Chicago Press, 1990), pp. 90–1.
115 Thomas Hill, *Dignity and Practical Reason in Kant's Moral Theory* (Ithaca and London: Cornell University Press, 1992), p. 76.
116 Thus, the aptly titled study of the tradition leading up to Kant's view of autonomy: Schneewind's *The Invention of Autonomy*.

Chapter 3   Autonomy's Autonomy

1 Bernard Carnois, *The Coherence of Kant's Doctrine of Freedom*, trans. David Booth (Chicago and London: University of Chicago Press, 1987), p. 67.

2 Recent English-speaking Kant scholarship has built impressively on an earlier German scholarly interest in the roots and sources of Kant's theory of autonomy: e.g., Richard Velkley, *Freedom and the End of Reason: On the Moral Foundation of Kant's Critical Philosophy* (Chicago and London: University of Chicago Press, 1989); Jerome Schneewind, *The Invention of Autonomy: A History of Modern Moral Philosophy* (Cambridge: Cambridge University Press, 1998). Both Velkley and Schneewind utilize the important works of Josef Schmucker and Dieter Henrich and supplement such earlier works as Paul Arthur Schilpp, *Kant's Pre-Critical Ethics*, 2nd edn (Evanston: Northwestern University Press, 1960) and Keith Ward, *The Development of Kant's View of Ethics* (Oxford: Basil Blackwell, 1972). Velkley has made available in English some of Dieter Henrich's important work in Henrich, *The Unity of Reason: Essays on Kant's Philosophy*, ed. Velkley, trans. Jeffrey Edwards, Louis Hunt, Manfred Kuehn, and Guenter Zoeller (Cambridge, MA and London: Harvard University Press, 1994). Also important are Henry Allison, *Kant's Theory of Freedom* (Cambridge: Cambridge University Press, 1990) and Bernard Carnois, *op. cit.*; Thomas E. Hill, Jr, "The Kantian Conception of Autonomy," in Hill, *Dignity and Practical Reason in Kant's Moral Theory* (Ithaca and London: Cornell University Press, 1992), pp. 76–96; and Christine Korsgaard, "Morality as Freedom," in Korsgaard, *Creating the Kingdom of Ends* (Cambridge: Cambridge University Press, 1996), pp. 159–87. Needless to say, the overall literature on Kant's theory of freedom is vast. Useful bibliographies are included in Roger Sullivan, *Immanuel Kant's Moral Theory* (Cambridge: Cambridge University Press, 1989); Paul Guyer (ed.), *The Cambridge Companion to Kant* (Cambridge: Cambridge University Press, 1992); and Howard Caygill, *A Kant Dictionary* (Oxford: Blackwell, 1995).

3 I borrow here from Schneewind's account of the difficulties posed for early modern moral philosophy by the need to make God a "member" of the modern moral community. *Op. cit.*, pp. 139–40, 239, 250ff., 510–13.

4 Kant's own ambiguous relationship to deism is helpfully explored by Allen Wood, "Kant's Deism," in Philip J. Rossi and Michael Wreen (eds), *Kant's Philosophy of Religion Reconsidered* (Bloomington and Indianapolis: Indiana University Press, 1991), pp. 1–21.

5 The "problem of 'autonomy,' or of genuine self-determination or self-rule . . . stretches over the historical problem of modernity as itself a category. . . ." Robert B. Pippin, *Modernism as a Philosophical Problem* (Oxford: Blackwell, 1991), p. 3.

6 Carnois, *op. cit.*, p. 45.

7 Schneewind, *op. cit.*, p. 3.

8 *Ibid.*, p. 491. In his summary of Kant's debt to Rousseau, Schneewind cites the frequently mentioned fact that the sole picture on the walls of Kant's house was a portrait of Rousseau, but he also cites a biographer's comment that the portrait "'was certainly a present from some friend or other, in consideration of whom Kant felt its preservation to be a duty'" (p. 490 n. 14).

9 Amos Funkenstein, *Theology and the Scientific Imagination: From the Middle Ages to the Seventeenth Century* (Princeton: Princeton University Press, 1986), pp. 346ff. Interestingly, Funkenstein argues in this important work that a crucial though insufficiently emphasized aspect of the "secularization" process was the simple fact that theology in early modern Europe was increasingly done by laymen. Robert Pippin amplifies Funkenstein's point: "These

laymen were impressed with the results of the new mathematization of physics, and the possible application of physics to all modes of knowledge, and so entertained the very non-Aristotelian, non-Scholastic hope for a unified system of knowledge, a system that would include theology. Thus it is possible to show that secularization, rather than always denoting a 'hidden' religious agenda in secular pursuits, can denote a hidden or explicit secular motive in theological discourse...." Pippin, *op. cit.*, p. 174 n. 21. The link between theology and the powerful theme of the "mathematization of physics" forms a recognizable bridge to Kant's aspirations. Likewise, the interplay between theology and secular disciplines foreshadows Kant's late work, *The Conflict of the Faculties*, which was designed in part to adjudicate the fields of inquiry appropriate for theological and for non-theological faculties. Kant, *The Conflict of the Faculties*, trans. Mary J. Gregor (Lincoln and London: University of Nebraska Press, 1992).

10   Richard Velkley, "The Crisis of the End of Reason in Kant's Philosophy and the *Remarks* of 1764–1765," in Ronald Beiner and William James Booth (eds), *Kant and Political Philosophy* (New Haven and London: Yale University Press, 1993), p. 78.

11   David Hume, *A Treatise of Human Nature*, ed. L. A. Selby-Bigge (Oxford: Clarendon Press, 1951), p. 415.

12   "Rousseau and Kant are the greatest early figures in a movement of thought that expresses a powerful protest, indeed often a feeling of revulsion, against the spirit and aim of modern philosophy and whose later flowering is Romantic thought and German speculative idealist philosophy. The thinkers in this by no means homogeneous 'movement' are united by their tendency to see in earlier modernity a spirit of 'low individualism,' grounded in passion and self-interest – a spirit that fails to combine legitimate demands of the human soul for freedom and autonomy with its 'higher needs' for 'wholeness,' 'community,' and profound dedication to the noble and the sacred. The objection was that the founders of the modern rational reform of society had placed the foundations of both philosophic inquiry and civil life chiefly in the pursuit of private satisfactions of mostly bodily needs and that they had understood 'freedom' principally as the freedom to pursue such satisfactions with minimal interference from state, religion, or even moral law. Again the problem is that the earlier modern view makes reason, or even the soul, chiefly an instrument of the body. ... The various protests against modern thought and life were all supported by the reading of Rousseau. ..." Velkley, *Freedom and the End of Reason*, pp. 32, 180 n. 50.

13   *Ibid.*, ch. 1; Schneewind, *op. cit.*, pp. 487–92. Lewis White Beck, "Kant's Two Conceptions of the Will in Their Political Context," in Beiner and Booth (eds), *Kant and Political Philosophy*, pp. 43ff.

14   Henrich, *op. cit.*, p. 66. For a masterful discussion of the origins of Kant's concept of moral obligation, framed in terms of the historical development of his viewpoint, see the essay in Henrich entitled "The Concept of Moral Insight and Kant's Doctrine of the Fact of Reason," pp. 55–87. See also Henrich's essay, "The Moral Image of the World," in Henrich, *Aesthetic Judgment and the Moral Image of the World: Studies in Kant* (Stanford: Stanford University Press, 1992), pp. 3–28.

15   Probably written in 1486, the "Oration" has God address Adam in the following way: "The nature of all other beings is limited and constrained

within the bounds of laws prescribed by Us. Thou, constrained by no limits, in accordance with thine own free will in whose hand We have placed thee, shalt ordain for thyself the limits of thy nature. ... We have made thee neither of heaven nor of earth, neither mortal nor immortal, so that with freedom of choice and with honor, as though the maker and molder of thyself, thou mayest fashion thyself in whatever shape thou shalt prefer." Pico Della Mirandola, "Oration on the Dignity of Man," trans. Elizabeth Livermore Forbes, in Ernst Cassirer, Paul Oskar Kristeller, and John Herman Randall, Jr (eds), *The Renaissance Philosophy of Man* (Chicago and London: University of Chicago Press, 1948), p. 225.

16   Kant, *Foundations*, p. 59. One way to understand Kant's theory of autonomy is to view it as a sustained and sophisticated development of the idea of freedom as "self-legislation," as opposed to freedom from constraint or outside interference, a distinction that had been coursing through early modern thought at least since Machiavelli. "For centuries the theologians of Christianity had been expected to perform the cultural task of restating and improving the comprehensive doctrine from which a common moral vocabulary was drawn and to provide a shared self-understanding. In the seventeenth and eighteenth centuries clerical thinkers were joined, usually to their dismay, by nonclerical philosophers who took it upon themselves to provide comprehensive views that would improve on the ideas of the theologians – or that even would replace them. Religious, political, social, and economic changes increasingly forced philosophers to face the question of the extent to which human beings are capable of self-governance. The development of moral philosophy in our period is best understood by seeing the complex problem of autonomy at its core." Schneewind, "Introduction" to Schneewind (ed.), *Moral Philosophy from Montaigne to Kant*, Vol. 1 (Cambridge: Cambridge University Press, 1990), p. 20.

17   Kant, *Foundations*, pp. 64–5.

18   *Ibid.*, p. 65.

19   Schneewind, *The Invention of Autonomy*, p. 509.

20   The Augustinian echoes produced by Kant's emphasis on the will are examined by Hannah Arendt in a section of *The Life of the Mind* entitled "Augustine, the First Philosopher of the Will." *The Life of the Mind* (New York and London: Harcourt Brace Jovanovich, 1978), pp. 84–110. Patrick Riley suggests that Augustine's account of the good will is "remarkably 'pre-Kantian'" – which, I suppose, is a way of saying Kant's view is basically Augustinian. Riley, "The Elements of Kant's Practical Philosophy," in Beiner and Booth (eds), *Kant and Political Philosophy*, p. 11. Riley elaborates helpfully on Arendt's account of the connection between Kant and Augustine.

21   Kant, *Religion*, p. 31, emphasis Kant's. I develop the issue of the relation between incentives and maxims in *Fallen Freedom: Kant on Radical Evil and Moral Regeneration* (Cambridge: Cambridge University Press, 1990), pp. 32ff.

22   Kant, *Religion*, p. 173. In remarks such as this, we perhaps see examples of what Yirmiahu Yovel has referred to as "the aging Kant ... getting even with the perpetrators of what he once called his 'youthful slavery' in the pietist school he attended as a child," where demonstrations of piety were insisted upon, regardless of sincerity of conviction. Yovel, *Spinoza and Other*

Heretics: The Adventures of Immanence (Princeton: Princeton University Press, 1989), p. 8. This formative early experience gave Kant a lifelong hatred of hypocrisy in religious matters. A helpful account in English of Kant's early schooling is Ann L. Loades, *Kant and Job's Comforters* (Newcastle upon Tyne: Avero, 1985), ch. 1.

23 The previously cited studies of Schmucker, Henrich, Velkley, and Schneewind trace this set of developments.

24 Kant, *Foundations*, p. 9. Dieter Henrich dates the origins of this conception of the good – and, indeed, the origins of the categorical imperative – a full twenty years prior to the publication of the *Foundations*. Henrich, *The Unity of Reason*, pp. 72ff., 95ff. Henrich bases his view on Kant's marginal notes (from the mid-1760s) to his own copy of his *Observations on the Feeling of the Beautiful and the Sublime*. In part through Henrich's influence, these notes or "reflections" have also informed the efforts of both Velkley (both works cited) and Schneewind, *The Invention of Autonomy*, to trace the development of Kant's moral philosophy.

25 Barbara Herman, *The Practice of Moral Judgment* (Cambridge, MA and London: Harvard University Press, 1993), p. vii. In both the title essay in this volume (pp. 73–93), and in her essay "On the Value of Acting from the Motive of Duty" (pp. 1–22), Herman very helpfully reconstructs the Kantian account of duty in a way that both discloses and avoids the pitfalls of much traditional interpretation of Kant's ethics. One of Herman's guiding interpretive claims is that accounts of Kant's moral theory become muddled due to the uncritical use of an empiricist conception of "motives," a criticism that dovetails neatly with Schneewind's tracing of the evolution of Kant's conception of autonomy. "Kant's argument is roughly this: if morality binds with practical necessity, it cannot work through the passive desires and interests that agents happen to have. Moral agents therefore cannot be described by an empiricist account of motivation. They must possess the capacity to be moved by principle (or by a conception of the good). A satisfactory grasp of the possibility of morality requires a revision of our understanding of agency. In arguing that willings of actions and ends (as described in maxims) are the appropriate objects of practical assessment, Kant not only introduces an alternative theory of action, but also argues for the methodological priority of a theory of value. It is not until the motive of duty is placed in the revised theory of action and agency that Kant's claims for it can make sense. For this reason, the familiar debate about the motive of duty must be futile" (Herman, p. viii). Representing a significant wing within recent interpreters of Kant's moral philosophy, Herman wants to argue that we would be better off simply dropping the whole idea of deontology in our approach to Kant. For a helpful cautionary note regarding such an approach, see Schneewind, "Kant and Stoic Ethics," in Stephen Engstrom and Jennifer Whiting (eds), *Aristotle, Kant, and the Stoics: Rethinking Happiness and Duty* (Cambridge: Cambridge University Press, 1996), pp. 288–90.

26 Kant, *Religion*, p. 4.

27 Adrian S. Piper, "Kant on the Objectivity of the Moral Law," in Andrews Reath, Barbara Herman, and Christine M. Korsgaard (eds), *Reclaiming the History of Ethics: Essays for John Rawls* (Cambridge: Cambridge University Press, 1997), p. 241.

28   Schneewind, *The Invention of Autonomy*, p. 484. See Henrich, *The Unity of Reason*, p. 68: "Kant felt it was his special merit that he had justified moral insight as a form of rational cognition. ... The rule by means of which moral insight finds its judgment is formulated by Kant in analogy to the law of theoretical reason."

29   Kant, *On the Old Saw: That Might be Right in Theory but it Won't Work in Practice*, trans. E. B. Ashton (Philadelphia: University of Pennsylvania Press, 1974), p. 47n.

30   Schneewind, *The Invention of Autonomy*, p. 518.

31   Kant, *Religion*, p. 19. Allison, *op. cit.*, pp. 39–40, 129–45. Whereas the Greene–Hudson translation of the *Religion* translates both *Wille* and *Willkür* as "will" (with a lower-case "w" following when the translated word is *Willkür*), the new translation by George Di Giovanni translates *Wille* as "will" and *Willkür* as "power of choice" – which, in fact, had been the occasional practice of Hoyt Hudson in his original translation published in 1934.

32   In personal correspondence some years ago, Schubert Ogden suggested to me that the traditional theological doctrine "distinguishing between the formal and material *imago Dei*...must be hovering somewhere in the background of Kant's distinction between *der Wille* and *die Willkür.*" Such a parallel, Ogden suggests, might offer a way of reconciling divine transcendence and human autonomy in Kant, in so far as the distinction between the formal and material *imago Dei* provides a basis for such a reconciliation in the biblical and theological traditions themselves. Certainly this may be so with respect to the systematic interests that preoccupy Ogden. However, my main concern is the momentum that early German idealism generated in the production of the position we associate with Feuerbach and Marx and, in general, in the production of a cultural sphere that increasingly found references to divine transcendence either mystifying or redundant. Either result makes such references dispensable: the former, because the culture can no longer truly understand what is being said; and the latter, because what is being said can be said better and just as fully in purely human terms.

33   Kant, *The Metaphysics of Morals*, trans. Mary Gregor (Cambridge: Cambridge University Press, 1991), p. 42. This work was originally published in 1797, and another context in which Kant mobilizes the *Wille/Willkür* distinction in a clear way is a similarly late (1793) work, *Religion within the Limits of Reason Alone*. Yet versions of the distinction in Kant's account of the will and human freedom can be traced back at least to the *Critique of Pure Reason*. See Allison, *op. cit.*, pp. 129–45, as well as the brief but helpful discussion in the entry on "Will" in Caygill, *A Kant Dictionary*, pp. 413–17. See also Ralf Meerbote, "*Wille* and *Willkür* in Kant's Theory of Action," in Moltke Gram (ed.), *Interpreting Kant* (Iowa City: University of Iowa Press, 1982), pp. 69–84.

34   In a typically competent and illuminating account, Lewis White Beck undertakes the interesting task of charting out some of the broader political implications of Kant's distinction between *Wille* and *Willkür* in "Kant's Two Conceptions of the Will in Their Political Context," pp. 38–49.

35   Kant, *Religion*, pp. 22–3, emphasis Kant's.

36   *Ibid.*, p. 21.

37 *Ibid.*, p. 21n.

38 I have attempted to give a fuller account of the activity of "maxim-making" in *Fallen Freedom*, ch. 2. See also Onora O'Neill, *Constructions of Reason: Explorations of Kant's Practical Philosophy* (Cambridge: Cambridge University Press, 1989), Part II.

39 John Silber once argued that it would be better to render Kant's position in terms of the dictum, "ought *presupposes* can." "It is both ambiguous and highly misleading to say that Kant believes that 'ought' implies 'can.' On the other hand, it is quite correct to say that Kant holds that 'ought' presupposes 'can.' If one is really obligated to do something, he must be able to do it. But it is also true that, if a person cannot do something, he is not obligated to do it. 'Cannot' implies no obligation." Silber, "Kant's Conception of the Highest Good as Immanent and Transcendent," *Philosophical Review* LXVII (1959), p. 476.

40 It is important to distinguish "rational structure" here from "human nature." Speaking of the principle of duty conveyed by the categorical imperative, Kant warns at one point in the *Foundations* that "it is extremely important to remember that we must not let ourselves think that the reality of this principle can be derived from the particular constitution of human nature. For duty is practical unconditional necessity of action; it must, therefore, hold for all rational beings (to which alone an imperative can apply), and only for that reason can it be a law for all human wills." *Foundations*, p. 43.

41 To be sure, Hegel's criticism of Kant's ethics is rendered in the broader context of his polemic against what he took to be Kant's "subjectivism," his inadequate conception of freedom, and the philosophical uselessness of the phenomena–noumena dichotomy. For helpful accounts, see Joachim Ritter, "Morality and Ethical Life: Hegel's Controversy with Kantian Ethics," in Ritter, *Hegel and the French Revolution: Essays on the Philosophy of Right*, trans. Richard Dien Winfield (Cambridge, MA and London: MIT Press, 1982), pp. 151–82; Timothy O'Hagan, "On Hegel's Critique of Kant's Moral and Political Philosophy," in Stephen Priest (ed.), *Hegel's Critique of Kant* (Oxford: Clarendon Press, 1987), pp. 135–59.

42 J. B. Schneewind, "Autonomy, Obligation, and Virtue: An Overview of Kant's Moral Philosophy," in Paul Guyer (ed.), *The Cambridge Companion to Kant*, p. 310.

43 Georg Lukács, *The Young Hegel: Studies in the Relations between Dialectics and Economics*, trans. Rodney Livingston (Cambridge, MA: MIT Press, 1976), pp. 18–30; Laurence Dickey, *Hegel: Religion, Economics, and the Politics of Spirit, 1770–1807* (Cambridge: Cambridge University Press, 1987), pp. 157ff.

44 D. Henrich, "Hutcheson und Kant," *Kant-Studien* 49 (1957–8), pp. 65–6. See the fuller discussion of this aspect of the development of Kant's ethical viewpoint in Velkley, *Freedom and the End of Reason*, pp. 49–52.

45 Relevant here is John Rawls' comment: "For Kant there is no essential difference between freedom of the will and freedom of thought. If our mathematical and theoretical reasoning is free, as shown in free judgments, then so is our pure practical reasoning as shown in free, deliberative judgments." Rawls, "Themes in Kant's Moral Philosophy," in Eckart Förster (ed.), *Kant's Transcendental Deductions* (Stanford: Stanford University Press, 1989), p. 108.

46   This issue of moral epistemology forms one of the major organizing themes of Schneewind's recent study, *The Invention of Autonomy*. "Proponents of conceptions of morality as self-governance all take it that moral agents must possess certain specific psychological capacities. Normal adults are able to be aware of or to know, with no external help, what morality directs or approves, and to bring themselves to live accordingly regardless of threats and rewards" (p. 9). In effect, Kant's moral theory fulfills the goals of this sort of moral theorist by coupling the universalizability principle to the ideal of universal access to moral principles.

47   In *Religion within the Limits of Reason Alone* (pp. 97, 126n.), Kant speaks explicitly of historical religions as "vehicles" of moral insight, while making it clear that their pedagogical impact does not compromise the rational basis of the moral insight thus conveyed.

48   Kant, *Practical*, p. 48. The highly problematic notion of a "fact of reason" is a kind of successor to Kant's deduction of the moral law in the *Foundations*. Henry Allison notes that the "general consensus appears to be that even though this deduction failed, it was at least a step in the right direction. Consequently, by abandoning the effort to provide a deduction of the moral law and relying instead on a brute appeal to a putative fact of reason, which in turn is supposed to provide the basis for a deduction of freedom, Kant in effect reverted to a precritical dogmatism of practical reason." Allison himself takes pains to counter this "general consensus," arguing instead that "Kant's turn to the fact of reason marks a genuine advance" and is "the best available strategy for authenticating the moral law and establishing the reality of transcendental freedom." Allison, *op. cit.*, p. 230. John Rawls similarly defends Kant's doctrine of a fact of reason, suggesting that here "Kant may be ahead of his critics." Rawls, *op. cit.*, p. 108. Alternatively, Beck suggests that Kant's notion of a fact of reason is riddled with confusion, citing three possible meanings that Kant's own text supports: consciousness of the moral law; the moral law itself; and autonomy. Lewis White Beck, *A Commentary on Kant's Critique of Practical Reason* (Chicago and London: University of Chicago Press, 1960), p. 167. (See also the following note.)

49   Beck, *A Commentary on Kant's Critique of Practical Reason*, pp. 164ff. The relevant transitions in Kant's thinking include the refinement of the earlier standpoint of the *Foundations* evident in the second *Critique*'s notion of the moral law as a "fact of reason" that entails the awareness of autonomy. As Christine Korsgaard has formulated the issue, in the *Foundations* "Kant's emphasis is on our consciousness of the spontaneity of reason in the production of ideas in general; in the *Critique of Practical Reason*, it is on our awareness of the moral law and of our ability to act from it (the Fact of Reason), which he says reveals our freedom to us. ..." Korsgaard adds that she believes "that Kant revised his argument because the spontaneous production of ideas only places us among the noumena as thinkers. To be among the noumena as *agents*, we must be able to *act from* pure ideas, and for this, the positive conception of freedom which is found only in the categorical imperative, as well as our ability to act from that conception, are necessary." Korsgaard, *Creating the Kingdom of Ends*, p. 217, n. 21, emphasis Korsgaard's. See also the discussion of a "fact of reason" in Henrich, *The Unity of Reason*, pp. 68ff.

50   Kant, *Practical*, p. 130.

51 George Schrader once suggested that Kant associated a metaphysical anchoring of the moral law with heteronomy: "If Kant had been clearer in his own mind as to the metaphysical foundation for the categorical imperative, he would have found it necessary to credit heteronomy with a fundamental role in the moral life. Freedom and reason, which Kant properly recognized as the necessary conditions of morality, became for him too exclusively ends-in-themselves." Schrader offers this observation in the course of arguing, against Kant, that "categorical obligation does not require an autonomous foundation." Schrader, "Autonomy, Heteronomy, and Moral Imperatives," in Robert Paul Wolff (ed.), *Foundations of the Metaphysics of Morals, with Critical Essays* (Indianapolis and New York: Bobbs-Merrill, 1969), p. 133.

52 Pierre Hassner, "Immanuel Kant," in Leo Strauss and Joseph Cropsey (eds), *History of Political Philosophy*, 3rd edn (Chicago and London: University of Chicago Press, 1987), p. 588. Hassner's formulation dovetails with Bernard Carnois' emphasis on the priority of freedom as first among equals in any consideration of the postulates of practical reason. Since freedom is necessarily entailed by our apprehension of the moral law which, in turn, is a fact of reason, "freedom occupies a privileged place among the ideas of pure reason. Over and again Kant underscores this point. In relation to the other ideas (God and immortality), the idea of freedom enjoys certain privileges...[for as] a conclusion derived immediately from a fact of reason, freedom is the object of a practical knowledge. ...By contrast, we neither know nor perceive the possibility and the reality of God and immortality, since they are not conditions of the moral law but merely conditions of the highest good, which is the necessary object of the free will." Carnois, *The Coherence of Kant's Doctrine of Freedom*, p. 67. This is why "Kant repeatedly warned us not to view moral faith as the foundation of the moral law," Henrich, *The Unity of Reason*, p. 80.

53 Kant, *Practical*, p. 43, emphasis added.

54 Kant, *Practical*, p. 76. Kant's ethics "includes the acknowledgment that 'respect for the law' is a primordial motivation. It is impossible to derive it from other impulses or desires, or even from reason in general. Instead, it derives directly from awareness of the validity of the law." Henrich, "The Moral Image of the World," p. 22.

55 Hill, *op. cit.*, p. 84, emphasis Hill's.

56 Kant, *Practical*, p. 76.

57 Kant, *Pure*, pp. 410–11.

58 For a helpful elaboration of the Third Antinomy and its resolution, see Allison, *op. cit.*, pp. 14ff.

59 There is the further problem associated with the fact that, elsewhere in the *Critique of Practical Reason* (pp. 77ff.), Kant forcefully argues that all other feelings (including love) are "pathological." Kant is obviously attempting to insulate moral agency from the polluting influences of sensuous inclinations, yet his stringency in pursuit of this cause does not keep him from invoking the notion of "feeling" when accounting for the mode in which the moral law conveys its impact. In this account of moral feeling, we thus have something like a cross-threading of the objective–rational and the intuitive–psychological that perhaps reflects the dynamic state of European moral philosophy at the close of the eighteenth century, coming from a

thinker who flirted with Scottish moral-sense theory before devising his more rationalist position.

60 Kant, *Pure*, A553/B581, p. 476.

61 Kant, *Practical*, p. 49. In the "Preface" to the second *Critique*, Kant attempts to rationalize the importing of the vocabulary of causality into the noumenal realm by simply repeating the distinction between phenomena and noumena, rather than by addressing the question of the intelligibility of the causal principle outside its proper domain: "The union of causality as freedom with causality as the mechanism of nature, the first being given through the moral law and the latter through natural law, and both as related to the same subject, man, is impossible unless man is conceived by pure consciousness as a being in itself in relation to the former, but by empirical reason as appearance in relation to the latter. Otherwise the self-contradiction of reason is unavoidable" (p. 6n.). But our problem is not that of reconciling two images of "man" but of understanding what "causality" could possibly mean outside the phenomenal sphere. Among the many efforts to relate causality (and temporality) to Kant's ethical outlook, a particularly helpful discussion is offered by Paul Stern, "The Problem of History and Temporality in Kantian Ethics," *Review of Metaphysics* 39 (1986), pp. 505–45.

62 The impossibility of ever eradicating the capacity of respect for the moral law is what is at issue in Kant's rejection of what he calls "devilishness" in *Religion within the Limits of Reason Alone*, for only a devil could reject the moral law *because* it is the moral law. See the helpful discussion in Sharon Anderson-Gold, "Kant's Rejection of Devilishness: The Limits of Human Volition," *Idealistic Studies* 14 (1984), pp. 35–48. See also my discussion in *Fallen Freedom: Kant on Radical Evil and Moral Regeneration*, pp. 73–7.

63 "Freedom, however, among all the ideas of speculative reason is the only one whose possibility we know a priori. We do not understand it, but we know it as the condition of the moral law which we do know." Kant, *Practical*, p. 4.

64 Kant, *Foundations*, p. 64.

65 Schneewind, *The Invention of Autonomy*, pp. 495–7.

66 Kant, *Religion*, p. 142, emphasis Kant's. (Unfortunately, the Greene–Hudson translation of the *Religion* has not included Kant's emphasis.)

67 Kant, *Pure*, A819/B847, p. 644.

68 *Ibid.*

69 *Ibid.*

70 Kant, *Religion*, p. 163.

71 Kant, *Pure*, A634/B662, pp. 526–7.

72 Kant, *Practical*, pp. 129ff. See the discussion of this point in ch. 2 above.

73 Kant, *Foundations*, p. 25.

74 S. Kierkegaard, *Fear and Trembling*, trans. Howard V. Hong and Edna H. Hong (Princeton: Princeton University Press, 1983).

75 Kant, *Religion*, pp. 100–1. See Yirmiahu Yovel, "Bible Interpretation as Philosophical Praxis: A Study of Spinoza and Kant," *Journal of the History of Philosophy* 54 (1972), pp. 189–212.

76 Schneewind, *The Invention of Autonomy*, p. 512.

77 Yovel, *Kant and the Philosophy of History* (Princeton: Princeton University Press, 1980), p. 116.

Chapter 4   Reason's Interest

1 Onora O'Neill, *Constructions of Reason: Explorations of Kant's Practical Philosophy* (Cambridge: Cambridge University Press, 1989), p. 4.

2 Kant, *Pure*, A707/B735, p. 573. I have used O'Neill's own translation here, in which she translates *Gebäude* as "building," where Kemp Smith uses "edifice." Cited in O'Neill, *op. cit.*, p. 11.

3 Kant, *Pure*, A738/B706, p. 593.

4 O'Neill, *op. cit.*, p. 3.

5 *Ibid.*, p. 12.

6 Guided by her concern for the political dimensions of Kant's imagery, O'Neill is particularly interested in the themes of authority, discipline, and submission running through the "Transcendental Doctrine of Method." For her, discipline in the form of "self-discipline" is intimately associated with the reflexive character of reason. "This is why the discussion of philosophical method *must* come at the end of a critique of reason. At the beginning we had no 'material' to discipline; now a hypothesis about how we might embark on the tasks of reason has supplied some material, but has not shown how this material is to be combined for the edifice of knowledge. It has, however, provided a vantage point for a reflexive task, which could not be undertaken initially, but only retrospectively, reflectively, toward the end... To undertake the self-critique of reason at the beginning would be to submit to some tribunal that lacks authority. Like Bacon, Kant rejects the jurisdiction of such tribunals." *Ibid.*, pp. 13–14.

7 Kant's "construction" imagery is also suggestive of lines across the full expanse of modern Continental thought connecting him with his life-long reader, Martin Heidegger, whose philosophical odyssey culminates in the idea that "language is the *house* of being."

8 Kant, *Pure*, A553/B581, p. 476.

9 In his important essay of 1786, "What is Orientation in Thinking?," Kant effectively reinforces his metaphors of construction with metaphors of spatial orientation. In pursuit of what he calls the "healthy maxims of reason" which avoid the dogmatism of traditional speculative metaphysics, Kant says that to "*orientate* oneself, in the proper sense of the word, means to use a given direction – and we divide the horizon into four of these – in order to find the others, and in particular that of *sunrise*." He then goes on to extend this image to orientation in a "mathematical sense" and orientation in "thought" itself. Kant, "What is Orientation in Thinking?," trans. H. B. Nisbet in Hans Reiss (ed.), *Kant: Political Writings*, 2nd edn (Cambridge: Cambridge University Press, 1991), pp. 238ff., emphasis Kant's.

10 One might also say that the metaphorical dimension in Kant's thinking shrinks the presumed gap between his conception of philosophy and Nietzsche's "emphasis on the rhetorical and aesthetic dimensions of language." This Nietzschean perspective underwrites a variety of contemporary efforts to devalue "the self-assertive and self-aggrandizing notion of reason that underlies Western 'logocentrism'" and to criticize "subject-centered reason itself." Consequently, any significant alteration in our view of the relation between Kant's conception of philosophy and philosophical language and Nietzsche's would have a strong ripple effect. Thomas McCarthy, "Introduction," in Jürgen Habermas, *The Philosophical Discourse of Mod-*

ernity, trans. Frederick Lawrence (Cambridge, MA: The MIT Press, 1987), pp. viii–x.

11 Kant, *Pure*, A805/B833; Letter to C. F. Stäudlin (1793) in Arnulf Zweig (ed. and trans.), *Kant: Philosophical Correspondence, 1759–99* (Chicago and London: University of Chicago Press, 1967), p. 205.

12 John Sallis, *The Gathering of Reason* (Athens: Ohio University Press, 1980), p. 47.

13 *Ibid.*

14 Kant, *Pure*, A302/B359, p. 303.

15 Roger Sullivan, *An Introduction to Kant's Ethics* (Cambridge: Cambridge University Press, 1994), p. 84.

16 Kant, *Pure*, A326/ B383, p. 318.

17 *Ibid.*, A409/ B436, p. 386, emphasis Kant's.

18 *Ibid.*, Bxv, p. 21.

19 Kant, *Prolegomena to Any Future Metaphysics*, trans. P. Carus (Indianapolis and New York: Bobbs-Merrill, 1950), pp. 87–8.

20 In a letter late in life (1798) to his friend Christian Garve, Kant wrote: "It was not from the investigation of the existence of God, of immortality, and so on, that I started but from the antinomy of pure reason, 'The world has a beginning ——; it has no beginning ——,' and so on, up to the fourth [*sic*] antinomy: 'Man has freedom' —— against this: 'There is no freedom; and everything belongs to natural necessity.' These were what first awoke me from the dogmatic slumbers and drove me to the critique of reason itself in order to end the scandal of reason's ostensible contradictions with itself." Quoted in Zweig, *op. cit.*, p. 99n.

21 Richard Velkley, *Freedom and the End of Reason* (Chicago and London: University of Chicago Press, 1989), p. 29.

22 Hans Blumenberg, *The Legitimacy of the Modern Age*, trans. Robert M. Wallace (Cambridge, MA and London: The MIT Press, 1983), p. 56, emphasis added.

23 Robert M. Wallace, "Translator's Introduction" to *Ibid.*, p. xxxi, n.q.

24 Kant, *Pure*, A464/B492, p. 423.

25 At such points as this, Susan Meld Shell's recent effort to relate Kant's philosophy to his own ambivalence about our "embodied" condition and to his intense preoccupation with his own health (including special attention to his bowels) is especially suggestive. *The Embodiment of Reason* (Chicago and London: University of Chicago Press, 1996).

26 Kant, *Practical*, p. 82.

27 Richard Velkley, *op. cit.*, p. 46.

28 *Ibid.*

29 Kant, *Practical*, pp. 124ff.

30 Pierre Hassner, "Immanuel Kant," in Leo Strauss and Joseph Cropsey (eds), *History of Political Philosophy*, 3rd edn (Chicago and London: University of Chicago Press, 1987), p. 587.

31 Kant, *Practical*, p. 124, emphasis added.

32 *Ibid.*, p. 125, emphasis added.

33 *Ibid.*

34 *Ibid.*, pp. 125–6.

35 *Ibid.*, p. 126, emphasis added.

36 Y. Yovel, *Kant and the Philosophy of History* (Princeton: Princeton University Press, 1980), p. 15. Yovel argues convincingly that there is an important difference between an "interest" and an "end" of reason. "The concept of end does not necessarily indicate a lack or a privation. It is a teleological concept, whose function is retained even after it has been actualized. ... An interest, on the other hand, is related to the *gap* that exists between the abstract goal and its actuality, between the archetypal model of rationality latent in our minds and its full explication" (p. 18, emphasis Yovel's).

37 Susan Neiman, *The Unity of Reason* (New York and Oxford: Oxford University Press, 1994), p. 179.

38 Kant, *Practical*, p. 151, emphasis added.

39 Neiman, *op. cit.*, p. 179, emphasis added.

40 *Ibid.*

41 *Ibid.*

42 Kant, *Practical*, p. 147. One might reasonably assume that the idea of the "interest" of reason has a better claim to the title of "root metaphor" in Kant's account of rationality, but Yovel offers the interesting notion that the "interest" of reason ceases to be a metaphor and becomes a "systematic concept" instead. In an aside that one wishes he had developed further, Yovel adds that the "interest" of reason "might be a metaphor in the deeper sense in which the substantive 'reason' is itself a metaphor, or in which such concepts as 'ground' or 'basis' are metaphoric. But this is a different issue altogether." Yovel, *op. cit.*, p. 16 n. 2.

43 Kant, "What is Orientation in Thinking?," pp. 240–1, emphasis Kant's.

44 Neiman, *op. cit.*, p. 3.

45 It is interesting to note that two recent books on Kant carry this title: Neiman's, just cited, and the collection of translated essays by Dieter Henrich edited by Richard Velkley, *The Unity of Reason: Essays on Kant's Philosophy* (Cambridge, MA and London: Harvard University Press, 1994).

46 Quentin Lauer, S. J., *Hegel's Concept of God* (Albany: State University of New York Press, 1982), p. 24.

47 Frederick Beiser, *The Fate of Reason: German Philosophy from Kant to Fichte* (Cambridge, MA and London: Harvard University Press, 1987); Andrew Bowie, *Schelling and Modern European Philosophy* (London and New York: Routledge, 1993), esp. chs 1–2. Perhaps the most telling indicator of a potential "historicizing" of reason in Kant is the brief but suggestive "History of Pure Reason" with which he concludes the *Critique of Pure Reason*. *Pure*, A852/B880–A856/B884, pp. 666–9. See the discussion in Yovel, *op. cit.*, pp. 247ff.

48 For a helpful effort to relate Hegel's concept of *Geist* to Kant's philosophy, see Robert Solomon, "Hegel's Concept of *Geist*," in Alasdair MacIntyre (ed.), *Hegel: A Collection of Critical Essays* (Garden City: Doubleday and Co., 1972), pp. 125–49, esp. pp. 131ff.

49 Kant, *Pure*, A808/B836, p. 637, emphasis Kant's.

50 *Ibid.*, A808/B836, pp. 637–8.

51 Kant, *Foundations*, p. 57.

52 *Ibid.*, pp. 39, 47.

53 *Ibid.*, p. 54.

54 For example, Christine Korsgaard maintains that Kant's position does not amount to an equivalence of all three versions of the categorical imperative,

as though the second and third versions are simply derived from the principle of universalizability informing the first. Such a view, she argues, ignores "the fact that each formulation is intended to represent some characteristic feature of rational principles. In particular, 'humanity' is argued to be the appropriate material for a rational principle, just as universality is its appropriate form. Furthermore, the addition of each new feature represents a step further into the metaphysics of morals, with the idea of autonomy providing the stepping-stone that will make the transition to a critique of practical reason possible." *Creating the Kingdom of Ends* (Cambridge: Cambridge University Press, 1996), pp. 106–7. For my purposes, the particularly interesting feature of the third version is the deepening of the social dimension already introduced by the second version, raising the possibility that the individual's pursuit of virtue is inseparable from the promotion of a certain sort of community. Whether this potential connection is simply masked, or in fact challenged, by Kant's division of his eventual *Metaphysics of Morals* between "The Doctrine of Right" and "The Doctrine of Virtue" is a good question.

55 Kant, *Foundations*, p. 49.
56 *Ibid.*, p. 51. In an interesting account, Thomas Hill has argued that the third formula of the categorical imperative "is in important respects an improvement over the much discussed first formula" and "a guide for moral living." In his argument on behalf of this claim, Hill brings into view numerous features of the third formula that remain hidden or opaque in Kant's own very compressed account. Hill, *Dignity and Practical Reason in Kant's Moral Theory* (Ithaca and London: Cornell University Press, 1992), pp. 58ff.
57 Kant, *Foundations*, pp. 51–2.
58 Sharon Anderson-Gold, "Kant's Ethical Commonwealth: The Highest Good as a Social Goal," *International Philosophical Quarterly* 26 (1986), p. 27.
59 J. B. Schneewind, "Voluntarism and the Foundations of Ethics," *Proceedings and Addresses of the American Philosophical Association* 70.2 (1996), p. 36.
60 Roger J. Sullivan, *Immanuel Kant's Moral Theory* (Cambridge: Cambridge University Press, 1989), p. 213.
61 J. B. Schneewind, "Autonomy, Obligation, and Virtue: An Overview of Kant's Moral Philosophy," in Paul Guyer (ed.), *The Cambridge Companion to Kant* (Cambridge: Cambridge University Press, 1992), p. 310.
62 Beck argues that precisely because Kant developed his doctrine of freedom and law in his ethical theory "more than Rousseau did, we are in a better position to clarify his political doctrines than we are to clarify those of Rousseau." Beck, "Kant's Two Conceptions of the Will in Their Political Context," in Ronald Beiner and William James Booth (eds), *Kant and Political Philosophy: The Contemporary Legacy* (New Haven and London: Yale University Press, 1993), p. 44. The growing interest in Kant's political philosophy and, in fact, in its potential centrality to his ethics, is readily evident in Roger Sullivan's use of Kant's political theory as the opening chapter of his lucid and useful primer, *An Introduction to Kant's Ethics*. More generally, see Patrick Riley, *Kant's Political Philosophy* (Totowa, N.J.: Rowman and Littlefield, 1983).
63 Kant, *Foundations*, p. 52. The question of the potential intrusion on individual autonomy produced by a conception of willing that must be universally

valid is explored in helpful detail by Andrews Reath, "Legislating for a
Realm of Ends: The Social Dimension of Autonomy," in Reath, Barbara
Herman, and Christine M. Korsgaard (eds), *Reclaiming the History of
Ethics: Essays for John Rawls* (Cambridge: Cambridge University Press,
1997), pp. 214–39.

64 Korsgaard, *op. cit.*, p. 193.
65 The potentially utopian element in Kant's theory of the realm of ends, and
the objections to the theory that such an element might justifiably elicit, are
helpfully analyzed by Thomas Hill, "Kant's Utopianism," in Hill, *op. cit.*,
pp. 67–75. The problem of utopianism, Hill suggests, "is the problem of
whether Kant draws illegitimate inferences concerning what we should do in
this imperfect world from premises about what perfectly rational beings
would do in an ideal world," p. 67.
66 Kant, *Religion*, pp. 85ff. In his pre-critical lectures on ethics dating from the
late 1770s, Kant says that the "realization of the full destiny, the highest
possible perfection of human nature – that is the kingdom of God on earth.
Justice and equity, the authority, not of governments, but of conscience
within us, will then rule the world. This is the destined final end, the highest
moral perfection to which the human race can attain; but the hope of it is
still distant; it will be many centuries before it can be realized." Kant,
Lectures on Ethics, trans. Louis Infield (New York: Harper Torchbooks,
1963), p. 253.
67 Kant, *Foundations*, p. 55.
68 Pierre Hassner, "Immanuel Kant," in Strauss and Cropsey (eds), *History of
Political Philosophy*, p. 585. The potential connection between the idea of
self-agreement and the ideal ethical community is implicitly reinforced by
Howard Caygill's provocative effort to relate the idea of an ethical kingdom
to perfected forms of judgment, particularly in light of Kant's *Critique of
Judgement*. See Caygill, "Kant and the Kingdom," in Phillip Blond (ed.),
Post-Secular Philosophy: Between Philosophy and Theology (London and
New York: Routledge, 1998), pp. 107–15.
69 Kant's legacy within contemporary political philosophy is of course best
known through the work and influence of John Rawls. For a helpful summary of the issues, see Bernard Yack, "The Problem with Kantian Liberalism," in Beiner and Booth (eds), *op. cit.*, pp. 224–44.

Chapter 5 Heaven Comes to Earth

1 Kant, Religion, p. 87.
2 *Ibid.*
3 *Ibid.*, p. 90, emphasis Kant's.
4 Hans W. Frei, *Types of Christian Theology*, ed. George Hunsinger and William C. Placher (New Haven and London: Yale University Press, 1992), p. 58.
5 Frederick C. Beiser, *The Sovereignty of Reason* (Princeton: Princeton University Press, 1996), p. 13.
6 See especially Kant's rather self-conscious effort to explain the title of the
book in his "Preface to the Second Edition," *Religion*, p. 11.
7 Garrett Green, "Kant as Christian Apologist: The Failure of Accommodationist Theology," *Pro Ecclesia* IV (1995), p. 304. The most comprehensive
study of the sources and composition of the *Religion* remains Josef Bohatec,

Die Religionsphilosophie Kants in der "Religion innerhalb der Grenzen der blossen Vernunft" (Hildesheim: Georg Olms, 1966) which, regrettably, has never been translated. An excellent guide in English to the topics and aims of the *Religion* is Michel Despland, *Kant on History and Religion* (Montreal and London: McGill-Queen's University Press, 1973), esp. chs 8–10.

8 James Collins, *The Emergence of Philosophy of Religion* (New Haven and London: Yale University Press, 1967), p. 91.

9 Kant, *Religion*, pp. 54ff.

10 *Ibid.*, p. 54. In an undeveloped but provocative remark, Kant alludes at one point to the idea that Jesus "breaks" the "power" of the evil principle to keep us in its hold, implying a constitutive rather than simply illustrative role for christology. An interpretation of Kant's christology emphasizing this aspect of his thinking is offered by Despland, *op. cit.*, pp. 197ff., 223ff. A helpful elaboration of Kant's christology is offered by Vincent A. McCarthy, *Quest for a Philosophical Jesus: Christianity and Philosophy in Rousseau, Kant, Hegel, and Schelling* (Macon, Georgia: Mercer University Press, 1986).

11 Kant, *Religion*, p. 39n. Kant's sense of the boundaries among historical/philological work, theological construction, and a philosophical examination of religion receives its fullest expression several years later in his *Conflict of the Faculties*, trans. Mary J. Gregor (Lincoln and London: University of Nebraska Press, 1992).

12 Kant, *Religion*, p. 11.

13 *Ibid.*, p. 122, emphasis Kant's.

14 In fact, it was the vividly polemical tone of Kant's "Concluding Remark" to his "On the Failure of All Attempted Philosophical Theodicies," published in 1791, that raised Kant's profile in the censor's office in Berlin and insured close scrutiny of his work. Having been reorganized along much more repressive lines following the death of Frederick the Great in 1786, with the anti-Enlightenment pastor Johann Wollner replacing the liberal von Zedlitz in 1788, the Prussian censor's office laid down strict new rules regarding the conformity of all teaching and writing with strict biblical guidelines. Kant's "Concluding Remark" of 1791 makes veiled but unmistakable references to the edict promulgating the new guidelines. "He who says to himself (or to God; in matters of religion this amounts to the same thing) that he believes something, without having perhaps given a single look at himself to ascertain whether he is indeed certain, or certain up to a point, of this conviction, tells a lie, and his lie is not only the most stupid one before the One who searches the heart, but it is also the most criminal one because it cuts under the ground of sincerity, the basis of every virtue. . . . It is easy to see how such blind and exterior *confessions* (easily accompanied by an equally untrue inner confession) can bring about progressively, especially if they are the source of worldly advantages, a certain duplicity in everyone's way of thinking." Kant, "On the Failure of All Attempted Philosophical Theodicies," translated by Michel Despland in Despland, *op. cit.*, pp. 294–5, emphasis Kant's. See the discussions in Bernard M. G. Reardon, *Kant as Philosophical Theologian* (London: Macmillan Press, 1988), pp. 80–3; and Allen Wood, "General Introduction," Kant, *Religion and Rational Theology*, trans. and ed. Wood and George Di Giovanni (Cambridge: Cambridge University Press, 1996), pp. xv–xxii. Kant provides his own very interesting summary of the confrontation with the censor's office, including the text of

Wollner's letter accusing him of "misusing" his philosophy "to distort and disparage many of the cardinal and basic teachings of the Holy Scriptures and of Christianity," in the "Preface" to *The Conflict of the Faculties*, pp. 8–21, published five years after the appearance of the *Religion*.

15 For a more extensive account of Kant's theory of radical evil, see my previous work, *Fallen Freedom: Kant on Radical Evil and Moral Regeneration* (Cambridge: Cambridge University Press, 1990). Other helpful sources include Emil Fackenheim, "Kant and Radical Evil," University of Toronto Quarterly 23 (1954); Olivier Reboul, *Kant et le Problème du Mal* (Montréal: Presses de l'université de Montréal, 1971); Jean-Louis Bruch, La Philosophie religieuse de Kant (Paris: Aubier, 1968); and Allen W. Wood, *Kant's Moral Religion* (Ithaca and London: Cornell University Press, 1970). The passing of the 200th anniversary of the publication of Kant's *Religion* occasioned the publication of a collection of essays that set Kant's theory of radical evil in the context of contemporary psychoanalytic theory. See Joan Copjec (ed.), *Radical Evil* (London and New York: Verso, 1996).

16 Kant, *Religion*, pp. 21–34.

17 *Ibid.*, p. 28.

18 See my account of the unfathomable "ground" of moral evil in Kant in "The Inscrutability of Moral Evil in Kant," *The Thomist* 51 (1987), pp. 246–69.

19 Kant, *Religion*, p. 3l. Kant's account of the "subordination" of one sort of incentive to another in the process of maxim-making is his clearest account of the fact that, for him, moral evil is not the "absence" of the moral incentive. As Kant puts it, the "difference between a good man and one who is evil cannot lie in the difference between the incentives which they adopt into their maxim (not in the content of the maxim), but rather must depend upon *subordination* (the form of the maxim), *i.e., which of the two incentives he makes the condition of the other*," emphasis Kant's. In terms of the distinction between *Wille* and *Willkür* I discussed in ch. 3, Kant is suggesting that the rational capacity to respect the moral law is never completely extinguished, even in the most wicked person. Among other things, this claim makes it possible on Kantian grounds always to hold an evil-doer responsible for his or her behavior as well as responsible in principle for undergoing a moral reformation. Moreover, Kant's emphasis here on the "form" rather than the "content" of the maxim is consistent with the general tendency of his moral theory to discern the formal qualities of moral agency.

20 *Ibid.*, p. 26.

21 *Ibid.*, pp. 27–8, 32. Kant's account of the moral "disposition" in the *Religion* is a significant fresh development in his moral theory, suggesting that he was sensitive to potential problems within his earlier accounts of moral agency in the *Foundations* and the second *Critique*. See Henry E. Allison, Kant's *Theory of Freedom* (Cambridge: Cambridge University Press, 1990), pp. 136–45.

22 Kant, *Religion*, p. 32, emphasis Kant's.

23 Sharon Anderson-Gold, "Kant's Rejection of Devilishness: The Limits of Human Volition," *Idealistic Studies* 14 (1984), pp. 35–48.

24 Kant, *Religion*, p. 86, emphasis Kant's.

25 *Ibid.*, emphasis Kant's.

26   This is, for example, the view of Y. Yovel, *Kant and the Philosophy of History* (Princeton: Princeton University Press, 1980).
27   Kant, *Religion*, p. 4.
28   *Ibid.*, pp. 4–5.
29   This point has potentially important implications for Allen Wood's well-known defense of a necessary tie between theism and Kant's moral theory. Since Wood's view is heavily dependent on his reading of the concept of the highest good in the *Critique of Practical Reason*, any alteration in the terms of the highest good would warrant a reevaluation of Wood's interpretation. Allen Wood, *Kant's Moral Religion*.
30   Kant, *Religion*, p. 86.
31   See my effort to distinguish and clarify the two in "The Problem of Salvation in Kant's *Religion within the Limits of Reason Alone*," *International Philosophical Quarterly* 37 (1997), pp. 319–28. A very helpful discussion of the individual's relation to corporate salvation that also includes insights into the problem of God's relation to the ethical commonwealth is offered by Sharon Anderson-Gold, "God and Community: An Inquiry into the Religious Implications of the Highest Good," in Philip J. Rossi and Michael Wreen (eds), *Kant's Philosophy of Religion Reconsidered* (Bloomington and Indianapolis: Indiana University Press, 1991), pp. 113–31.
32   Kant, *Religion*, p. 18, emphasis Kant's.
33   *Ibid.*, p. 43, emphasis and biblical references Kant's.
34   *Ibid.*
35   *Ibid.*, p. 115.
36   *Ibid.*, pp. 97, 106. How this historical "gradualism" can be reconciled with the atemporal nature of the noumenal locus of freedom and, thus, of morality itself is a deep problem never fully addressed by Kant. Indeed, beginning with "The History of Pure Reason" with which the first *Critique* concludes, Kant's philosophy badly needs some sort of splice between the worlds of "is" and "ought" that might account for the idea of moral "progress" which permeates his outlook. An interesting attempt to locate the needed splice in Kant's account of reflective judgment in the *Critique of Judgement* is offered by Adina Davidovich, *Religion as a Province of Meaning* (Minneapolis: Fortress Press, 1993).
37   "The history of the human race as a whole can be regarded as the realisation of a hidden plan of nature to bring about an internally – and for this purpose also externally – perfect political constitution as the only possible state within which all natural capacities of mankind can be developed completely." Kant, "Idea for a Universal History with a Cosmopolitan Purpose," trans. H. B. Nisbet in Hans Reiss (ed.), *Kant: Political Writings* (Cambridge: Cambridge University Press, 1991), p. 50.
38   Kant, *Religion*, pp. 21–3. For further discussion, see Michalson, *Fallen Freedom*, pp. 37ff.
39   Kant, *Religion*, p. 22, emphasis Kant's.
40   *Ibid.*, emphasis Kant's.
41   Sharon Anderson-Gold, "Kant's Ethical Commonwealth: The Highest Good as a Social Goal," *International Philosophical Quarterly* 26 (1986), p. 25.
42   Kant, "Idea for a Universal History with a Cosmopolitan Purpose," p. 44.
43   *Ibid.*

44 *Ibid.*, pp. 44–5, emphasis Kant's. Judith Shklar offers a nice summary of Kant's strategy here: "Clearly Kant meant to circumvent Machiavelli's argument that because men are evil they should be ruled by princes of his special kind. Since Kant knew most men to be as Machiavelli pictured them, he had to evade his conclusions, if he was to justify free government. Men are always ready for free institutions if the latter do not depend on virtue, if they are fueled by selfish impulses properly balanced, just as Madison had explained." Shklar, *Ordinary Vices* (Cambridge, MA and London: Harvard University Press, 1984), p. 234.

45 W. H. Walsh has pointed out that there is an implicit tension between Kant's notion of the "unsocial sociability of men" and the rational hope that we participate together with God in the promotion of the highest good. The doctrine of the highest good, Walsh reminds us, reflects the moral agent's need for assurance "that his own moral efforts will not be in vain," but the assurance introduced by the idea of the unsocial sociability of men "is that other people's selfish actions may unwittingly turn out to have good results. So far from encouraging the virtuous to persist in their moral aims, this could tempt them to abandon them altogether, secure in the conviction that God will make everything right in the end." Walsh, *Kant's Criticism of Metaphysics* (Chicago and London: University of Chicago Press, 1975), p. 235.

46 Kant, *Religion*, p. 88, emphasis Kant's.

47 *Ibid.*, p. 22.

48 Pierre Hassner, "Immanuel Kant," in Leo Strauss and Joseph Cropsey (eds), *History of Political Philosophy*, 3rd edn (Chicago and London: University of Chicago Press, 1987), p. 592.

49 Anderson-Gold, "Kant's Ethical Commonwealth," p. 25.

50 Kant, *Religion*, p. 89, emphasis added. For helpful additional perspective, see Philip J. Rossi, "Autonomy and Community: The Social Character of Kant's 'Moral Faith,'" *The Modern Schoolman* 61 (1984), pp. 169–86.

51 Yovel, *op. cit.*, pp. 29, 72.

52 Anderson-Gold, "Kant's Ethical Commonwealth," p. 24.

53 E.g., Kant, *Practical*, p. 113: "Consequently, though the highest good may be the entire *object* of a pure practical reason, i.e., of a pure will, it is still not to be taken as the *determining ground* of the pure will; the moral law alone must be seen as the ground for making the highest good and its realization or promotion the object of the pure will," emphasis Kant's.

54 *Ibid.*, p. 129, emphasis Kant's.

55 Kant, *Religion*, p. 5. See also p. 130.

56 In discussing the highest good, Kant in fact distinguishes between "highest" understood as "supreme" (*supremum*) or understood as "perfect" (*consummatum*): the former simply yields virtue, while the latter yields virtue proportioned with happiness (*Practical*, pp. 114ff.). Obviously, it is the second sense that leaves the moral agent in a difficult – perhaps impossible – situation, just as it is the second sense that puts momentum into Kant's moral argument for the existence of God. For further analysis of this ambiguity in the term "highest," see my article "The Non-Moral Element in Kant's Moral Proof of the Existence of God," *Scottish Journal of Theology* 39 (1986), pp. 501–15.

57 Lewis White Beck, *A Commentary on Kant's Critique of Practical Reason* (Chicago and London: University of Chicago Press, 1960), pp. 244–5, emphasis Beck's. A particularly forceful argument against the relevance of the highest good as a source of moral motivation is offered by Thomas Auxter, "The Unimportance of Kant's Highest Good," *Journal of the History of Philosophy* 17 (1979), pp. 121–34.
58 Yovel, *op. cit.*, pp. 72, 74, emphasis Yovel's.
59 Kant, *Religion*, p. 89.
60 *Ibid.*, p. 32, emphasis Kant's.
61 *Ibid.*, p. 40.
62 *Ibid.*, pp. 40–1. For further discussion, see Michalson, *Fallen Freedom*, ch. 5.
63 Michalson, *Fallen Freedom*, pp. 95ff.
64 Kant, *Religion*, p. 89.
65 *Ibid.*
66 *Ibid.*, p. 89. One could say that in this aspect of his thinking, Kant is trying to solve the problem of how autonomous rational agents can create a genuine community that, far from infringing on individual autonomy, actually fulfills it. With some slight modifications – beginning with the replacement of "autonomy" by "authenticity" – this Kantian project finds an interesting contemporary parallel in the recent work of Charles Taylor, *The Ethics of Authenticity* (Cambridge, MA and London: Harvard University Press, 1991), even as Taylor tries to overcome what he takes to be the limitations of the sort of liberalism that we associate with a contemporary Kantian such as John Rawls.
67 In *The General Will Before Rousseau* (Princeton: Princeton University Press, 1986), Patrick Riley convincingly describes the historical trajectory of this transformation leading up, not only to Rousseau, but to Kant and Hegel and well.
68 Yirmiahu Yovel, "The God of Kant," *Scripta Hierosolymitana* XX (1968), p. 121.
69 Kant, *Religion*, p. 130, emphasis Kant's.
70 Susan Neiman, *The Unity of Reason* (New York and Oxford: Oxford University Press, 1994), p. 178. Referring to an unresolved "tension" in Kant's thought, Neiman argues that a complete secularization of religious belief is for him finally impossible, because of the ultimate gap between reason and nature. "If the need to find reason in the world itself seems outdated, Kant's acknowledgment that we cannot do so is deeply modern. And it is this acknowledgment that is missed by the attempt to view the Highest Good in purely secular terms. Nothing else in Kant's work exposes so clearly the gap that he believes to separate reason from nature. Morality, the product of pure practical reason, is free of all natural conditions, happiness is wholly dependent on the natural world. Our desire to become the authors of our own happiness is a desire to overcome that separation. But despite suggestions to the contrary, Kant's notion of the Highest Good is not a means by which to do so. ... Rational faith is the means that permits us to live with the consciousness of this separation, allowing us to hope that the world will become a place more appropriate to reason's needs." *Ibid.*, pp. 178–9.
71 Kant, *Religion*, p. 90.
72 *Ibid.*, pp. 90–1, emphasis Kant's.

73 *Ibid.*, pp. 43, 60–1.
74 *Ibid.*, p. 90, emphasis Kant's.
75 *Ibid.*
76 *Ibid.*, p. 6n.
77 Roger Sullivan, *Immanuel Kant's Moral Theory* (Cambridge: Cambridge University Press, 1989), p. 217.
78 Schneewind, "Voluntarism and the Foundations of Ethics," in *Proceedings and Addresses of the American Philosophical Association* 70.2 (1996), pp. 34ff.
79 Kant, *Religion*, p. 91n.
80 Kant, *Judgement*, p. 125, emphasis Kant's.
81 Kant, *Religion*, p. 89.
82 The undeveloped nature of Kant's *Opus Postumum* makes it difficult to consider in much detail the alternative possibilities embedded in Kant's observation in that context that *"a being which has only rights and no duties is God. . . .* The concept of God is . . . the concept of a being that can *obligate all moral beings* without itself [being] obligated, and, hence, has rightful power over them all. . . . A being which is never obligated, but would be obligating for every other rational being, is the highest being in a moral sense." Kant, *Opus Postumum*, trans. Eckart Förster and Michael Rosen (Cambridge: Cambridge University Press, 1993), pp. 203, 207, emphasis Kant's. Such a conception of God would seem to contradict the notion, characteristic of the *Religion*, that God is a fellow member of the ethical commonwealth.
83 Kant, *Foundations*, p. 5.
84 Schneewind, *The Invention of Autonomy* (Cambridge: Cambridge University Press, 1998), pp. 510–11. In his reconstruction of the history lying behind Kant's claim in the *Foundations* that it is "self-evident" that God and humanity fall under the same moral obligation, Schneewind (p. 511) remarks that, in light of the highly controversial nature of this idea in the eighteenth century, Kant "might have argued" for such a position, but "it is surely surprising that he could have thought" such an idea self-evident. "An unquestioned assumption that the moral community must include God would, however, make it seem self-evident to him that there must be a moral law that applies to all rational beings, not to humans only, and a pure a priori moral philosophy to explain it. Kant is plainly making that assumption."
85 In arguing flatly that Kant simply "renounces the postulate of the immortality of the soul" in the *Religion*, Yovel adds that it "should be renounced by Kant in *any* case. For if virtue is not a holy will but a good disposition in conflict – and the adversary in this conflict is always the natural inclinations – then the attainment of virtue would also require the immortality of the *body*, a strange Schellingian notion that could never have entered Kant's mind." Yovel, "The God of Kant," pp. 116–17.

Chapter 6   Conclusion

1 Robert Pippin, *Modernism as a Philosophical Problem* (Oxford: Blackwell, 1991), p. 8.

2   Jürgen Habermas, *The Philosophical Discourse of Modernity*, trans. Frederick Lawrence (Cambridge, MA: The MIT Press, 1987), p. 302, emphasis added.

3   Dieter Henrich, "The Concept of Moral Insight and Kant's Doctrine of the Fact of Reason," trans. Manfred Kuehn, in Henrich, *The Unity of Reason: Essays on Kant's Philosophy*, ed. Richard Velkley (Cambridge, MA and London: Harvard University Press, 1994), p. 80.

4   Hans Blumenberg, *The Legitimacy of the Modern Age*, trans. Robert M. Wallace (Cambridge, MA and London: The MIT Press, 1983), p. 59.

5   Michel Despland, *Kant on History and Religion* (Montreal and London: McGill-Queen's University Press, 1973), p. 3. Despland is here summarizing the results of the work early in the twentieth century of Hermann Schmalenbach, who attempted to explain Kant's religious outlook by means of Rudolf Otto's recently published *The Idea of the Holy*. It is of more than passing interest that Despland's list of the features characterizing Schmalenbach's account of Kant's "religiousness" includes Kant's "sense of the *deus absconditus*," presumably a way of referring to the absent God who leaves us to work out our own moral fate. Schmalenbach "documented the kinship of Kant's piety with that of the Old Testament and of Calvinism . . . [and] established that Kant's personal religiousness is not rooted in the Enlightenment." Despland concludes: "Nothing has since come to refute the main body of Schmalenbach's conclusions." Whatever the merits of this view, my own approach to Kant obviously depends upon a distinction between the non-religious implications of his actual philosophical position and the lingering pietistic quality of his overall sensibility. If one picks up the arguments in isolation from the sensibility, the non-theistic implications of his outlook are easier to trace – though of course something profoundly important about the man himself is lost.

6   Susan Neiman, *The Unity of Reason: Rereading Kant* (New York and Oxford: Oxford University Press, 1994), p. 178.

7   Kant, *Religion*, p. 3.

8   Bernard Yack, *The Longing for Total Revolution: Philosophic Sources of Social Discontent from Rousseau to Marx and Nietzsche* (Berkeley: University of California Press, 1986), p. 99.

9   Blumenberg, *The Legitimacy of the Modern Age*, p. 78.

10   J. B. Schneewind, *The Invention of Autonomy: A History of Modern Moral Philosophy* (Cambridge: Cambridge University Press, 1998), p. 512.

11   "First, let us consider the inner man to see how a righteous, free, and pious Christian, that is, a spiritual, new, and inner man, becomes what he is. It is evident that no external thing has any influence in producing Christian righteousness or freedom, or in producing unrighteousness or servitude." Martin Luther, "The Freedom of a Christian," trans. W. A. Lambert and Harold J. Grimm, in John Dillenberger (ed.), *Martin Luther: Selections from His Writings* (Garden City, New York: Anchor Books, 1961), pp. 53–4. See the comments linking Luther and Kant in Howard Caygill, *A Kant Dictionary* (Oxford: Blackwell, 1995), p. 88.

12   Karl Marx, *The German Ideology*, ed. C. J. Arthus (New York: International Publishers, 1970), p. 97.

13   Dick Howard, *From Marx to Kant* (Albany: State University of New York Press, 1985).

14 "The rejection of theodicy is the first condition of emancipation. From this point of view, [Kant's] secularization of the Highest Good is part of the general secularization of human ideals that took place during the Enlightenment and reached its height in Feuerbach and Marx." Neiman, *op. cit.*, p. 178.

15 Garrett Green, "Kant as Christian Apologist: The Failure of Accommodationist Theology," *Pro Ecclesia* IV (1995), p. 302.

16 David Tracy, "Lindbeck's New Program for Theology: A Reflection," *The Thomist* 49 (1985), p. 465.

17 For a very helpful analysis of this experiential dimension and some of its implications, see Wayne Proudfoot, *Religious Experience* (Berkeley: University of California Press, 1985). I should add that, although Kant and Schleiermacher share a general commitment to theological mediation, their relationship is quite complex. A helpful guide to this relationship is Richard Crouter's "Introduction" to his translation of Schleiermacher, *On Religion: Speeches to Its Cultured Despisers* (Cambridge: Cambridge University Press, 1996), pp. 1–73, esp. pp. 18ff.

18 Hans W. Frei, *The Identity of Jesus Christ* (Philadelphia: Fortress Press, 1975), p. xi, emphasis added.

19 A particularly powerful example of the subversion of the Cartesian–Kantian conception of selfhood within contemporary feminist thought is the work of Mary Daly. While, by her own account, Daly's radical standpoint has now moved well beyond its original philosophical and theological context, portions of her work exemplify how, for some, privatistic accounts of selfhood and faith would become part of the problem, rather than the natural and inevitable conceptuality for framing the mediating project. See, for example, Daly's development of the relationship between modes of being and modes of knowing in *Beyond God the Father: Toward a Philosophy of Women's Liberation* (Boston: Beacon Press, 1973) and *Pure Lust: Elemental Feminist Philosophy* (Boston: Beacon Press, 1984), esp. ch. 4.

20 Two studies of Kant that link him with suspicions of our embodied nature are Robin May Schott, *Cognition and Eros: A Critique of the Kantian Paradigm* (Boston: Beacon Press, 1988), and Susan Meld Shell, *The Embodiment of Reason: Kant on Spirit, Generation, and Community* (Chicago and London: University of Chicago Press, 1996). Portions of this part of my discussion are adapted from my article "Cartesianism," in Alister McGrath (ed.), *The Blackwell Encyclopedia of Modern Christian Thought* (Oxford: Blackwell, 1993), pp. 67–71.

21 Cornel West, "The Politics of American Neo-Pragmatism," in West and John Rajchman (eds), *Post-Analytic Philosophy* (New York: Columbia University Press, 1985), pp. 268–9.

22 Drawing from Foucault's work, Sharon Welch develops the connections between the hermeneutical insights of liberation theology and the power/knowledge nexus in a particularly clear way. Welch, *Communities of Resistance and Solidarity: A Feminist Theology of Liberation* (Maryknoll, New York: Orbis Books, 1985), esp. ch. 2. See also the collection of essays in Rebecca S. Chopp and Sheila Greeve Davaney (eds), *Horizons in Feminist Theology: Identity, Tradition, and Norms* (Minneapolis: Fortress Press, 1997).

23 See, for example, Elisabeth Schüssler-Fiorenza, *In Memory of Her: A Feminist Reconstruction of Christian Origins* (New York: Crossroad Publishing Company, 1983); Jon Sobrino, *Christology at the Crossroads: A Latin American Approach* (Maryknoll, New York: Orbis Books, 1978). Still very helpful as a general introduction to Latin American liberation theology is the classic work of Gustavo Gutierrez, *A Theology of Liberation*, trans. Sister Caridad Inda and John Eagleson (Maryknoll, New York: Orbis, 1971, 2nd rev. edn, 1988).

24 On the other hand, the extent to which Kant's concept of the ethical commonwealth might be a resource for politically charged theologies remains largely unexplored. Given my reading of the ethical commonwealth as Kant's implicit way of transforming the otherworldliness of the postulate of immortality into a this-worldly concern for morally enhanced historical existence, the connection with the aims of liberation theology is not altogether far-fetched – though, obviously, the liberal individualism of Kant's position would have to be nudged in a more communitarian direction.

25 These sorts of attacks on the Cartesian–Kantian tradition are in many ways the spin-off effects of the tradition's own distintegration from within. By this I mean to refer to the way Continental thought generated its own self-criticism through the writings of Nietzsche, the phenomenology of Husserl, and the several moments in the philosophy of Heidegger. For many of those influenced by this internal criticism, the Cartesian–Kantian subject needs to be "de-centered" in the name of a more general ontology not so closely tied to a misleading preoccupation with personal consciousness and philosophical anthropology. In its more recent, radical forms, associated particularly with the work of Jacques Derrida, this post-Heideggerian position "deconstructs" the very notion of a "subject" and utterly subverts the Cartesian motif of "representation," producing revolutionary results for biblical interpretation. With neither a "subject" behind it, nor the capacity to "represent" either truths or meanings, the biblical text can have no "message" in the traditional sense. The very idea of the text existing in relation to a reality external to it is placed in jeopardy, along with the classic conception of ontology that gave traditional theism its framing context.

26 George Lindbeck, *The Nature of Doctrine: Religion and Theology in a Postliberal Age* (Philadelphia: Westminster Press, 1984). See the summary of the loose grouping of theologians identified with postliberal theology in Sheila Greeve Davaney and Delwin Brown, "Postliberalism," in *The Blackwell Encyclopedia of Modern Christian Thought*, ed. Alister E. McGrath, pp. 453–6.

27 An especially good example of Wittgenstein's debunking of a certain kind of epistemological skepticism is the work translated as *On Certainty*, trans. Denis Paul and G. E. M. Anscombe, ed. Anscombe and G. H. von Wright (New York: Harper and Row, 1969).

28 Though not usually grouped with the postliberals, Fergus Kerr has similarly adapted Wittgenstein's philosophy in order to subvert what he takes to be misleading conceptions of selfhood informing much modern theology. Kerr, *Theology after Wittgenstein* (Oxford: Blackwell, 1986).

29 Lindbeck, *op. cit.*, p. 33.

30 *Ibid.*, p. 34.

31   In Lindbeck's case, the fate of the motifs of "inner" and "outer" is made even more complex by his adaptation of arguments drawn from cultural anthropology, especially the well-known work of Clifford Geertz. See especially Lindbeck's account of what he calls a "cultural–linguistic" view of religion which places priority on what is "outside" the believer. Ibid., pp. 32ff.

32   Ibid., p. 132.

33   Ibid., p. 118. For a powerful extension of the idea of theology viewed as "Christian self-description," understood in relation to varying philosophical commitments and varying degrees of reliance on philosophical anthropology, see Hans W. Frei, Types of Christian Theology, ed. George Hunsinger and William C. Placher (New Haven and London: Yale University Press, 1992), chs 3–4. Frei's work has been highly influential in the emergence of a postliberal theological program, and his magisterial work, The Eclipse of Biblical Narrative (New Haven and London: Yale University Press, 1974), informs postliberal theology's insights into biblical hermeneutics in significant ways.

34   Lindbeck, op. cit., p. 34.

35   E.g., ibid., pp. 33–4.

36   Ibid., pp. 130–1.

37   Schubert M. Ogden, The Reality of God (New York: Harper and Row, 1966), pp. 20, 37, 140.

38   David Tracy, Blessed Rage for Order: The New Pluralism in Theology (New York: The Seabury Press, 1975), p. 34. Tracy's views have evolved considerably since the publication of this work, yet it is clear that he continues to maintain a fundamental commitment to mediation, in contrast, say, to Lindbeck.

39   Ibid., p. 33.

40   David Tracy, "Lindbeck's New Program for Theology: A Reflection," p. 465. See my more extended effort to clarify what is at stake in the relation between Lindbeck and Tracy, "The Response to Lindbeck," Modern Theology 4 (1988), pp. 107–20.

41   The most sustained effort to demonstrate this shift in perspective through an exercise in biblical interpretation probably remains Hans W. Frei, The Identity of Jesus Christ.

42   It should be noted that Lindbeck does not reject apologetics outright, saying that "a postliberal approach need not exclude an ad hoc apologetics, but only one that is systematically prior and controlling in the fashion of post-Cartesian natural theology and of later liberalism." Lindbeck, op. cit., pp. 131–2. For an elaboration of just what an "ad hoc" apologetics might be, see William Werpehowski, "Ad Hoc Apologetics," Journal of Religion 66 (1986), pp. 282–301. Relevant here in a provocative way is Brian Gerrish's effort to close the presumed distance between postliberalism and the theology of Schleiermacher. See his essay "Nature and the Theater of Redemption: Schleiermacher on Christian Dogmatics and the Creation Story," in Gerrish, Continuing the Reformation: Essays on Modern Religious Thought (Chicago and London: University of Chicago Press, 1993), pp. 196–216, esp. pp. 206ff.

43   An insightful guide to more fundamentally theological issues, offered by one largely sympathetic to the aims of postliberalism, is Kathryn E. Tanner, God

and Creation in Christian Theology: Tyranny or Empowerment (Oxford: Blackwell, 1985).

44 Gerard Loughlin, "Readings of the Bible," a review of Frei's Types of Christian Theology, Times Literary Supplement (February 26, 1993), p. 26.

45 Tracy, for one, insists quite plausibly that the mediating tradition has been much more creative than Lindbeck seems to allow regarding fresh models of selfhood. "Lindbeck's New Program for Theology: A Reflection," pp. 463–4. Tracy's claims on behalf of the mediating tradition's inventiveness with respect to philosophical anthropology has an analogue in Ogden's claims concerning the renewal of metaphysics through the influence of Whitehead and Hartshorne.

46 George Hunsinger, How to Read Karl Barth: The Shape of His Theology (New York and Oxford: Oxford University Press, 1991), p. 35.

47 This has been engagingly argued by Alasdair MacIntyre in "The Debate about God: Victorian Relevance and Contemporary Irrelevance," in MacIntyre and Paul Ricoeur, The Religious Significance of Atheism (New York: Columbia University Press, 1969), pp. 3–55. See also the analysis of problems nagging the liberal project in Van A. Harvey, "The Pathos of Liberal Theology," Journal of Religion 56 (1976), pp. 382–91.

Bibliography

Works by Kant

For a list of Kant's works and the relevant translations, see the notes to chapter 1.

Other Works

Allison, Henry E., *Idealism and Freedom: Essays on Kant's Theoretical and Practical Philosophy* (Cambridge: Cambridge University Press, 1996).

——, *Kant's Theory of Freedom* (Cambridge: Cambridge University Press, 1990).

——, *Kant's Transcendental Idealism: An Interpretation and Defense* (New Haven and London: Yale University Press, 1983).

——, *Lessing and the Enlightenment* (Ann Arbor: University of Michigan Press, 1966).

Ameriks, Karl, "Kant's Deduction of Freedom and Morality," *Journal of the History of Philosophy* 19 (1981), pp. 53–79.

Ameriks, Karl and Dieter Sturma (eds), *The Modern Subject: Conceptions of the Self in Classical German Philosophy* (Albany: State University of New York Press, 1995).

Anderson-Gold, Sharon, "God and Community: An Inquiry into the Religious Implications of the Highest Good," in Rossi and Wreen (eds), pp. 113–31.

——, "Kant's Ethical Commonwealth: The Highest Good as a Social Goal," *International Philosophical Quarterly* 26 (1986), pp. 23–32.

——, "Kant's Rejection of Devilishness: The Limits of Human Volition," *Idealistic Studies* 14 (1984), pp. 35–48.

Arendt, Hannah, *The Life of the Mind* (New York and London: Harcourt Brace Jovanovich, 1978).

Aune, Bruce, *Kant's Theory of Morals* (Princeton: Princeton University Press, 1979).

Auxter, Thomas, "The Unimportance of Kant's Highest Good," *Journal of the History of Philosophy* 17 (1979), pp. 121–34.

Barth, Karl, "An Introductory Essay," Ludwig Feuerbach, *The Essence of Christianity*, trans. George Eliot (New York: Harper and Row, 1957).

——, *Protestant Thought from Rousseau to Ritschl*, trans. Brian Cozens (New York: Simon and Schuster, 1969).

——, "Rudolf Bultmann: An Attempt to Understand Him," *Kerygma and Myth*, Vol. 2, trans. Reginald H. Fuller, ed. Hans Werner Bartsch (London: SPCK, 1962).

Beck, Lewis White, *A Commentary on Kant's Critique of Practical Reason* (Chicago and London: University of Chicago Press, 1960).

——, *Early German Philosophy: Kant and His Predecessors* (Cambridge, MA and London: Harvard University Press, 1969).

——, "Kant's Two Conceptions of the Will in Their Political Context," in Beiner and Booth (eds), pp. 38–49.

Beiner, Ronald and William James Booth (eds), *Kant and Political Philosophy: The Contemporary Legacy* (New Haven and London: Yale University Press, 1993).

Beiser, Frederick C., *The Fate of Reason: German Philosophy from Kant to Fichte* (Cambridge, MA and London: Harvard University Press, 1987).

——, *The Sovereignty of Reason: The Defense of Rationality in the Early English Enlightenment* (Princeton: Princeton University Press, 1996).

Bennett, Jonathan, *Kant's Dialectic* (Cambridge: Cambridge University Press, 1974).

Berg, Jonathan, "How Could Ethics Depend on Religion?," in *A Companion to Ethics*, ed. Peter Singer (Oxford: Blackwell, 1991), pp. 525–33.

Bernstein, J. M., *The Philosophy of the Novel: Lukács, Marxism and the Dialectics of Form* (Minneapolis: University of Minnesota Press, 1984).

Blumenberg, Hans, *The Legitimacy of the Modern Age*, trans. Robert M. Wallace (Cambridge, MA and London: The MIT Press, 1983).

Bohatec, Josef, *Die Religionsphilosophie Kants in der "Religion innerhalb der Grenzen der blossen Vernunft"* (Hildesheim: Georg Olms, 1966).

Bowie, Andrew, *Schelling and Modern European Philosophy* (London and New York: Routledge, 1993).

Bruch, Jean-Louis, *La Philosophie religieuse de Kant* (Paris: Aubier, 1968).

Buckley, Michael J., S.J., *At the Origins of Modern Atheism* (New Haven and London: Yale University Press, 1987).

Carnois, Bernard, *The Coherence of Kant's Doctrine of Freedom*, trans. David Booth (Chicago and London: University of Chicago Press, 1987).

Cascardi, Anthony J., *The Subject of Modernity* (Cambridge: Cambridge University Press, 1992).

Cassirer, Ernst, *Kant's Life and Thought*, trans. James Haden (New Haven and London: Yale University Press, 1981).

——, *The Philosophy of the Enlightenment*, trans. Fritz C. A. Koelln and James P. Pettegrove (Princeton: Princeton University Press, 1951).

Caygill, Howard, "Kant and the Kingdom," in *Post-Secular Philosophy: Between Philosophy and Theology*, ed. Phillip Blond (London and New York: Routledge, 1998), pp. 107–15.

——, *A Kant Dictionary* (Oxford: Blackwell, 1995).

Collins, James, *The Emergence of Philosophy of Religion* (New Haven and London: Yale University Press, 1967).

——, *God in Modern Philosophy* (Chicago: Regnery, 1959).

Connerton, Paul, *The Tragedy of Enlightenment: An Essay on the Frankfurt School* (Cambridge: Cambridge University Press, 1980).

Copleston, Frederick, S.J., *A History of Philosophy*, Vol. 6, Part II (Garden City: Image Books, 1964).

Crouter, Richard, "Introduction," Friedrich Schleiermacher, *On Religion: Speeches to Its Cultured Despisers*, trans. and ed. Crouter (Cambridge: Cambridge University Press, 1996), pp. 1–73.

Cushman, Robert E., "Barth's Attack upon Cartesianism and the Future in Theology," *Journal of Religion* 36 (1956), pp. 207–24.

Davaney, Sheila Greeve and Delwin Brown, "Postliberalism," in McGrath (ed.), pp. 453–6.

Davidovich, Adina, *Religion as a Province of Meaning* (Minneapolis: Fortress Press, 1993).

Despland, Michel, *Kant on History and Religion* (Montreal and London: McGill-Queen's University Press, 1973).

Dickey, Laurence, *Hegel: Religion, Economics, and the Politics of Spirit, 1770–1807* (Cambridge: Cambridge University Press, 1987).

Eagleton, Terry, *The Ideology of the Aesthetic* (Oxford: Blackwell, 1990).

England, F. E., *Kant's Conception of God* (London: George Allen and Unwin, 1929).

Engstrom, Stephen and Jennifer Whiting (eds), *Aristotle, Kant, and the Stoics: Rethinking Happiness and Duty* (Cambridge: Cambridge University Press, 1996).

Fackenheim, Emil L., "Immanuel Kant," in Smart, Clayton, Sherry, and Katz (eds), pp. 17–40.

——, "Kant and Radical Evil," *University of Toronto Quarterly* 23 (1954).

Feuerbach, Ludwig, *The Essence of Christianity*, trans. George Eliot (New York: Harper and Row, 1957).

Förster, Eckart, "Introduction," Kant, *Opus Postumum*, trans. Förster and Michael Rosen, ed. Forster (Cambridge: Cambridge University Press, 1993), pp. xv-lv.

——(ed.), *Kant's Transcendental Deductions* (Stanford: Stanford University Press, 1989).

Frei, Hans W., *The Eclipse of Biblical Narrative* (New Haven and London: Yale University Press, 1974).

——, "Feuerbach and Theology," *Journal of the American Academy of Religion* 35 (1967), pp. 250–6.

——, *The Identity of Jesus Christ* (Philadelphia: Fortress Press, 1975).

——, "Niebuhr's Theological Background," in *Faith and Ethics: The Theology of H. Richard Niebuhr*, ed. Paul Ramsey (New York: Harper and Row, 1957), pp. 9–64.

——, *Types of Christian Theology*, ed. George Hunsinger and William C. Placher (New Haven and London: Yale University Press, 1992).

Funkenstein, Amos, *Theology and the Scientific Imagination: From the Middle Ages to the Seventeenth Century* (Princeton: Princeton University Press, 1986).

Gadamer, Hans-Georg, *Hegel's Dialectic*, trans. P. Christopher Smith (New Haven and London: Yale University Press, 1976).

Gerrish, Brian A., *Continuing the Reformation: Essays on Modern Religious Thought* (Chicago and London: University of Chicago Press, 1993).

Gibbons, Sarah L., *Kant's Theory of Imagination* (Oxford: Oxford University Press, 1994).

Glasse, John, "Barth on Feuerbach," *Harvard Theological Review* 57 (1964), pp. 69–96.

Godlove, Terry F., Jr, "Moral Actions, Moral Lives: Kant on Intending the Highest Good," *The Southern Journal of Philosophy* 25 (1987), pp. 49–64.

Goldmann, Lucien, *The Philosophy of the Enlightenment: The Christian Burgess and the Enlightenment*, trans. Henry Maas (Cambridge, MA: The MIT Press, 1973).

Green, Garrett, "Editor's Introduction," J. G. Fichte, *Attempt at a Critique of All Revelation*, trans. Green (Cambridge: Cambridge University Press, 1977).

——, "Kant as Christian Apologist: The Failure of Accommodationist Theology," *Pro Ecclesia* IV (1995), pp. 301–17.

Green, Ronald M., *Kierkegaard and Kant: The Hidden Debt* (Albany: State University of New York Press, 1992).

Gregor, Mary, "Translator's Introduction" to Kant, *Metaphysics of Morals* (Cambridge: Cambridge University Press, 1991).

Guyer, Paul (ed.), *The Cambridge Companion to Kant* (Cambridge: Cambridge University Press, 1992).

——, "Thought and Being: Hegel's Critique of Kant's Theoretical Philosophy," in *The Cambridge Companion to Hegel*, ed. Frederick C. Beiser (Cambridge: Cambridge University Press, 1993), pp. 171–210.

Habermas, Jürgen, *The Philosophical Discourse of Modernity*, trans. Frederick Lawrence (Cambridge, MA: The MIT Press, 1987).

Hacking, Ian, *The Emergence of Probability* (Cambridge: Cambridge University Press, 1975).

Harvey, Van A., *Feuerbach and the Interpretation of Religion* (Cambridge: Cambridge University Press, 1995).

——, "The Pathos of Liberal Theology," *Journal of Religion* 56 (1976), pp. 382–91.

Hassner, Pierre, "Immanual Kant," in *History of Political Philosophy*, 3rd edn, ed. Leo Strauss and Joseph Cropsey (Chicago and London: University of Chicago Press, 1987), pp. 581–621.

Hegel, G. W. F., *Early Theological Writings*, trans. T. M. Knox (Philadelphia: University of Pennsylvania Press, 1971).

Henrich, Dieter, *Aesthetic Judgment and the Moral Image of the World* (Stanford: Stanford University Press, 1992).

——, "Hutcheson und Kant," *Kant-Studien* 49 (1957–8), pp. 49–69.

——, *The Unity of Reason: Essays on Kant's Philosophy*, trans. Jeffrey Edwards, Louis Hunt, Manfred Kuehn, and Guenter Zoeller, ed. Richard Velkley (Cambridge, MA and London: Harvard University Press, 1994).

Herman, Barbara, *The Practice of Moral Judgment* (Cambridge, MA and London: Harvard University Press, 1993).

Hill, Thomas E., Jr, *Autonomy and Self-Respect* (Cambridge: Cambridge University Press, 1991).

——, *Dignity and Practical Reason in Kant's Moral Theory* (Ithaca and London: Cornell University Press, 1992).

Höffe, Otfried, *Immanuel Kant*, trans. Marshall Farrier (Albany: State University of New York Press, 1994).

Howard, Dick, *From Marx to Kant* (Albany: State University of New York Press, 1985).

Kaufman, Gordon D., *God the Problem* (Cambridge, MA: Harvard University Press, 1972).

Kerford, G. B. and D. E. Walford (trans.), *Kant: Selected Pre-Critical Writings and Correspondence with Beck* (Manchester: University of Manchester Press, 1968).

Kerr, Fergus, *Theology after Wittgenstein* (Oxford: Blackwell, 1986).

Kierkegaard, Soren, *Fear and Trembling*, trans. Howard V. Hong and Edna H. Hong (Princeton: Princeton University Press, 1983).

Körner, Stephen, *Kant* (Middlesex and Baltimore: Penguin Books, 1955).

Korsgaard, Christine, *Creating the Kingdom of Ends* (Cambridge: Cambridge University Press, 1996).

Kroner, Richard, *Kant's Weltanschauung*, trans. John E. Smith (Chicago and London: University of Chicago Press, 1956).

Lauer, Quentin, S. J., *Hegel's Concept of God* (Albany: State University of New York Press, 1982).

Lehmann, Paul, *Ethics in Christian Context* (New York: Harper and Row, 1963).

Levi, Albert, *Philosophy as Social Expression* (Chicago and London: University of Chicago Press, 1974).

Lindbeck, George, *The Nature of Doctrine: Religion and Theology in a Post-liberal Age* (Philadelphia: Westminster Press, 1984).

Loades, Ann L., *Kant and Job's Comforters* (Newcastle upon Tyne: Avero, 1985).

Löwith, Karl, *From Hegel to Nietzsche*, trans. David E. Green (Garden City, New York: Doubleday Anchor Books, 1967).

Lukács, Georg, *The Young Hegel*, trans. Rodney Livingston (Cambridge, MA: The MIT Press, 1976).

Luther, Martin, *On the Bondage of the Will*, trans. J. I. Packer and O. R. Johnston (Westwood, N. J.: Fleming H. Revell, 1957).

MacIntyre, Alasdair, "The Debate about God: Victorian Relevance and Contemporary Irrelevance," in MacIntyre and Paul Ricoeur, *The Religious Significance of Atheism* (New York: Columbia University Press, 1969), pp. 3–55.

——, *A Short History of Ethics* (New York: Macmillan, 1966).

Mariña, Jacqueline, "Kant on Grace: A Reply to his Critics," *Religious Studies* 33 (1997), pp. 379–400.

Marx, Karl, *The German Ideology*, ed. C. J. Arthus (New York: International Publishers, 1970).

Masterson, Patrick, *Atheism and Alienation* (Middlesex: Penguin Books, 1973).

McCarthy, Thomas, "Introduction," in Habermas, pp. vii–xvii.

McCarthy, Vincent A., *Quest for a Philosophical Jesus: Christianity and Philosophy in Rousseau, Kant, Hegel, and Schelling* (Macon, Georgia: Mercer University Press, 1986).

McCormack, Bruce, *Karl Barth's Critically Realistic Dialectical Theology: Its Genesis and Development, 1909–1936* (New York and Oxford: Oxford University Press, 1995).

McGrath, Alister E. (ed.), *The Blackwell Encyclopedia of Modern Christian Thought* (Oxford: Blackwell, 1993).

Meerbote, Ralf, "*Wille* and *Willkür* in Kant's Theory of Action," in *Interpreting Kant*, ed. Moltke Gram (Iowa City: University of Iowa Press, 1982).

Michalson, Gordon E., Jr, "Cartesianism," in McGrath (ed.), pp. 67–71.

——, *Fallen Freedom: Kant on Radical Evil and Moral Regeneration* (Cambridge: Cambridge University Press, 1990).

——, *The Historical Dimensions of a Rational Faith: The Role of History in Kant's Religious Thought* (Washington, D.C.: University Press of America, 1977).

——, "The Non-Moral Element in Kant's Moral Proof of the Existence of God," *Scottish Journal of Theology* 39 (1986), pp. 501–15.

——, "The Problem of Salvation in Kant's *Religion within the Limits of Reason Alone*," *International Philosophical Quarterly* 37 (1997), pp. 319–28.

Nagel, Thomas, *The View from Nowhere* (New York and Oxford: Oxford University Press, 1986).

Neiman, Susan, *The Unity of Reason* (New York and Oxford: Oxford University Press, 1994).

Ogden, Schubert M., *Christ without Myth* (New York: Harper and Row, 1961).

——, *The Reality of God* (New York: Harper and Row, 1966).

O'Hagan, Timothy, "On Hegel's Critique of Kant's Moral and Political Philosophy," in Priest (ed.), pp. 135–59.

O'Neill, Onora, *Constructions of Reason: Explorations of Kant's Practical Philosophy* (Cambridge: Cambridge University Press, 1989).

——, "Vindicating Reason," in Guyer (ed.), pp. 280–308.

Outka, Gene, "Religious and Moral Duty: Notes on *Fear and Trembling*," in *Religion and Morality*, ed. Outka and John P. Reeder, Jr (Garden City: Doubleday, 1973), pp. 204–54.

Paton, H. J., *The Categorical Imperative: A Study in Kant's Moral Philosophy* (London: Hutchinson and Co., 1947).

Piper, Adrian S., "Kant on the Objectivity of the Moral Law," in Reath, Herman, and Korsgaard (eds), pp. 240–69.

Pippin, Robert B., *Modernism as a Philosophical Problem* (Oxford: Blackwell, 1991).

Priest, Stephen (ed.), *Hegel's Critique of Kant* (Oxford: Clarendon Press, 1987).

Proudfoot, Wayne, *Religious Experience* (Berkeley: University of California Press, 1985).

Rawls, John, "Kantian Constructivism in Moral Theory," *Journal of Philosophy* 77 (1980), pp. 515–72.

——, "Themes in Kant's Moral Philosophy," in Förster (ed.), pp. 81–113.

Reardon, Bernard M. G., *Kant as Philosophical Theologian* (London: Macmillan Press, 1988).

Reath, Andrews, "Introduction" to Kant, *Critique of Practical Reason*, trans. Mary Gregor (Cambridge: Cambridge University Press, 1997).

——, "Legislating for a Realm of Ends: The Social Dimension of Autonomy," in Reath, Herman, and Korsgaard (eds), pp. 214–39.

Reath, Andrews, Barbara Herman, and Christine M. Korsgaard (eds), *Reclaiming the History of Ethics: Essays for John Rawls* (Cambridge: Cambridge University Press, 1997).

Reboul, Olivier, *Kant et le Problème du Mal* (Montréal: Presses de l'université de Montréal, 1971).

Riley, Patrick, "The Elements of Kant's Practical Philosophy," in Beiner and Booth (eds), pp. 9–37.

——, *The General Will Before Rousseau* (Princeton: Princeton University Press, 1986).

——, *Kant's Political Philosophy* (Totowa, N.J.: Rowman and Littlefield, 1983).

Ritter, Joachim, "Morality and Ethical Life: Hegel's Controversy with Kantian Ethics," in Ritter, *Hegel and the French Revolution: Essays on the Philosophy of Right*, trans. Richard Dien Winfield (Cambridge, MA and London: The MIT Press, 1982).

Rossi, Philip J., "Autonomy and Community: The Social Character of Kant's 'Moral Faith,'" *The Modern Schoolman* 61 (1984), pp. 169–86.

——, *Together Toward Hope: A Journey to Moral Theology* (Notre Dame, IN: University of Notre Dame Press, 1983).

Rossi, Philip J. and Michael Wreen (eds), *Kant's Philosophy of Religion Reconsidered* (Bloomington and Indianapolis: Indiana University Press, 1991).

Sala, Giovanni, *Kant und die Frage nach Gott* (Berlin: Walter de Gruyter, 1989).

Sallis, John, *The Gathering of Reason* (Athens: Ohio University Press, 1980).

Schilpp, Paul Arthur, *Kant's Pre-Critical Ethics*, 2nd edn (Evanston: Northwestern University Press, 1960).

Schneewind, Jerome B., "Autonomy, Obligation, and Virtue: An Overview of Kant's Moral Philosophy," in Guyer (ed.), pp. 309–41.

——, "The Divine Corporation and the History of Ethics," in *Philosophy and History*, ed. Schneewind, Richard Rorty, and Quentin Skinner (Cambridge: Cambridge University Press, 1984), pp. 173–91.

——, *The Invention of Autonomy* (Cambridge: Cambridge University Press, 1998).

——, "Kant and Stoic Ethics," in Engstrom and Whiting (eds), pp. 285–301.

—— (ed.), *Moral Philosophy from Montaigne to Kant*, Vol. 1 (Cambridge: Cambridge University Press, 1990).

——, "Voluntarism and the Foundations of Ethics," *Proceedings and Addresses of the American Philosophical Association* 70.2 (1996), pp. 25–42.

Schott, Robin May, *Cognition and Eros: A Critique of the Kantian Paradigm* (Boston: Beacon Press, 1988).

Schrader, George, "Autonomy, Heteronomy, and Moral Imperatives," in *Foundations of the Metaphysics of Morals, with Critical Essays*, ed. Robert Paul Wolff (Indianapolis and New York: Bobbs-Merrill, 1969), pp. 117–33.

——, "Kant's Presumed Repudiation of the 'Moral Argument' in the *Opus Postumum*: An Examination of Adickes' Interpretation," *Philosophy* XXVI (1951), pp. 228–41.

Shell, Susan Meld, *The Embodiment of Reason* (Chicago and London: University of Chicago Press, 1996).

Shklar, Judith N., *Ordinary Vices* (Cambridge, MA and London: Harvard University Press, 1984).

Silber, John, "The Ethical Significance of Kant's *Religion within the Limits of Reason Alone*," in Kant, *Religion within the Limits of Reason Alone*, trans. and ed. T. M. Greene and H. H. Hudson (New York: Harper and Row, 1960), pp. lxxix–cxlii.

——, "The Importance of the Highest Good in Kant's Ethics," *Ethics* LXXIII (1963), pp. 179–97.

——, "Kant's Conception of the Highest Good as Immanent and Transcendent," *Philosophical Review* LXVII (1959), pp. 469–92.

Smart, Ninian, John Clayton, Patrick Sherry, and Steven T. Katz (eds), *Nineteenth Century Religious Thought in the West*, Vol. 1 (Cambridge: Cambridge University Press, 1985).

Smith, John E., "Hegel's Critique of Kant," *Review of Metaphysics* 26 (1973), pp. 438–60.

Solomon, Robert, "Hegel's Concept of *Geist*," in *Hegel: A Collection of Critical Essays*, ed. Alasdair MacIntyre (Garden City, New York: Doubleday and Company, 1972).

Stern, Paul, "The Problem of History and Temporality in Kantian Ethics," *Review of Metaphysics* 39 (1986), pp. 505–45.

Stout, Jeffrey, *The Flight from Authority* (Notre Dame, IN: University of Notre Dame Press, 1981).

Sullivan, Roger J., *Immanuel Kant's Moral Theory* (Cambridge: Cambridge University Press, 1989).

——, *An Introduction to Kant's Ethics* (Cambridge: Cambridge University Press, 1994).

Tanner, Kathryn E., *God and Creation in Christian Theology: Tyranny or Empowerment* (Oxford: Blackwell, 1985).

Taylor, Charles, *The Ethics of Authenticity* (Cambridge, MA and London: Harvard University Press, 1991).

——, *Hegel* (Cambridge: Cambridge University Press, 1975).

——, *Sources of the Self* (Cambridge, MA: Harvard University Press, 1989).

Taylor, Mark C. (ed.), *Deconstruction in Context: Literature and Philosophy* (Chicago and London: University of Chicago Press, 1986).

Thielicke, Helmut, *The Evangelical Faith*, Vol. 1, trans. G. Bromiley (Grand Rapids: William B. Eerdmans, 1974).

Tillich, Paul, *Perspectives on 19th and 20th Century Protestant Theology*, ed. Carl E. Braaten (New York: Harper and Row, 1967).

Toulmin, Stephen, *Cosmopolis: The Hidden Agenda of Modernity* (Chicago and London: University of Chicago Press, 1990).

Tracy, David, *The Analogical Imagination: Christian Theology and the Culture of Pluralism* (New York: Crossroad, 1981).

——, *Blessed Rage for Order: The New Pluralism in Theology* (New York: The Seabury Press, 1975).

——, "Lindbeck's New Program for Theology: A Reflection," *The Thomist* 49 (1985), pp. 460–72.

Treash, Gordon, "Translator's Introduction" to Kant, *The One Possible Basis for a Demonstration of the Existence of God* (Lincoln and London: University of Nebraska Press, 1994).

Velkley, Richard, "The Crisis of the End of Reason in Kant's Philosophy and the *Remarks* of 1764–1765," in *Kant and Political Philosophy: The Contemporary Legacy*, ed. Ronald Beiner and William James Booth (New Haven and London: Yale University Press, 1993).

——, *Freedom and the End of Reason* (Chicago and London: University of Chicago Press, 1989).

Vogel, Manfred H., "The Barth–Feuerbach Confrontation," *Harvard Theological Review* 59 (1966), pp. 27–52.

Walker, Ralph, *Kant* (London: Routledge and Kegan Paul, 1978).

Walsh, W. H., *Kant's Criticism of Metaphysics* (Chicago and London: University of Chicago Press, 1975).

Ward, Keith, *The Development of Kant's View of Ethics* (Oxford: Blackwell, 1972).

Welch, Claude, *Protestant Thought in the Nineteenth Century:* Vol. 1, *1799–1870* (New Haven and London: Yale University Press, 1972).
——, *Protestant Thought in the Nineteenth Century:* Vol. 2, *1870–1914* (New Haven and London: Yale University Press, 1985).
Werpehowski, William, "Ad Hoc Apologetics," *Journal of Religion* 66 (1986), pp. 282–301.
West, Cornel, "The Politics of American Neo-Pragmatism," in *Post-Analytic Philosophy*, ed. West and John Rajchman (New York: Columbia University Press, 1985), pp. 259–75.
Wood, Allen W., "General Introduction," Kant, *Religion and Rational Theology*, trans. and ed. Wood and George Di Giovanni (Cambridge: Cambridge University Press, 1996), pp. xi–xxiv.
——, "Kant's Deism," in Rossi and Wreen (eds), pp. 1–21.
——, *Kant's Moral Religion* (Ithaca and London: Cornell University Press, 1970).
——, *Kant's Rational Theology* (Ithaca and London: Cornell University Press, 1978).
——, "Rational Theology, Moral Faith, and Religion," in Guyer (ed.), pp. 394–416.
——, "Translator's Introduction," Kant, *Lectures on Philosophical Theology*, trans. Wood and Gertrude M. Clark (Ithaca and London: Cornell University Press, 1978), pp. 9–18.
Yack, Bernard, *The Longing for Total Revolution: Philosophic Sources of Social Discontent from Rousseau to Marx and Nietzsche* (Berkeley: University of California Press, 1986).
——, "The Problem with Kantian Liberalism," in Beiner and Booth (eds), pp. 224–44.
Yovel, Yirmiahu, "Bible Interpretation as Philosophical Praxis: A Study of Spinoza and Kant," *Journal of the History of Philosophy* 54 (1972), pp. 189–212.
——, "The God of Kant," *Scripta Hierosolymitana* XX (1968).
——, *Kant and the Philosophy of History* (Princeton: Princeton University Press, 1980).
—— (ed.), *Kant's Practical Philosophy Reconsidered* (Dordrecht: Kluwer Academic Publishers, 1989).
——, *Spinoza and Other Heretics: The Adventures of Immanence (Princeton: Princeton University Press, 1989).*
Zammito, John, *The Genesis of Kant's Critique of Judgment* (Chicago and London: University of Chicago Press, 1992).

Index

Ptolemy, 138
Pufendorf, Samuel, 49, 154 n. 88

radical evil, 26, 32, 42, 101, 103–5,
107–12, 114–15, 121, 152 n. 63,
172 n. 15
Rawls, John, 162 n. 45, 163 n. 48,
170 n. 69, 175 n. 66
*Religion within the Limits of Reason
Alone*, 46, 64, 66, 70, 74, 92, 124
and ethical commonwealth, 24, 97,
101–22
and radical evil, 26, 32, 101, 103–5
rigorism, 108
Riley, Patrick, 154–5 n. 91, 159 n. 20,
175 n. 67
Ritschl, Albrecht, 4
Rousseau, Jean-Jacques, 22, 31, 38,
60–1, 68, 91, 116, 157 n. 8,
158 n. 12, 169 n. 62, 175 n. 67

Sallis, John, 83–4
Schleiermacher, Friedrich, 129,
142 n. 9, 178 n. 17, 180 n. 42
Schmalenbach, Hermann, 177 n. 5
Schmucker, Josef, 157 n. 2, 160 n. 23
Schneewind, Jerome, 26, 65, 67, 96,
144 n. 28, 148 n. 10, 154 n. 88,
154 n. 90, 155 n. 98, 157 n. 2,
157 n. 3, 157 n. 8, 160 n. 23,
160 n. 24, 160 n. 25, 176 n. 84
Schrader, George, 164 n. 51
Schultz, Franz Albert, 102
Shell, Susan Meld, 167 n. 25
Shklar, Judith, 174 n. 44
Silber, John, 162 n. 39
Spinoza, Baruch, 33, 45, 149 n. 24,
153 n. 75
Stapfer, J. F., 102
Stoicism, 37
Sullivan, Roger, 84, 169 n. 62
Swedenborg, Emanuel, 31

Taylor, Charles, 141 n. 3, 142 n. 9,
175 n. 66

teleology, 5, 36–7, 86–7, 96, 109, 128,
168 n. 36; *see also* totality
theodicy, 30, 38, 59, 178 n. 14
Thielicke, Helmut, 10
Thomism, 15
Tillich, Paul, 17, 129, 132, 134,
145 n. 37
totality (totalization), 36–8, 42, 48,
78, 82, 84–6, 90, 93–9, 107,
111–13; *see also* teleology
Toulmin, Stephen, 9, 156 n. 114
Tracy, David, 134–5, 180 n. 38,
180 n. 40, 181 n. 45
transcendence, 18, 20–1, 23, 82–3,
97, 117, 124–6, 136–8,
161 n. 32
and autonomy, 2, 6–8, 12, 14, 33,
61–2, 77–8, 154 n. 90
and ethical commonwealth, 25, 101,
109, 112, 114, 120, 126
and Hegel, 3, 93, 141 n. 3
and Kant's moral argument, 29, 35,
41, 42, 48, 52–3
and Kierkegaard, 55–6

"Universal Natural History and
Theory of the Heavens," 30

Velkley, Richard, 31, 146 n. 51,
148 n. 10, 148 n. 16, 154 n. 90,
157 n. 2, 160 n. 23, 160 n. 24
voluntarism, 49–50, 51, 73, 119,
154 n. 88, 155 n. 91

Walker, Ralph, 45
Walsh, W. H., 174 n. 44
Weber, Max, 61
Welch, Sharon, 178 n. 22
Whitehead, Alfred North, 15,
181 n. 45
will, 18, 63–73, 77, 88, 94, 104, 106,
109, 111, 120–1, 148 n. 16,
159 n. 20, 161 n. 33, 169–70 n. 63
Wille, 65–6, 105, 161 n. 31, 161 n. 32,
161 n. 33, 161 n. 34, 172 n. 19